The Peoples of the
British Isles

Related books of interest

**The Peoples of the British Isles:
A New History From 1688 to Present**
Thomas William Heyck and Meredith Veldman

**The Peoples of the British Isles:
A New History From 1688 to 1914**
Thomas William Heyck and Meredith Veldman

**The Peoples of the British Isles:
A New History From 1870 to Present**
Thomas William Heyck and Meredith Veldman

The New Nature of History: Knowledge, Evidence, Language
Arthur Marwick

The Peoples of the
British Isles

A New History   **Fourth Edition**

From Prehistoric Times to 1688

Samantha A. Meigs
University of Indianapolis

Stanford E. Lehmberg
University of Minnesota

OXFORD
UNIVERSITY PRESS

OXFORD
UNIVERSITY PRESS

Oxford University Press is a department of the University of Oxford.
It furthers the University's objective of excellence in research, scholarship,
and education by publishing worldwide.

Oxford   New York
Auckland   Cape Town   Dar es Salaam   Hong Kong   Karachi
Kuala Lumpur   Madrid   Melbourne   Mexico City   Nairobi
New Delhi   Shanghai   Taipei   Toronto

With offices in
Argentina   Austria   Brazil   Chile   Czech Republic   France   Greece
Guatemala   Hungary   Italy   Japan   Poland   Portugal   Singapore
South Korea   Switzerland   Thailand   Turkey   Ukraine   Vietnam

Oxford is a registered trade mark of Oxford University Press
in the UK and certain other countries.

Published in the United States of America by
Oxford University Press
198 Madison Avenue, New York, NY 10016

© Oxford University Press 2016

Library of Congress Cataloging-in-Publication Data
Meigs, Samantha A., 1958–
    The peoples of the British Isles : a new history / Samantha Meigs, Stanford E. Lehmberg. —
Fourth edition.
       volumes cm
    Stanford E. Lehmberg's name appears first on the third edition.
    Authors of volumes 2–3 are Thomas William Heyck and Meredith Veldman.
    Includes bibliographical references and index.
    Contents: v. 1. From prehistoric times to 1688 — v. 2. From 1688 to 1914 — v. 3. From 1870
to the present.
    ISBN 978-0-19-065669-0 (v. 1 : alk. paper) — ISBN 978-0-19-061552-9 (v. 2 : alk. paper) —
ISBN 978-0-19-061553-6 (v. 3 : alk. paper) — ISBN 978-0-19-061554-3 (v. 2 and v. 3 : alk. paper)
    1. Great Britain—History. 2. Ethnology—Great Britain. 3. Ireland—History. 4. Ethnology—
Ireland. I. Lehmberg, Stanford E. II. Heyck, Thomas William, 1938–III. Veldman, Meredith.
IV. Title.
    DA30.L44   2014
    941—dc23
                                                                                    2014017285

ISBN 978-0-19-065669-0

9 8 7 6 5 4

Printed in Canada on acid-free paper

Contents

List of Illustrations ix
List of Maps xiii
Preface xv

1 Prehistoric Britain **1**
Geography 1
Prehistoric Britain 4
Stone Forts and Megaliths 5
The Prehistoric Peoples of the British Isles 10
The Iron Age (Beginning ca. 750 BCE) 12
Suggested Reading 17

2 Roman Britain **18**
The Beginning of the Roman Conquest 18
The Claudian Invasion 19
Boudicca and the Revolt of the Iceni 19
Extension of the Roman Conquest 21
The End of Roman Occupation 24
Impact of the Romans 24
Britain after the Romans 27
Suggested Reading 27

3 Early Christian Britain **29**
The Arrival of Christianity in Britain 29
Early Christianity in Wales 30
The Saints of Ireland: Patrick and Brigid 31
Columcille and the Celtic Monasticism 35
Legacies of Celtic Monasticism 39
Suggested Reading 44

4 Early Medieval Britain and Ireland and the Impact of the Vikings **45**
The Viking Raids 45
British Political Structures: The Scots, the Anglo-Saxons, and the Irish 48
Viking Expansion and Settlement 49
The Second Wave of Viking Invasions and the Anglo-Saxon Succession 56
The Succession of 1066 58
Overall Impact of the Vikings: The Celtic Regions 58
Anglo-Saxon Society and Culture 61
Suggested Reading 65

5 Norman Britain **66**
Who Were the Normans? 66
The Normanization of Britain 68
Norman Influences in Scotland 71

The Normanization of Ireland 73
The Normans in Wales 75
Consolidation of Norman Power in England 77
Suggested Reading 78

6 **Britain in the High Middle Ages** **80**
The Agricultural Revolution 80
The Urban Revolution 81
Twelfth Century Religious Life 84
The Reign of Henry II 87
Plantagenet Rule in Britain: The Sons of Henry II 91
Suggested Reading 94

7 **Identity Formation in the Four Kingdoms** **95**
National Monarchy 95
Wars of Expansion: Wales 97
Wars of Expansion: Scotland 102
Wars of Expansion: Ireland 106
Suggested Reading 110

8 **Britain in the Later Middle Ages** **111**
The Crises of the Fourteenth Century: Religion, War, and Plague 111
The English Succession 115
The Fifteenth Century: A Time of Transformation 118
The Late Middle Ages in Ireland 124
Scotland 128
Wales 131
The End of the Middle Ages 133
Suggested Reading 133

9 **The British Renaissance** **135**
The Wars of the Roses and the Shifting Succession 135
Scotland and the Early Stuarts 139
James IV and the Scottish Renaissance 143
Ireland's Politics and the Gaelic Revival 147
The Irish Renaissance Lords 150
The English Renaissance: Henry VIII 153
Suggested Reading 155

10 **The Age of Reformation** **157**
Henry VIII and the Origins of the English Reformation 157
Cranmer, Cromwell, and the Start of the English Reformation 160
The Broader Context of the Reformation in England 164
The Impact of the Reformation in England 164
Henry VIII's Last Years 166
The Scottish Reformation 167
The Continental Context of the Scottish Reformation 168
The Reformation in Ireland 176
The Reformation in Wales 179
Suggested Reading 180

11 Elizabethan Politics and Jacobean Tensions **181**
The Elizabethan Religious Settlement 181
Elizabethan Domestic Politics 183
The Internal Catholic Threat 187
International Politics 188
The Irish Problem 191
James VI of Scotland/I of England 193
Accession to the English Throne 199
Ireland 201
Scotland 203
James's Later Parliaments 204
Suggested Reading 205

12 Charles I and the Three Kingdoms **207**
Charles and the Age of Crisis 207
The Eleven Years Tyranny 210
Crisis in Scotland and Ireland 211
The Wars of the Three Kingdoms 214
Scotland 215
Charles's Trial and Execution 220
The Commonwealth and Protectorate 220
Suggested Reading 223

13 From Restoration to Revolution **224**
Charles II, the Merry Monarch 224
Restoration in the Other Kingdoms 227
Restoration London 228
Science and Culture 231
The Popish Plot 234
Charles's Death 235
Accession of James II of England/VII of Scotland 236
The Reign of William and Mary 238
Scotland 240
Ireland 241
Aftermath 242
Suggested Reading 243

Appendix: Genealogical Tables **245**

Illustration Credits **251**

Index **255**

List of Illustrations

Chapter 1

Newgrange, a Neolithic corbelled stone structure located in the
Boyne Valley in Ireland 7
Stonehenge (aerial view) 8
Standing stones of Callanish 9
Knockfarrel Iron Age hillfort near Dingwall, Scotland 10
Interior of stone house at Skara Brae, located in the
Orkney Islands of Scotland 12
Replica of Iron Age dwelling from Butser Ancient Farm 14

Chapter 2

Statue of Boudicca on London Bridge 20
Roman baths at Bath, England 22
Hadrian's Wall, showing one of the adjoining forts 23

Chapter 3

Shrine of St. Patrick's bell 32
The *Cathach*, Psalter of St. Columcille 36
Beehive cell, Skellig Mhicil, Ireland 39
St. Martin's Cross, Iona, Scotland 41
The *Lindisfarne Gospels*, written in Northumbria about 720 42
The *Book of Kells* 43

Chapter 4

Irish round tower 46
The Ardagh Chalice, early eighth century 47
Viking Dublin, showing excavations taking place 51
Rune stone, Iona, Scotland 52
Tombstones of the Lords of the Isles, Iona, Scotland 53
Animatronic figure from Jorvik Viking Center, York, England 55
The Bayeux Tapestry 59
The Pitney Brooch 63
Sutton Hoo ship burial 64

Chapter 5

A ceremony of homage and fealty as depicted in a medieval
English manuscript 67
Effigy of Richard de Clare, "Strongbow," in Christ Church Cathedral, Dublin ... 74
Ruins of Hugh de Lacy's Castle, Trim, Ireland 75
The *Domesday Book* 77

Chapter 6

Effigies of Henry II and Eleanor of Aquitaine, Fontevrault Abbey, France 88
Thomas Becket 90

Chapter 7

Edward I in Parliament 96
Llywelyn the Great and his sons, Gruffydd and Dafydd 98
Caernarfon Castle, Wales 101
The English coronation chair, Westminster Abbey 104
The Declaration of Arbroath 106

Chapter 8

Effigy of Edward III, Westminster Abbey 113
Effigies of Henry IV and his queen, Joan of Navarre 116
English archers at Agincourt 117
Henry V 118
Woodcut illustration from Hans Holbein's *Dance of Death* 122
Page from Wycliffe's Bible 123
Speed's Map of Ireland (1610), detail showing the dress of the "tame" town
    Irish and the "wild" Gaelic Irish 127
Statue of Owain Glyn Dwr, Corwen, Wales 132

Chapter 9

Richard III, portrait by an unknown artist 137
Forensic reconstruction of the features of Richard III 138
James IV of Scotland by an unknown artist 143
Woodcut of the MacSweeney chieftain and his court 149
Lough Gur, Ireland 153
Field of the Cloth of Gold, anonymous artist 154

Chapter 10

Henry VIII, copied from a portrait by Hans Holbein 158
Sir Thomas More 160
Thomas Cromwell, by Hans Holbein 161
The ruins of Glastonbury Abbey 162
The six wives of Henry VIII 163
Edward VI by Hans Holbein 170
Mary Tudor, by an unknown artist 171
The Burning of Archbishop Cranmer 172
Title page of John Knox's "The First Blast of the Trumpet against the
    Monstrous Regimen of Women" (1571) 173
Mary, Queen of Scots, by an unknown artist 174

Chapter 11

Elizabeth I when a Princess 182
Elizabeth I by Marc Gheeraerts 184
Cony catcher's pamphlet, by Robert Greene (1592) 185
Woodcut illustration of the execution of Mary, Queen of Scots 188
James I, by Daniel Mytens 193
Woodcut illustration of the Lancashire witches 196
Title page of James I's *Daemonologie* 197
Title page of James I's *Basilikon Doron* 198

Chapter 12

Charles I, by Daniel Mytens 208
James Graham, first Marquess of Montrose after Honthorst 216
Archibald Campbell, first Marquess of Argyll 217
Statue of Oliver Cromwell, lord protector of England, Ireland, and Scotland .. 221

Chapter 13

Charles II from the studio of John Michael Wright 225
Samuel Pepys 226
St. Paul's Cathedral, view from the southeast 230
Panorama of London, showing the skyline as it appeared following the
    great rebuilding 231
Robert Boyle, 1689 232
Charter of the Royal Society, detail 233
James II, by Sir Godfrey Kneller 236
Cartoon showing the rumor that James II's son (by his second, Catholic wife)
    was not legitimate, but was smuggled into the queen's bedroom in a
    warming pan 238
James Francis Stuart 239
William of Orange, by Sir Peter Lely 239
John Graham, first Viscount Dundee, seventh Laird of Claverhouse 241

List of Maps

Traditional counties and shires of the British Isles xiv
Geographic features of the British Isles 2
Hillforts and stone circles of the British Isles 6
Towns of Roman England 25
Traditional Irish (Celtic) monasteries of the British Isles 40
Viking settlement in the British Isles 50
Towns of medieval England 82
Cathedrals and monasteries of the British Isles 85
Medieval Welsh principalities, circa 1100 99
Irish families and lordships 125
Scottish clans and chieftaincies 130
Religions of Europe, circa 1600 189
Irish plantations (1580s to 1620s) 202
Early modern London, showing the extent of the Great Fire in 1666 229

Traditional Counties & Shires
of the British Isles

Traditional counties and shires of the British Isles. This map shows the historic counties and shires of the British Isles as they had evolved by the end of the seventeenth century. Some spellings have changed, but essentially this map represents the local political units of Britain as they existed until 1972.

Preface to the Fourth Edition

The fourth edition of volume one of *The Peoples of the British Isles* marks a full revision of text, illustrations, and maps. In the intervening years since the revisions of the third edition, historical interpretations have changed, students have changed, the position of Britain in a European perspective has changed, and the interrelationship between England and the other premodern kingdoms of the British Isles (Scotland, Ireland, and Wales) has changed. Keeping all these changes in mind, the strengths of the traditional narratives of British history are balanced here with a fuller integration of new historical interpretations and a more complete coverage of the histories of each of the regions of the British Isles, as well as situating the role of premodern Britain in a larger European and Atlantic context. As was the case with earlier editions, the emphasis of this series has always been on *all* the peoples of the British Isles, men and women, rich and poor, noble and laborer. In a short text it is impossible to include every element of this expanse of time, but I have tried to capture the breadth of experience contained in the formative years of prehistory through 1688. Although some points of emphasis of the volume have necessarily changed, I hope that the original author, Stanford E. Lehmberg, would have been pleased with the revisions of the fourth edition. He was a fine scholar who provided a refreshingly holistic viewpoint of premodern British history with his original text of volume one of *The Peoples of the British Isles*.

I have been honored to work on this volume, and I would like to thank T. W. Heyck for first proposing my involvement in this series. I would also like to express my thanks to the reviewers—Brian Cowan of McGill University, Charles Briggs of the University of Vermont, Dana Rabin of the University of Illinois at Urbana–Champaign, and Elizabeth Ewan of the University of Guelph—who provided many useful insights as to how the volume could best be structured for use in the classroom, and especially to Meredith Veldman, whose close reading of the text and perceptive suggestions have greatly improved the text. I would like to thank my brother for reading countless pages of drafts, and I would like to note my appreciation to various colleagues who have provided support and to everyone at Lyceum Books for helping to bring this project to completion.

Samantha A. Meigs
March 2016

Chapter 1

Prehistoric Britain

If we could imagine away all the modern structures and changes to the landscape of Britain brought about by people during the last five thousand years or so, we would be left with an approximate perception of how things might have looked to the inhabitants of prehistoric Britain. Almost certainly, it was a landscape full of symbolism, with tight interconnections between the geographical features of the land and the life experience of the inhabitants. What remains of this early era suggests a careful siting of buildings and monuments, often in locations that seem counterintuitive to us. Forts seem to face the "wrong" direction, stone monoliths were erected far from quarries, and strange arrangements of stones were constructed with seemingly no purpose. It is clear that these things were not accidental. They were designed to a purpose, but for the historian looking backward across time the view is hazy and uncertain. We do not know with certainty who exactly made up the aboriginal population of Britain. We know a little about their settlement patterns, their burial customs, and their idea of art and decoration, but we do not know what their language sounded like, what religious beliefs they embraced, or what daily life was like and how it changed over time. To try to fill in the sizable gaps in our knowledge, we must look closely at what does remain of the landscape and durable constructions and try to make sense of them.

GEOGRAPHY

For all of its small size (about fifty thousand square miles), Britain has an enormously varied geologic and geographic terrain. Rugged mountains define northern and southern territorial regions in Scotland and Wales, and barren moorland emphasizes the physical (as opposed to political) line of demarcation between Scotland and England. England divides roughly into two zones, with an imaginary line drawn from the river Exe (near Exeter) in the southwest to the river Tees in the northeast. Below this line is most of the fertile land of England, crossed by the many navigable rivers that have played an important role throughout England's history. North of the line, the terrain is rugged, more suited to pasturage than farming. The craggy Pennines give rise to a very different set of social and economic conditions from those in the south.

Wales has always had strong local identities corresponding at least in part to geography. The Cambrian Mountains dominate the western coastline, and

Geographic features of the British Isles. This map illustrates the terrain of the British Isles. Geography and topography have greatly influenced settlement, politics, social organization, linguistic divisions, and identities within all four kingdoms (England, Ireland, Scotland, and Wales).

the Severn River separates Wales geographically from the English Cotswolds. Not surprisingly, Celtic-style lordships and law held sway longer in the more inaccessible mountainous regions than in the more accessible arable terrain.

Similarly, Scotland has a variety of different geophysical characteristics that greatly affected the experience of life and the history of the different regions. Most people are familiar with the terms *Lowland* and *Highland*, although they are often confused about exactly which areas each encompasses. Both terms are fraught with cultural and political meaning, but in a purely geographical context, areas north and west of the Highland Boundary Fault are considered Highland and those south and east are Lowland, although the flat coastal lands to the east are often considered more Lowland than Highland. Thus, the rich fertile farmland of Aberdeenshire belongs to the Lowlands, whereas the rugged hill country of the Trossachs is properly Highland, although considerably farther south. Also, usually not included in the Highland/Lowland designation are the northern islands of Shetland and Orkney, although the Hebrides have often been considered part of the Highlands. Despite the ambiguities, observable differences in terrain, agriculture, and settlement patterns have resulted in the continued use of the terms Highland and Lowland, suggesting not only geographical differences, but also political, social, economic, and cultural differences that persisted across time and were exacerbated by language, shifting political allegiances, and post-Reformation religious changes.

Ireland has its own physical complexity, usually described as a saucer with hills and mountains around the perimeter and soggy bogland in the middle. Although Ireland has rivers whose names are familiar to most people—the Shannon, the Liffey, and the Boyne—they are not interconnected and did not serve as arteries for commerce as the rivers did in England or on the Continent. For Ireland, the port towns were the most important economic centers, with Dublin, Cork, Wexford, Waterford, Belfast, and Galway each playing a part in the story of Ireland's past. Dublin has been the capital of Ireland since Viking days and has had a checkered relationship with England, only fifty miles away across the Irish channel. Because so much of Ireland's history has been tied to England, it is very easy to perceive the island only in terms of its geographical proximity to the English mainland. However, in premodern times, the cultural ties to Scotland were stronger. Only eighteen miles separate Ulster from Kintyre, and up until the early modern period, Gaelic Ireland and the Highlands and islands of Scotland were closely connected through a shared language and interrelated ruling families. Moreover, the west coast of Ireland was always closely connected with continental Europe through seafaring trade and politics, a continuing influence that should not be overlooked in the complexities of Irish history.

Thus, the British Isles are a kaleidoscope of landscapes and identities, with marked visual differences among the rocky uplands of the English midlands; the rolling hills of the south; the bleak, stony coastline of Cornwall; and the markedly individual identity of all of the islands, including the Isle of Man and the Channel Islands—as well as the differing characteristics of all the river estuaries that provided some of the "roadways" of the past. In addition to geography, these identities were shaped by language, culture, religion, and an ever-shifting set of boundaries and marches. No wonder the people of the British Isles would be characterized by their regional identities and strong individualism.

PREHISTORIC BRITAIN

Although we are lacking in written documentation pertaining to the British Isles prior to the Roman era (ca. 55 CE) there is an abundance of archaeological evidence from which to build the story of the prehistoric peoples of the British Isles. The earliest evidence of settlement may date back as far as the lower Paleolithic (approximately 350,000 BCE), but by the upper Paleolithic (35,000–8500 BCE), sites became much more plentiful, with at least forty known in Britain (25% of which are located in Wales). The nature of these sites (scattered and various in typology) make generalized interpretation extremely difficult. However, by the Neolithic period (starting around 10,000 BCE), the retreating glaciers of the Ice Age made Britain much more favorable for human settlement, and the number of archaeological sites increased accordingly. It is during this period that groups of varying geographic and linguistic background began to establish territories in the British Isles. Archaeologists identify these groups primarily by their farming habits, material culture, and often by their burial practices.

Most archaeologists agree that by around 4000 BCE settlers had arrived from the Continent and were practicing a variety of farming methods similar to those indicated in European sites. Contrary to some older interpretations, it does not appear that these continental settlers introduced agriculture into Britain, but rather that the changing climatic conditions may have influenced the underlying subsistence base. It is also quite possible that these new settlers may have brought specific agricultural methods with them that were then adapted by the indigenous population. Not surprisingly, evidence of cereal crops predominates in sites dating to circa 4000 BCE, with the specific types varying by locale. Emmer wheat was grown in the chalklands, whereas the hardier barley was the primary cereal crop in the rockier, less fertile lands of the north. The amount of land brought under cultivation seems to have expanded during this period, perhaps as a result of new land-clearing techniques. All regions show evidence of animal husbandry, with cattle predominant, followed by sheep, and some evidence of pigs, curiously variable by specific region. Even with what seems to have been an expansion in settled agricultural life, hunting and gathering still formed an important part of daily life and economy. Archaeological evidence shows seeds in settlement sites ranging from blackberries, sloes, and crab apples to nuts, particularly hazelnuts. Many small animal bones, often carbonized, testify to the importance of hunting. Some are bones from expected food sources: red deer, wild boar, and hares, but other bones such as those from wild cats, bears, and wolves provide a glimpse into some of the dangers that lurked nearby these sparsely settled agricultural villages.

The types of structures in which these early inhabitants lived varied considerably by location. There is some evidence of single-family dwellings, particularly in the south and southwest of England. More commonly, houses existed in collective ditched enclosures with ramparts affording some measure of protection, presumably from human as well as animal predators. Perhaps the best known examples of this type of structure include Windmill Hill in north Wiltshire and Maiden Castle in Dorset.

Excavations at early British settlement sites show that the inhabitants practiced numerous trades and crafts such as woodworking, pottery making, flint working, and textile production. Distinctive variations in methods of construction, materials, and decorative techniques help identify the different tribal groups that produced them. No doubt there were cases of acculturation where styles were passed from one group to another, but usually it is clear that certain features were characteristic of specific groups. One of the best examples of this can be seen in the appearance and spread of Celtic features in decorative motifs that perhaps originated in continental La Tène society. Located near modern day Switzerland, La Tène is often seen as one of the earliest examples of a definably Celtic civilization.

The identification and assumed migration of the Celts are subjects marked by controversy and lack of agreement among scholars. One modern archaeologist has even argued that the term Celt is virtually meaningless. Part of the problem has been a reliance on Roman written sources that considerably postdate the arrival of the Celts in Britain. Older theories assumed that the Celts traveled from the Continent to Ireland and thence to Britain (specifically the western coastal areas of Scotland), but more recent archaeological and linguistic study has indicated the probability of different waves of migration that likely included direct movement from the Continent into southern England as well as northern movement between Ireland and Scotland. What is clear is that the people usually referred to as Celts brought with them identifiable and distinctive architectural styles as well as burial customs and decorative motifs. Scottish evidence provides us with especially clear-cut examples showing the differences between Celtic design and that of the indigenous population, usually (incorrectly) lumped together as Picts.

STONE FORTS AND MEGALITHS

It is unclear which of various migrating groups were responsible for building the great megaliths that dot the landscape of the British Isles. Quite possibly the distinctive types of architecture reflect diverse styles or motivations of different groups, although representative examples of standing stones, hillforts, cairn burials, wedge burials, souterrains, and chambered tombs all commingle. Dating is usually based on traces of carbon. Therefore, it is very difficult to date structures that do not contain carbon material. Even when these structures contain buried or cremated remains containing carbon the structure may not date to the same time as the burial.

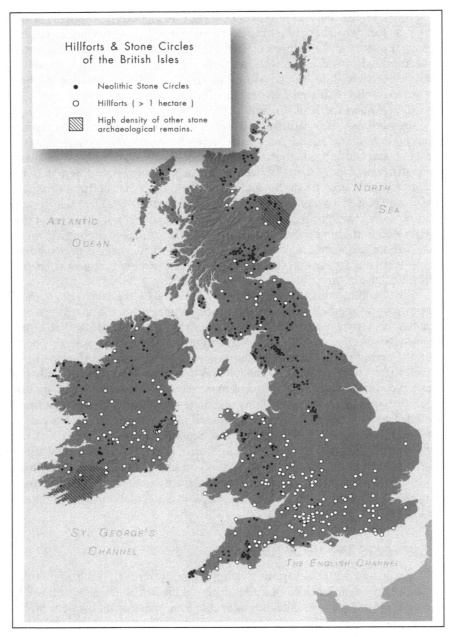

Hillforts and stone circles of the British Isles. This map shows the distribution areas of Iron Age hillforts and stone circles in the British Isles. It is interesting to note where the two types of monuments coincide and where they do not. We do not know who built them, but the distinction in distribution suggests possible differences in the outlooks and needs of the builders. Stone circles would seem to be associated with sacred spaces, whereas the hillforts appear to be fortified military bases.

Although some of these structures were associated with burials, it is clear that we do not fully understand the reasons for their construction. For example the awe-inspiring chambered tombs of the three great complexes along the Boyne Valley in Ireland—Newgrange, Knowth, and Dowth—were plainly designed as more than simple tombs. Although cremated remains were found in the most impressive structure, Newgrange, that is not its most noteworthy feature. Built with an enormous knowledge of advanced architecture and astronomy, the drystone central chamber (which has not leaked in five thousand years!) is illuminated by the rising sun for fifteen minutes only at dawn on the day of the midwinter solstice. When the sun's rays enter the narrow passageway, they fall nearly perfectly on a carved design on the chamber's wall. For some scholars that nearly perfect alignment contributes proof of the great antiquity of the structure, which perhaps predates the pyramids of Egypt. Based on modern calculations, five thousand years ago the sun would have hit precisely in the center of the design.

Other excavations in the Boyne Valley reveal that the central building in the Knowth complex works similarly except that it catches the light at sunset during the autumn equinox. It is at least conceivable that the entire complex of the

Newgrange, a Neolithic corbelled stone structure located in the Boyne Valley in Ireland. The date of construction of Newgrange remains uncertain, probably circa 3200 BCE. Although human remains were found inside, its primary purpose was likely not as a tomb, but rather as a sacred site. At dawn on the Midwinter Solstice, the sun shines through the passageway in the picture, illuminating the interior and providing evidence of the advanced astronomical knowledge of the builders.

Boyne Valley served some astronomical and/or religious purpose, and the burials came later. The probably contemporaneous Maeshowe, located in Orkney, is a similar structure (a corbelled drystone chambered cairn that is also illuminated on the winter solstice). It is unknown if the builders had any direct knowledge of each other, although it seems likely. It also seems likely that the structures served similar ritual or community purposes.

Similarly, scholars have shown that the great stone circles and avenues of standing stones that have long fascinated observers have astronomical meaning. Stonehenge is perhaps the most famous of these, but it is by no means the only example. Stone circles exist in many locations—from the nearby Avebury complex to the circle at Castlerigg in the Lake District. Arguably the most evocative circles are the most remote: the Ring of Brodgar in the Orkneys (which originally contained sixty-six stones) and the standing stones of Callanish on the Isle of Lewis. It is possible that the northern examples are the oldest and that the building of such monuments moved from north to south, but that is uncertain, along with their precise usage.

The geographical locations of these massive stone structures and the difficulty with which building materials would have been brought to the sites make it clear that we do not have all of the pieces to solve the riddles associated with the megaliths. The people who built them did so with great precision and effort, but their motivations elude us. If the chambered tombs and stone circles that presumably relate to religious functions are not puzzling enough, the location of stone hillforts and their relationship to politics and warfare raise even more questions.

Stonehenge (aerial view), a prehistoric monument located on Salisbury Plain, near the middle of the south coast of England. This stone circle has become an iconic symbol of ancient Britain. Now a destination for tourists and associated with druidic observances, the monument illustrates its unknown builders' knowledge of astronomy and engineering.

Standing stones of Callanish, Neolithic stone circle, located on the isle of Lewis in the Outer Hebrides of Scotland. The remoteness of this site gives dramatic evidence of the importance of henge monuments to the societies that created them. Astronomical alignments are also associated with this site.

Scholars usually date these structures to the Iron Age, and they are likely connected with the celticization of the British Isles. Tradition tells us that there were many waves of successive invaders, perhaps rival groups of Celts from mainland Europe or other parts of the British Isles. One of the oldest of the Irish epics, the *Lebor Gabála Erenn* or *Book of Invasions*, mentions four waves of invaders: the Fir Bolg, the Formorians, the Tuatha de Dánann, and the Milesians, mythological races that in some way may correspond to successive historic settlements. The builders of the hillforts were plainly worried about invasion, expending a great amount of time and resources in building huge defensible structures on hills and near the coastline. Although these structures are found throughout Britain, the greatest concentration of the hillforts can be found in Wales, the northern and western regions of Scotland, and the western coast of Ireland. Interestingly, many of the coastal hillforts, such as Dún Aonghasa on the Aran Islands, face out toward the Atlantic. When visiting the windblown and desolate site, looking out across the Atlantic from the fortress on cliffs fifty feet high, one cannot help but wonder who the enemy might have been. To add to the mystery, some of the hillforts are vitrified. They were apparently heated to extremely high temperatures (whether by design or through attack is unknown) so that the great blocks of stone melted and fused. Excavations undertaken at various hillfort sites suggest a mixed usage of these structures. Danebury in Hampshire seems to have been used as both a village compound and a fortification for food; others, such as Craig Phadraig near Inverness, which may have served as the capital of the Picts, may have been communal centers for both trade and politics.

Knockfarrel Iron Age hillfort near Dingwall, Scotland. Detail of vitrified stones. Many hillforts situated around the Moray Firth in Scotland show evidence of vitrification (melting and fusing of the stones at very high temperatures). It is unknown what caused the high heat: natural fires, part of military conquest, or perhaps a process (now unknown) intended to strengthen the fortifications.

THE PREHISTORIC PEOPLES OF THE BRITISH ISLES

One of the earliest groups of people identified in Britain, the so-called *Beaker folk*, were named from the distinctive shape of the pottery containers they used. These beaker pots are found in England, Ireland, and the south of Scotland, and it is unclear whether the sites are indicative of migratory settlement or trade. These people were probably not indigenous to Britain, but it is unknown where they came from or when they arrived in Britain. Earliest estimates place them as Neolithic, and it is possible that they were the makers of at least some of the megalithic structures. In addition to their pottery, the Beaker folk are identifiable in the archaeological record through their burial customs: single inhumation, usually in round barrows, as opposed to the long barrow group burials of the possibly contemporaneous Windmill Hill culture. The Beaker folk used bronze articles, such as drinking vessels and jewelry, but it is likely that these articles were exported from the Continent and not produced locally.

The first known workers in bronze in the British Isles were the people identified as the *Wessex culture*. They seem to have first been established in southwest England, a logical location given the necessity of tin in the process of bronze making. The time period generally referred to as the Bronze Age in Britain is from circa 2000 to 1000 BCE. During that time the Wessex culture produced beautiful bronze objects that have been found at burial sites alongside objects from as far away as Egypt and Greece, indicating a startling degree of international trade. During this same period the Irish were producing beautiful gold work, especially jewelry such as pennanular brooches (used to secure cloaks), earrings, and the distinctive gold torques (neck rings) worn by the Irish elites. The people of the Wessex culture practiced cremation rather than inhumation, erecting inverted urns over the burial site. This practice has led to an alternative designation of this group as the *Urnfield culture*.

Perhaps one of the most evocative sites of early settlement in the British Isles is Skara Brae, located in the remote Orkney Islands. Part of its fascination lies in the fact that it was once a lost village, entirely covered by sand and only rediscovered in 1850, when a great storm removed enough of the sand that covered the stone structures to make them visible. What had lain underneath millennia of sand deposits was a village consisting of houses made entirely of stone. (There is virtually no wood on the windswept Orkney Islands.) It is unknown who the inhabitants of these houses might have been, and they apparently lived there for only a few centuries (probably approximately from 3200 to 2200 BCE).

What makes the structures so striking and so immediate is the strong sense that they were ordinary homes occupied by ordinary people. They lack the grandeur of the standing stones, hillforts, and chambered cairns, but in many ways this site bring us closer to the prehistoric inhabitants of Britain than any of the more monumental structures. They still seem to be comfortable structures, resistant to the winds and well laid out. There are eight houses in the complex, each self-contained, but all connected by passageways, providing a clear picture of inhabitants able to move from one to another living space, regardless of weather conditions outside. Each house has a fireplace and raised stone platform (presumably a bed), and perhaps most intriguing, a stone dresser facing the door. It is fascinating to wonder what kind of personal treasures might have been placed on the dresser. We do not know for sure because when the inhabitants left they took their treasures with them. What they left behind (besides the stone structures) were mountains of refuse. The houses had no windows, and between the walls of adjacent buildings were piles of garbage. Perhaps these served as a kind of insulation, but in any case they provide much evidence for archaeologists concerning the diet of the inhabitants of Skara Brae. From their trash we know they had cattle, grew grain, and had a diet rich in fish and shellfish. But what the site cannot answer is who they were and why they left.

Interior of stone house at Skara Brae, located in the Orkney Islands of Scotland. Skara Brae, consisting of eight stone-built houses, remarkably well-preserved by windblown sand, is the most complete Neolithic settlement in Europe. We do not know who inhabited the houses or why they left, but the remote site with its tidy houses, beds, and chests is highly evocative.

THE IRON AGE (BEGINNING CA. 750 BCE)

Whatever the earlier waves of invasions may have been, the Celts were almost certainly the last group of prehistoric invaders to arrive in Britain, leaving an indelible mark of language and culture on the regions they inhabited. Our documentary sources come from the Romans and are largely unflattering and often misinformed. Caesar tells us that the Belgae from Gaul had settlements in Britain, and the Romans who invaded Britain during the Claudian and Antonine campaigns describe tall, red-haired, warlike people, with the women equal to the men in stature and ferocity. These were likely the people we now call Celts, but they would probably have identified themselves by their specific tribal allegiances rather than as a collective group.

By the time of the Romans, these tribal groups were organized into essentially a clan structure. Leadership was defined by lineage and consisted of a warrior aristocracy, with hereditary specialists such as artisans (and most likely hereditary professionals such as doctors, jurists, and poets delineated in later Irish traditions and law codes), farmers, and free and unfree servants. They spoke linguistically related dialects of Goidelic languages, characterized as *P-Celtic* (Welsh, Cornish, and Breton) and *Q-Celtic* (which evolved into Irish, Scots Gaelic, and Manx). Because they did not record their history and literature in written form, later historians have been forced to use a combination of archaeological evidence, hostile Roman sources, and later insular documentation to try to piece together the culture of the pre-Christian British Celts. Caesar commented that they relied on the training of the memory to preserve their traditions and way of life, and modern research into the oral tradition indicates that they likely had a much higher accuracy and ability to preserve complex information than once was thought. Thus, it is quite possible that the material contained in the earliest recorded Irish histories and epics (such as the previously mentioned *Lebor Gabala Erenn* [*Book of Invasions*] and the *Táin Bó Cúailgne* [*The Cattle Raid of Cooley*]) reasonably depicts the highly aristocratic, war-minded, and cultured Celts first encountered by the Romans. The similarly themed Welsh chronicles, known collectively as the *Annales Cambriae*, and the great Welsh epic *The Mabinogion*, although surviving only in later manuscript versions, point to similarities between ancient Welsh society and culture and that of the Irish.

In the absence of contemporary written documentation, much of the history of the early Celts in Britain has been pieced together through archaeological evidence. It is possible that the Celts were the builders of the hillforts (although it is also possible that they used previously existing sites) and their weapons show an advanced knowledge of iron making. Additionally, they continued to work in bronze and gold. The Battersea bronze shield, found near London, is an example of the intricate bronze work of this period (ca.1000 BCE). The Celts in Britain used both bronze and gold coins as well as iron bars as currency and conducted trade with the Gauls in France. Celtic metalwork has also been found in the Mediterranean.

One of the best examples of an Iron Age Celtic settlement is Danebury, in the chalklands of Wessex. This site was first excavated in the 1960s and has yielded a wealth of information about Iron Age Britain. This hillfort was clearly used for communal defense. It was situated on a hill and had three rings of concentric ramparts. It was near a spring for water, a pasture for sheep, meadows for cattle, and a forest for fuel and building materials. Archaeological evidence shows that the site was continuously inhabited from the sixth to the first century BCE. Within the walls (enclosing about thirteen acres) were found more than eighteen thousand postholes and five thousand storage pits. This was no haphazard collection of huts, but rather an extremely organized and well-conceived settlement. There were roads and paths within the wall of the hillfort, and the buildings seem to have been situated according to use, with groups of houses, workshops, storage buildings, and so forth. Near the center of the site was a larger, more elaborate structure that has been conjectured to have been a temple. The buildings at Danebury were well constructed, with thatched circular houses of wattle and daub, furnished inside with planking and caulking made of moss and resin that would have made them dry and resistant to wind. Artifacts, or evidence of artifacts, show that the inhabitants had ovens, looms, and a wide range of other domestic equipment. The number of storage pits and their contents provide evidence of a thriving community, with good agriculture and animal husbandry. It is not known for sure how many people lived at the Danebury complex, but it has been estimated that the population was somewhere between 200 and 350.

With knowledge from archaeological sites, an interesting project in experimental archaeology was undertaken in 1970. It is the Butser Ancient Farm Research Center and open-air museum, which was developed as a sort of laboratory in which to test premises from archaeological excavations. The center was relocated twice and now stands at the site of Windmill Hill. Through the years, scholars have reconstructed an Iron Age farm and houses, enclosures, and other structures using only the tools and methods that would have been available to Iron Age communities. Founded under the auspices of the Council for British Archaeology, this project has been central to our understanding of Iron Age Britain. Volunteers have grown crops such as those that would have been used in the Iron Age including spelt and emmer wheat. The Butser experiment indicated that grain yields were very high (as much as 1.1 tons per acre), and thus perhaps it was possible that the ancient Britons had enough grain surplus to export, something mentioned in Roman documents, but viewed skeptically until this project.

Tools were also tested at Butser, and knowledge was gained through actual experience that could not have been attained otherwise. For example, it had been thought that sickles were used to harvest grain as they were in later periods, but the experimental archaeologists soon determined that plucking the

Replica of Iron Age dwelling from Butser Ancient Farm, an outdoor open-air museum and experimental archaeology research site located near Petersfield in Hampshire, England. The research work at Butser has provided many clues about how people lived and farmed during the Iron Age.

grains by hand was much more efficient. Similarly, documentation had suggested that Iron Age farmers used cows to pull the light plow called an *ard*, but this had been dismissed as unlikely. The Butser farmers brought in Dexter cows (the closest relative to the now extinct Celtic shorthorn), tried using them with the ard, and found that it worked very well. The cows had both the needed strength and docility; moreover, they would have provided milk for the owner's family.

Textile production was another subject for study at Butser. It became clear that the deep holes located by the sidewall of Iron Age houses worked perfectly to support the legs of a vertical loom and allowed the cloth to be made wider by extending the amount of space from the bottom of the loom to the height that could be reached for weaving. Soay sheep from the Scottish island of St. Kilda were also brought to Butser. Because of the remote island location, the bloodline of the sheep had continued unchanged for at least two thousand years, and they approximate very nearly the sheep used by Iron Age Celts. Experiments with their wool revealed much about ancient textile production. Like Icelandic sheep, Soay sheep produce wool that is plucked rather than shorn and handles differently through both the spinning and weaving processes. The fabric produced at Butser closely matches fabric samples that have been found at burial sites.

The discoveries at Butser vary from major importance (two to three men could indeed build a Celtic house) to minor (mysterious indentations inside the door sills of Iron Age houses were probably made by chickens rolling in the dirt after a rainstorm), but all give us information that we would not have otherwise. It should be observed that experimental archaeology is rarely definitive—it does not tell us that people of the past did things a certain way, but it does tell us that they could have done it that way, and sometimes that is enough to answer a question or lead to further research.

Other archaeological evidence that has been extremely useful in trying to understand Iron Age Britain is the wide range of artifacts found in burial sites. The Celts favored inhumation and often included an assortment of grave goods at burial sites, such as shields, swords, and spears (presumably for male burials) and jewelry and textile tools (for female burials). The British sites do not have the sheer magnificence of some of those of the continental Celts such as the Hochdorf burial or that of the so-called Lady of Vix (usually cited as the best examples of La Tène burials). At the site at Hochdorf in Germany, which can be dated to 530 BCE, the body of a chieftain was accompanied by gold and amber jewelry, a dagger, a comb and clippers, fishhooks, and clothing decorations. Even more impressively, the body of the Lady of Vix, interred in a chariot burial that can be dated to around 500 BCE in the south of France, was accompanied by a remarkably rich collection of artifacts including numerous examples of jewelry and an enormous bronze krater. Although the British examples are more modest, they show a similar pattern of chariot burials and the inclusion of jewelry, weapons, and household artifacts with the deceased. An unusual site is the Snettisham Hoard in East Anglia, which seems not to have been a burial site, but rather a repository for valuables. Inside an enclosure ditch were five separate hoards of gold ingots and broken jewelry (evidently intended to be melted and recast) along with sixty-three gold torques and an assortment of other gold objects. Archaeologists are unsure how and why the collection was amassed (perhaps votive offerings or a tribal treasury), but it provides a fascinating catalogue of Iron Age gold work.

One other category of Iron Age burial site that has produced more questions than answers is the bog burials that have been found across Britain. Scandinavian examples are perhaps better known, but Britain has at least eighty documented examples. Unfortunately some of these were found in the eighteenth and nineteenth centuries and evidence from these sites no longer exists. However, the chance finding of a body in Lindow Marsh in 1984 combined with new methods in forensic archaeology produced a dramatic case study that caught the media's attention at the time and continues to puzzle those who have studied it. The subject was a young male whose remains consisted of a torso, head, and foot. A leg and part of a lower body found a few years later probably belong with the other remains. He was subjected to all manner of scientific observation: CT scans, MRIs, endoscopy, radiography, and other tests. Forensic reconstruction has given us a model of his face: a handsome dark-haired Celt in his mid-twenties. What the scientists did not expect was the manner of his death. He had been struck on the head, two blows that were sufficiently violent to chip one of his molars, his neck was broken (apparently by a sinew garotte that was still in place), and he had been stabbed in the carotid artery.

The elaborate and unnecessarily multiplied causes of death made it plain that this was unlikely to have been a simple murder. Scandinavian bog burials have often been associated with executions, and that is a possibility for Lindow Man (or Pete Marsh as he was nicknamed by the British media). Perhaps even more disturbing is the possibility that he may have been a ritual sacrifice. His stomach contained fragments of charred bread (which literary evidence tells us was sometimes used for drawing lots) and mistletoe pollen (associated with magical rites of the druids or pagan priests). The body shows no evidence that he resisted his fate, and his hands (with carefully manicured fingernails typical of an elite who did no manual labor) show no evidence of having been bound, suggesting that he may have been a willing participant. One historian has argued, based on his hands and the mistletoe, that he might have been a druid himself, although this hypothesis has not met general acceptance. It is unknown exactly when he died; carbon dating of the body and the surrounding peat yields different dates. It is possible that the burial might have been as late as the period of Roman occupation, but more likely it is an Iron Age burial.

The mysteries surrounding the death of Lindow Man remind us of how little we know of the religious practices of the Iron Age Celts. We know that there were temple sites that both predate and postdate the Romans, and there is some indication of a cult of severed heads associated with certain sacred wells, springs, and rivers. Most of our information about Celtic gods and goddesses comes from the Continent, from later literary sources, and from biased Roman sources; therefore, it is extremely inconclusive. Although archaeology has told us a great deal about the daily life of the Iron Age Celts, much of their mental landscape remains conjectural.

When the Romans first arrived in Britain it is quite possible that the Celts knew more about the Romans than the Romans knew about the Celts. We know that there was active Romano-British trade prior to Caesar's time (particularly the tin trade of Cornwall and the trade involving other goods from the south of Britain).There is also at least some probability that the tribes that descended from the Belgae on both sides of the channel maintained some communication and trade relations with each other. Part of Caesar's motivation in launching his invasion was the fear that British Celts might be providing refuge and resources to the Gauls. Nonetheless, when Caesar embarked for Britain in 55 BCE with ten thousand men and five hundred cavalry it was an expedition into essentially unknown territory.

SUGGESTED READING

Bottigheimer, Karl. *Ireland and the Irish: A Short History.* New York: Columbia University Press, 1982.

Bradley, Richard. *The Prehistoric Settlement of Britain.* Henley-on-Thames, UK: Routledge & Kegan Paul, 1978.

Brown, Dale. *The Celts: Europe's People of Iron.* Alexandria, VA: Time-Life, 1994.

Chadwick, Nora. *The Celts.* London: Penguin Books, 1971.

Crossley-Holland, Kevin, and Andrew Rafferty. *The Stones Remain: Megalithic Sites of Britain.* London: Rider, 1989.

Cunliffe, Barry. *The Celts: A Very Short Introduction.* Oxford: Oxford University Press, 2003.

Darvill, Timothy. *Prehistoric Britain.* New Haven, CT: Yale University Press, 1987.

Hawkins, Gerald. *Stonehenge Decoded.* Garden City, NY: Hippocrene Books, 1965.

Herity, Michael, and George Eogan. *Ireland in Prehistory.* London: Routledge, 1977.

James, Simon. *The World of the Celts.* London: Thames & Hudson, 1993.

Kearney, Hugh. *The British Isles: A History of Four Nations.* Cambridge: Cambridge University Press, 1989.

O'Kelly, Michael J. *Early Ireland: An Introduction to Irish Prehistory.* Cambridge: Cambridge University Press, 1989.

Ross, Anne, and Don Robins. *The Life and Death of a Druid Prince: The Story of Lindow Man, an Archaeological Sensation.* New York: Summit Books, 1989.

Chapter 2

Roman Britain

This chapter explores the coming of the Romans to the British Isles, their immediate impact on the different regions, and the long-term legacies brought by the Romans. With the Romans, we begin the historic period of the peoples of the British Isles because the Romans produced written sources, albeit often biased and limited to very specific geographical regions.

THE BEGINNING OF THE ROMAN CONQUEST

Caesar's motivation for invading the British Isles is not altogether clear. He had defeated the Belgae in Gaul two years earlier, in 57 BCE, and may have thought of the British campaign as merely an extension of that conquest. It is also possible that he had heard of the mineral wealth of the British Isles, and he certainly was interested in any military exploit that would counter the successes of his rival Pompey in the east. The campaign nearly proved to be a disaster. Caesar was unable to find a suitable harbor, the mighty cliffs of Dover were well defended by the native inhabitants, and a storm wrecked many of his ships soon after they landed on a beach near Deal. It is a tribute to Caesar's great leadership that he was able to hold things together until repairs were made and his troops evacuated to Gaul. From his point of view, though, it was not a complete loss. The Kentish chiefs had submitted (fearing the numbers of Roman invaders) and perhaps most importantly he had learned firsthand how the Celts fought and what kind of supplies might be available. He planned another campaign for the following year.

In July 54 BCE Caesar again set sail, this time with eight hundred ships and twenty-five thousand legionaries. He landed unopposed, defeated the Britons at Stour, and was now able to penetrate north of the Thames. Although some of his ships were again damaged, he was able to pursue his victory and partly through exploiting intertribal hostilities and partly through military strength he was able to gain the support of the Trinovantes in Essex, along with some other smaller tribal groups, and attack the stronghold of his most powerful opponent, Cassivellanus, chieftain of the Catuvellauni. The confrontation was inconclusive. An uprising in Gaul demanded Caesar's attention and Cassivellanus was in no hurry to have his strength tested by the Roman legionaries. It suited both men for the British chieftain to accept the status of client king, agreeing to pay tribute to Rome and acknowledge Roman supremacy while in reality maintaining his effective local sovereignty and power. When Caesar sailed away with his troops, it is quite likely that he intended to return and secure a real victory, but other events intervened. In 44 BCE Caesar was assassinated and Britain was free of Roman military influences for almost a century.

THE CLAUDIAN INVASION

In 43 CE the Emperor Claudius decided on a new invasion. His predecessor, Caligula, evidently had had some thought of a second British conquest, going so far as to muster a Roman army on the Gaulish side of the channel. Unstable as ever, Caligula suddenly called off the invasion, saying, according to legend, that the ocean had now been conquered and his soldiers were ordered to pick up the *spoils* (seashells) on the beach. Caligula was assassinated shortly thereafter, and according to at least one historian of Roman Britain, Claudius may have felt the need to restore some degree of respect for the army and the office of the emperor. In any case, he knew he could use a military victory to bolster his own rather shaky hold on the throne, and it seemed to be in the interests of Roman security to subdue the overly independent British chieftains. He mustered four legions (the II Augusta, IX Hispana, XIV Gemina, and XX Valeria Victrix), all hardened veterans, along with loyal auxiliaries and set sail for Britain. The timing of this invasion was good from the Roman point of view. The client king of the Belgae, Cunobelinus (Shakespeare's Cymbeline), had just died, leaving a power struggle among several of the rival British tribes. After a decisive Roman victory near Durobrivae (Rochester), many of the tribes agreed to submit. Claudius came in person (staying only sixteen days), established a new Roman capital at Camulodunum (Colchester), and received the submissions of the tribal chieftains, among them Praesutagus of the Iceni tribe. Claudius sailed back to Rome, confident of the success of the British conquest.

BOUDICCA AND THE REVOLT OF THE ICENI

The illusion of easy success was shattered in 61 CE by a massive rebellion of the Iceni tribe under the startling leadership (by Roman standards) of the queen of the Iceni, Boudicca (or Boadicea). She was the widow of Praesutagus, who had offered his submission to the Romans. When he died in 59 CE he left behind a will. It was drawn up in Roman style, not binding by Celtic law but addressing what he clearly (and rightly) thought would be the likely annexation of his land by the Romans upon his death. His will left half of his land to the Roman emperor and half to his two teenage daughters. By this time Claudius had been assassinated and a new Roman emperor was on the throne, Nero. Nero had sent a new governor-general (Suetonius Paulinus) to Britain the year before Praesutagus's death. His orders were to subdue the still-rebellious British and extend the Roman conquest.

Statue of Boudicca on London Bridge. The 1850 statue of the warrior queen, located at Victoria Embankment at Westminster Bridge, commemorates the rising of the British Iceni tribe against the Romans in 60–61 CE. Boudicca has become an important symbol of British identity.

Wales and Scotland were seen as the greatest problems. It was assumed that the south was safely under Roman control, but that had already proven to be wrong when a major revolt by the druid priests at Anglesea shook Roman confidence. Roman sources describe the havoc: "Druid priests raised their arms to heaven, shouting prayers and curses. Along with them were fanatical women, dressed in black, their hair disheveled and torches in their hands who ran about screaming and shouting in an ecstasy of fury." Suetonius quickly gained the upper hand as the legionaries stabbed and trampled underfoot the druids and women. The sacred oak groves of the druids were then burned, and one cannot help but wonder if the superstitious Romans were still hearing the druid curses when news came of the new revolt of Boudicca and the Iceni.

In spite of Praesutagus's will, the kingdom of the Iceni had been invaded by the Romans (probably acting without orders from Suetonius). In the mayhem that followed, his widow, Queen Boudicca, was stripped and flogged and her two teenage daughters were raped before her eyes. We know nothing of Boudicca prior to these events. One Roman source noted that "the Britons were accustomed to female war leaders," and certainly the Celtic literary tradition contains martial queens. In any case, we have a dramatic, if unsubstantiated description by the Roman Dio Cassio of Boudicca taking command:

> She was very tall, and her aspect was terrifying, for her eyes flashed fiercely and her voice was harsh. A mass of red hair fell down to her hips, and around her neck was a twisted gold necklace: over a tunic of many colors she wore a thick mantle fastened with a brooch—this was her invariable attire. Now she clutched a spear to help her strike fear into all beholders, and spoke to the rebel tribes.

The Iceni warriors did not question her authority to lead and they went on to soundly defeat the Romans at the town of Camulodunum (Colchester). Boudicca and her army then began retaking land that had been held by the Romans, gathering new support from other British tribes. By the time Suetonius finally arrived with the Ninth legion it was essentially too late. Boudicca swept on to London and her troops triumphantly set fire to the city. Archaeological evidence provides clear proof of the impact of the rebellion. Suetonius fell back on Verulamium (St. Albans) and Boudicca's army followed in pursuit. According to Tacitus, the confidence of the British was the source of their undoing: "They were so full of confidence they had even brought along their wives to witness their victory, stationing them on wagons arranged around the extreme edge of the battlefield." The Romans had dug a deep trench, and from it they burst in a great wedge formation. Boudicca's army turned to retreat and found its own wagons blocking the way. The Romans cut down all the Britons they could find—both the warriors and the wives—and Tacitus says that more than eighty thousand Britons were killed that day. Boudicca herself was neither killed nor taken alive. Dio Cassio says that "she fell ill and died," but Tacitus says more bluntly that "the queen ended her life with poison," a not unlikely response to the fear of being taken by the Romans as a humiliated captive.

EXTENSION OF THE ROMAN CONQUEST

Although the Iceni rebellion had seriously challenged the Roman conquest of Britain, it did not end the Roman occupation or expansion. Under the Flavian emperors (from CE 69 to 96) Roman authority was extended into Wales and to the Scottish borders. Fortresses were built to protect the Roman garrisons in strategic locations (including settlements that would become Lincoln, York, Carleon, Cardiff, and Carmarthen). Under Agricola, governor of Britain in the 80s, the Roman expansion was extended as far into Scotland as Loch Lomond. There he secured approaches from the Highlands by a line of eight forts. The Romans marched farther northward and in 84 CE met resistance from the Scottish tribes at the Battle of Mons Graupius. It is still under debate where this was located. The Romans at this battle used the unusual strategy of sending in auxiliaries first (probably viewing them as more expendable) and holding the hardened legionaries in reserve. It was a decisive victory for the Romans, now securing their northern flank. Agricola himself soon returned to Rome, but he left behind an enormous legacy. In addition to the forts (at least sixty) and the roads he had built (at least thirteen hundred miles), he had extended policies aimed at the cultural Romanization of the Britons. Tacitus (his not unbiased son-in-law) noted that

> Agricola encouraged individuals and helped communities to build temples, fora, and houses. . . . Further he trained the sons of the chiefs in the liberal arts and expressed a preference for British natural ability over the trained abilities of the Gauls. The result was that the people who used to reject the Roman language began to aspire to rhetoric. Further the wearing of our national dress came to be esteemed and the toga came into fashion. And so little by little, the Britons were seduced into alluring vices: arcades, baths, and sumptuous banquets. In their simplicity they called such vices "civilization," when in reality they were part of their enslavement.

In other parts of the empire the Romans had used urbanization as one of their governing tactics. However, the landscape and culture of the British Isles did not as easily promote the building of *coloniae* (settlements of Roman citizens) or *municipia* (settlements with more limited Roman rights). The higher incidence of Roman-style towns in the south, complete with temples, baths, and

Roman baths at Bath, England. Although many of the more elaborate forms of Roman architecture cannot be found in Britain, the Roman baths at Bath provide us with a good illustration of some of the influences of Roman civility that existed there during the Roman period. The site has been restored and visitors can explore the Bath house, temple, springs, and museum.

the occasional villa, reflects both land better suited to urban settlement than the rugged terrains of Wales and Scotland and a longer more or less continuous Roman cultural influence.

In the north and west, Agricola's victories were followed closely by a major change in Roman policy. In Rome Emperor Domitian was faced with attacks on the German frontiers and the British legionaries were needed there. He withdrew the entire Second legion, leaving Britain to be governed by greatly reduced forces. The conclusion was obvious: the extent of the British occupation had likewise to be reduced. Tacitus, saddened by the loss of Agricola's gains, commented, "the conquest of Britain was completed and immediately let go."

Although the decision had been made to effectively abandon the north, disturbances continued along the Clyde-Forth frontier. By around 105 CE the Emperor Trajan had moved the frontier farther south (along the Tyne to the Solway Firth). His successor, Hadrian, traveled to Britain himself to assess the situation. He brought with him a new legion, the VI Victrix, to replace the IX Hispana. (The Ninth is the so-called lost legion that vanished completely from history, perhaps destroyed by a northern insurrection or perhaps moved elsewhere in the empire and then destroyed.) Hadrian determined that the best course of action was to build a great wall across the northern frontier to protect the southern provinces from northern rebellion. This involved moving approximately two million tons of rock and dirt. The work was done by the legionaries themselves, resulting in a wall eight feet thick and fifteen feet high. There were fortified observation posts spaced a mile apart and sixteen forts interspersed along the wall. Behind the line a ditch was dug, twenty feet wide and ten feet deep. The wall required 9,500 men to garrison it. Still the disturbances continued and a few years later Antonius Pius (Hadrian's successor) built a new wall farther north (the Antonine Wall, along the Clyde-Forth line). The fortifications along the Antonine Wall were closer together and more heavily garrisoned than

Hadrian's Wall, showing one of the adjoining forts. The Romans built the seventy-three-mile-long wall between 122 and 128 CE in an attempt to secure their northern frontier during the Conquest of Britain. In 142 another wall (the Antonine Wall) was built farther to the north.

those of Hadrian's Wall. It was abandoned shortly thereafter (presumably because of more disturbances and a lack of Roman manpower), reoccupied, and then abandoned permanently in 162 CE.

THE END OF ROMAN OCCUPATION

Efforts were made to hold the frontier at Hadrian's Wall, but by the second century the Romans were having serious troubles both at home and throughout their far-flung empire. Septimius tried to reconquer British territory in the north but could not defeat the Caledonian guerrilla-style warfare. When he died at York, his son Caracalla abandoned Scotland and later granted rights of citizenship to all Roman subjects, including those of Britain.

The remaining period of Roman occupation was characterized by ongoing raids from the north, periodic efforts to subdue them, and a gradual withdrawal of Roman troops to other areas of the empire where they were more needed. In 410 CE the British appealed to the Emperor Honorius to protect them from the Saxons. They were told to provide for their own defense. Roman Britain as a political entity had come to an end.

IMPACT OF THE ROMANS

Economically, socially, and culturally, however, Roman influences in Britain had been indelibly established. Especially in the south, new towns had been founded based on a structural and social organization unknown to the pre-Roman inhabitants of Britain. London was the most significant in terms of population, extent, and trade, but towns such as St. Albans, Cirencester, Gloucester, and Winchester were to be of great importance in subsequent British history. (Note that the place-name suffix *cester* or *chester* provides evidence of Roman origins, deriving from the Latin word *castrum* or camp.) Lincoln (Lindum) was one of the few coloniae in Britain, and Bath (Aquae Sulis) is in many ways a model Roman town. Roman establishments at Canterbury (Durovernum Cantiacorum) and York (Eboracum) provided the foundation for later archbishoprics.

Although the Roman roads and aqueducts in Britain are small in scale compared to continental examples, nonetheless they show the introduction of new technologies brought by the Romans. There is archaeological evidence at Silchester (Calleva Atrebatum) of a hydraulic pump, and water lines and drain systems can be traced in most of the Roman towns. Public latrines and bathhouses were established, and as Tacitus observed, the natives soon became fond of such civilities. Amphitheaters were also built for entertainments. The one at Canterbury is estimated to have been built to hold an audience of seven thousand. We know that they housed plays and other performances, and in Britain it is likely they were also the setting for combats and races. (The more specifically designed circus does not seem to have existed in Roman Britain.)

In addition, Roman towns contained shops and governmental buildings. We know that there were many imported items in Britain, but there also seems

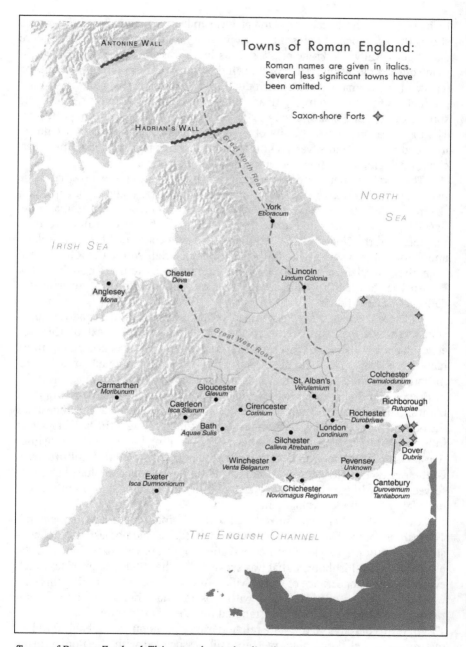

ANTONINE WALL

Towns of Roman England:

Roman names are given in italics. Several less significant towns have been omitted.

HADRIAN'S WALL

Saxon-shore Forts ✦

Great North Road

NORTH

SEA

IRISH SEA

York
Eboracum

Chester
Deva

Lincoln
Lindum Colonia

Anglesey
Mona

Great West Road

Colchester
Camulodunum

Carmarthen
Moribunum

Gloucester
Glevum

St. Alban's
Verulamium

Caerleon
Isca Silurum

Cirencester
Corinium

Richborough
Rutupiae

Rochester
Durobrivae

Bath
Aquae Sulis

London
Londinium

Silchester
Calleva Atrebatum

Dover
Dubris

Winchester
Venta Belgarum

Pevensey
Unknown

Exeter
Isca Dumnoniorum

Cantebury
*Durovernum
Tantiaborum*

Chichester
Noviomagus Reginorum

THE ENGLISH CHANNEL

Towns of Roman England. This map shows the distribution and placement of the most important towns of Roman England, along with their modern place-names. Note that the majority of them are clustered around the southern coast of England. The ones to the north and west were usually located on roads created for strategic and trade purposes. There were no Roman towns established in Ireland or north of the Antonine Wall.

to have been a significant amount of local industry. Archaeological evidence shows the existence of goldsmiths' shops, and bronze and silver articles were also made locally. We know of glassworks in Lancashire and pottery works in many different locations. The finest of all these products were imported, but the legacy of the Romans was the introduction of new materials, techniques, and products. A tomb found in St. Albans (likely belonging to Adminius, one of the sons of Cunobelinus) shows the mixture of material culture in Roman Britain. The tomb was located at the site of a pagan Celtic shrine, but the grave goods included an ivory and silver reclining couch, a thirty-piece Roman dinner set, chain mail, and four amphorae of imported Roman wine.

The establishment and continuation of both internal and external trade networks was somewhat dependent on shifting political realities, but many of the markets and trade routes persisted even after the end of formal Roman rule. Specialized items such as Purbeck marble and Whitby jet continued to have markets, and the trade in hides, textiles, and slaves continued between Ireland and Britain and in some cases to the Continent as well. Where the Romans had been they also left a legacy of coinage. Roman coins found throughout the British Isles attest to the ubiquity of their use and often provide evidence for dating of other artifacts.

Culturally, one of the biggest impacts of the Romans was the gradual expansion of the use of Latin by the native population. To some extent this was encouraged by the Roman government, but a certain degree of acceptance must have come simply from the necessary use of a common language in daily life. Although Latin did not become the foundation of the British language as it did in France and Spain, nonetheless evidence of its spread can be seen in place-names, personal names, and in words related to the concepts and industries introduced into Britain by the Romans. Interestingly enough, the lack of Roman influences in Ireland may well have been a contributing influence in the distinctive and significant development of the Irish language and literary culture. Irish Gaelic represents the oldest vernacular tradition in Europe, developed and preserved at least in part because of a lack of other contending literary influences until fairly late in its development.

Other cultural changes introduced by the Romans were fairly ephemeral. The fashion for wearing the toga mentioned by Tacitus did not last, and the construction of Roman-style villas never really caught on. One exception was the beautiful villa at Fishbourne that was excavated in the 1960s and provides much evidence of the appearance of British villas. As elsewhere in the empire, this villa was built around a central garden, with mosaics and other architectural decoration. Another villa, at Woodchester, had more than sixty rooms.

In terms of religion, the state religion was never popular (probably for obvious reasons) and the various mystery cults associated with the Roman army (such as the cults of Fortuna and Mithras) vanished with the armies. There is some evidence that observances at the temples of Isis and Minerva may have briefly persisted. The continued use of some temple sites may simply indicate that, although Roman temples may have been built there, these sites were still regarded as sacred to Celtic gods and goddesses and so observance was revived when the Romans left.

Arguably the most significant impact of the Romans in the British Isles was the introduction or extension of Christianity. The exact date of its foundation is uncertain. References exist that attribute the founding of Christianity in Britain to sources other than the Romans, with apocryphal traditions of visits by St. Peter and Joseph of Arimathea. Tertullian remarked cryptically in 206 CE that "parts of Britain inaccessible to the Romans [Ireland and/or Scotland?] have been subjected to Christ," and Bede records the martyrdom of three Christian Britons during the time of Diocletian. However, tantalizing as these references may be, they are impossible to prove. What we know for certain is that three British archbishops are identified as attending the Council of Arles in 314 CE, and both archaeological and literary evidence show that the Church was well established in Britain by the fourth century, bringing about a rapid transformation in society, as will be discussed in chapter 3.

BRITAIN AFTER THE ROMANS

In her book of fiction *The Lantern Bearers* (1959), Rosemary Sutcliff provides us with a poignant image of the departure of the Romans from Britain, with her British-born legionary hero deserting at the last moment and remaining behind to light the beacon at Rutupiae to give the illusion that Britain was still protected by the Romans. Sutcliff has her fictional hero comment: "We are the lantern bearers . . . [it is] for us to keep something burning, to carry what light we can forward against the darkness and the wind." Of course, there was no single dramatic moment of departure and no proof that those left behind had any such feelings. Yet, Sutcliff's words ring true when one looks at Britain in the years after the end of Roman occupation. It fell to the native chieftains to deal with the Saxon invasions, and the shadowy figures of Ambrosius and Arthurus (conflated in later romances into the heroic King Arthur) probably belong to the fifth century if they existed at all. The story of the actual Arthur, the location of his city of Camelot, and his wars and legal reforms will probably always remain more the fabric of legend than of history (although many archaeologists and historians have tried to find provable evidence of the historic Arthur), but the survival of the tradition is arguably more important than its historical foundation. In the earliest accounts (not to be confused with the later twelfth century romances) King Arthur became the symbol of identity for the Britons, the lantern bearers who carried forward many of the legacies of the Romans, but now emerged as a new people, forging their own identity and history.

SUGGESTED READING

Allason-Jones, Lindsay. *Women in Roman Britain*. London: British Museum Press, 1989.
Birley, Anthony. *The People of Roman Britain*. New York: Batsford, 1979.

Cunliffe, Barry. *Fishbourne: A Roman Palace and Its Garden*. Baltimore, MD: Johns
　　Hopkins University Press, 1971.
————. *Roman Bath Discovered*. New York: Routledge, 1984.
Fry, Plantagenet Somerset. *Roman Britain*. Totowa, NJ: David & Charles, 1984.
Henig, M. E. *Religion in Roman Britain*. New York: St. Martin's Press, 1984.
Hingley, Richard. *Rural Settlement in Roman Britain*. London: Batsford, 1989.
Lacy, Norris J., ed. *The New Arthurian Encyclopedia*. New York: Garland, 1996.
Maxwell, G. S. *The Romans in Scotland*. Edinburgh: Mercat Press, 1989.
Morris, John. *Londinium: London in the Roman Empire*. London: Weidenfeld &
　　Nicolson History, 1982.
Salway, Peter. *The Oxford Illustrated History of Roman Britain*. Oxford: Oxford
　　University Press, 1993.
Scullard, H. H. *Roman Britain: Outpost of the Empire*. London: Thames & Hudson,
　　1979.
Todd, Malcolm, *Roman Britain*, 3rd ed. London: Wiley-Blackwell, 1999.

Chapter 3

Early Christian Britain

With the demise of the Roman Empire much of the infrastructure and, at least to some degree, the shared social and cultural patterns that had bound together the regions under Roman rule faltered and declined. In the absence of any overarching political organization, regions turned to tribal leadership and regional cultural practices. Local languages and law codes predominated and decentralization was a characteristic theme of the transitional period between late antiquity and the early Middle Ages. The one major exception to this pattern was the emergence of Christianity and Christian scholarship as a unifying force. Although agreement as to church laws and common practices required many years to achieve, the early Christian focus on preserving and extending the knowledge and beauty of the ancient world was a glimmer of light in a dark time in history. Thomas Cahill titled his 1995 book *How the Irish Saved Civilization*. It can be argued that his concept is an overstatement, but there is much accuracy in the idea that the early Christians in Britain, the islands on the northern edge of the world, contributed greatly to the survival and reemergence of learning and with their efforts provided a new force of centralization in Western Europe.

THE ARRIVAL OF CHRISTIANITY IN BRITAIN

Although it seems as if it should be a simple question, the date when Christianity arrived in the British Isles is very difficult to establish. It would be logical to assume that it came with the Romans, but both written sources and traditions would seem to indicate otherwise. The most persistent tradition of Christianity arriving in Britain with Joseph of Arimathea, the wealthy Jew who gave his own tomb to Christ, is intriguing but unprovable.

Glastonbury, where Joseph supposedly settled, was a major prehistoric settlement, and it had been taken over by the Romans during the Claudian conquests, primarily because of its proximity to silver and lead deposits that they used for export and for building the great spa at Bath. Glastonbury was conveniently located near the Bristol Channel, and it stood near the road from Exeter to Lincoln. It was not a major center of Roman settlement, although Roman artifacts, some with Christian inscriptions, have been found in the vicinity. It is quite possible that Glastonbury may have been a sacred pagan site, and some of the traditions associated with Joseph and with the later Arthurian mythos may have been conflated accounts of local sanctity joined with the Christian apocrypha. Of Joseph himself, there is no proof, although one historian points out the interesting fact that the supposed route of the saint's journey from Marseilles to Limoges, to Brittany, and to Cornwall is precisely the route of the early tin trade. One particular local tradition makes Joseph a tin merchant (presumably learning his trade after arrival) and recounts how Jesus, during his "lost years," became his apprentice and so was present in Britain himself. Traditions surrounding the wonder-working Holy Thorn (supposedly the very thorn tree that sprouted where Joseph's staff was planted) and the Chalice Well (associated with the traditions of the Holy Grail, the communion cup used by Christ at the Last Supper) seem to date only from the twelfth century, when the abbey was undoubtedly promoting itself as a pilgrimage site. By the late Middle Ages, Glastonbury was deeply embedded in the Arthurian romances as the place where unspoiled Christianity (as represented by the Holy Grail) had been established and the place where the Isle of Avalon, the quasi-sacred final resting place of King Arthur and Queen Guinevere, could be found.

Although we know that the legend of Glastonbury is undoubtedly just that, there is a possibility that its persistence in local folk tradition may indicate some surviving memory that Christianity arrived in Britain very early. As previously mentioned, there is the tantalizing comment by Tertullian in 206 CE that Christianity had been established in "regions inaccessible to the Romans." Bede, the great eighth century ecclesiastical historian, tells us of three British martyrdoms during the Great Persecutions of the Roman Emperor Diocletian (beginning in 303 CE), including those of Aaron and Julius of Caerleon and Alban, who gave his name, St. Albans, to the Roman city of Verulamium. Some historians suggest that these martyrdoms might actually have occurred earlier, circa 208–09 CE. We know definitely that there were British representatives at the Council of Arles in 314 and again at Rimini in 359 CE. Clearly by the time Constantine officially sanctioned Christianity in the Roman Empire in 313 CE there were established flourishing Christian communities in the British Isles.

Unfortunately, Tertullian does not tell us which regions inaccessible to the Romans he meant. Although Roman occupation had penetrated into Wales and lowland Scotland, there were certainly many regions in both places remaining inaccessible, and Ireland, completely untouched by the Romans aside from minor trade, is also a contender. The third and fourth centuries are sparsely represented in our sources, but even so there is evidence of contact with the Continent and the development of several different centers of Christianity in the British Isles.

EARLY CHRISTIANITY IN WALES

Although it is clear that Christianity was established early in the Celtic-speaking regions of Wales, Ireland, Scotland, Cornwall, and Brittany, it must be emphasized that there was no monolithic "Celtic" religion common to all of them. Especially because the word Celtic has often been used (and misused) by

New Age enthusiasts, it is essential to understand that many later ideas have been grafted onto what we know of this early period. Our sources are unclear, often dating to hagiographies written several hundred years after the supposed life of a saint. These sources are also not unbiased because accounts were often written to uphold later ownership or traditions associated with churches and shrines. A good example is the account of the patron saint of Wales, St. David, of whom we know only the most shadowy details. The stories of his miracles and his establishment of a church independent of Canterbury come from a twelfth century manuscript and likely reflect more of the religious and political realities of that period than those of the early Middle Ages.

Hagiographies of other Welsh saints follow many of the same traditions that we see with British and continental saints. It was claimed that, when St. Sampson (a Welsh-born saint) was consecrated as bishop, fire (presumably holy) came from his mouth. St. Cadoc was believed to be able to help women to conceive. The shrine of the probably seventh century St. Winifred was much venerated by the Welsh throughout the Middle Ages. Hers was a gory story. Her would-be lover, Caradoc, was enraged when she rejected him and told him she was going to become a nun. In anger he decapitated her. Her uncle, St. Beuno, brought her back to life, but the place where her head had landed produced a holy spring (called Holywell), which became the most visited shrine in Wales, famous for its many miracles.

Although the stories are more folkloric than historic, we do know that there were a number of very active Welsh missionaries. Between the fifth and eighth centuries Christianity spread beyond the urbanized areas of the southeast where it was more firmly established, probably due at least in part to the efforts of Welsh monks. One historian has argued that, even though the concept of "Celtic Christianity" is misleading, there may have been a seafaring Atlantic connection that brought together British Celts, Bretons, and Galicians. Certainly there is evidence that the Welsh missionaries in wooden boats brought their message to the pagan populations of Cornwall, Devon, Somerset, and possibly Ireland and likely were strongly involved in the conversion of those regions.

THE SAINTS OF IRELAND: PATRICK AND BRIGID

Perhaps the best known religious figure of early Christian Britain is St. Patrick. His Vita is well known. He was born to a Christianized Roman family in Britain around the year 387 on the estate of Bannavern Taburniae. Where exactly this place may have been is still debated, perhaps either in Scotland or Wales. His grandfather (or father or uncle according to various traditions) was a priest. When he was sixteen he was captured by the Irish as a slave and spent six lonely years as a shepherd. In his *Confessio*, Patrick wrote, "On a certain night I heard in my sleep a voice saying to me 'you are fasting well, and you are very soon going to your homeland' . . . soon afterwards I heard the voice say to me 'look, your ship is ready.'" A real ship stood nearby. Patrick fled to the ship and landed in either Britain or Gaul. The tradition of his landing in Lerins

(Gaul) is plausible. A monastery had been established there around 400, and its style of monasticism accords well with what we know of Patrick's views. Although born Christian, Patrick would have been educated and ordained before undertaking his Irish mission.

The traditional date given for Patrick's arrival in Ireland is 432 CE, but it is possible that the date is more symbolic than actual, coinciding with the Council of Ephesus. What many people do not know is that Patrick was the second bishop of Ireland, not the first. Palladius was the first, and he was sent with orders from Pope Celestine in 431 to be bishop to "those of the Irish who believe in Christ," clearly indicating that Christianity had arrived in Ireland prior to this time. Palladius's time in Ireland was brief. Little is known about him, but he almost certainly was not Irish and he departed in less than a year, perhaps establishing a mission at Galloway in Scotland prior to his return to Rome. Thus, the popular image of Patrick as the founder of Christianity in Ireland does not accord with the sources, and the brief mission of Palladius simply highlights the question of how the earliest Christians in Ireland became Christianized.

Even if he was not the founder of Christianity in Ireland, St. Patrick's status as the patron saint of Ireland seems well warranted as evidenced by his predominant role in Irish tradition. Realistically, many of the stories associated with him are later additions and some are conflations with other saints' lives or other traditional stories. For example, the often-repeated story of St. Patrick driving

Shrine of St. Patrick's bell. Relics of the early Irish saints often consisted of articles that they used rather than corporeal remains. A simple bell was often used to call people together for mass. Later on these artifacts were often encased in elaborate gold and silver shrines, both to protect the article and to provide a focus of veneration.

the snakes out of Ireland is connected with a generic folk motif in which the holy man defeats the power of evil as represented by the serpent. Sober science tells us that it was the Ice Age and not the saint that rid Ireland of reptiles. However, even if the specific stories may or may not have been contemporaneous or true, the sheer volume of traditions surrounding St. Patrick testify to his immense impact on Ireland. There are myriad places and place-names associated with him (St. Patrick's Purgatory, Croagh Patrick, Downpatrick, and many others) that are traceable to later centers of Irish spirituality. Although the conversion process of the Irish is obscure, the prominent motif in the stories, the conversion of the Irish through Patrick's ability to defeat the competing magic of the Irish druids, probably reflects some degree of political and social reality.

We know from a combination of archaeological, literary, and historical sources that Irish society was rigidly stratified. With no impact from Roman structures, political organization remained tribal, with supreme local authority resting in the clan chief, who presided over his small kingdom of retainers including warriors, professionals (the *aes dána* or hereditary educated elites), farmers, servants, and slaves. The aes dána were defined by both rank and specialty—a high poet required at least fifteen years of education to be an *ollamh* (a professor who could teach), and although our sources are not clear for the pre-Christian era, it is likely that the education of the pre-Christian priests would have been similar. (Incidentally, the term druid comes from Roman sources concerning Gaul and is so fraught with historical debate that it is usually avoided by modern Irish scholars.) What is clear is that conversion of the Irish was dependent on the acceptance of the faith by both the chieftains and the aes dána, as representatives of the highest authority in Gaelic society.

The best known story recounts the conversion of the pagan King Laoghaire. He was the high king of Tara (the epicenter of the sacred pagan sites of the Boyne Valley). The story goes that Laoghaire had been warned of Patrick's coming by his druids. Fearing the pending destruction of the established order, the king sent out emissaries to assassinate him. Patrick and his followers recited the *lorica* (or breastplate charm) that later became known as "The Deer's Cry" ("Christ be before me, Christ be behind me, Christ be beside me, etc.") and miraculously they passed by the assassins, appearing to them only as a herd of deer. Arriving at the Hill of Slane on the eve of Bealltaine (the pagan spring festival), which coincided with the Easter Vigil, Patrick kindled a fire on the mountain that extinguished the fires built by the druids. A druidic duel ensued (reminiscent of that between Moses and Pharaoh's priests recorded in Exodus) in which Patrick defeated all the tricks that were tried by the pagan druids. At last, Laoghaire accepted defeat and acknowledged his conversion.

The story is no doubt just a story, but it captures what very likely was the pattern of conversion among the Irish. In Ireland, unlike many other regions of Europe, there is no record of martyrdoms, which strongly suggests a top-down conversion model. The rapidity with which both the chieftains and the aes dána became associated with the growing Christian church (a trend clearly documented in the early Irish annals, which were compilations of records kept in the monasteries but often documenting secular affairs as well) also indicates a commonality of purpose and perhaps outlook that was quickly established. As an interesting footnote, a possible historical verification of Patrick's connection with the Easter Fire can be seen in a documentable change in church liturgy. Previous to this time, embers from the altar fires that were extinguished on Good Friday were kept carefully preserved until Easter, but by the seventh century the blessing of a newly kindled fire at Easter had become an established practice on the Continent, likely introduced by Irish monks.

The interconnection between probable pagan traditions and early Christianity in Ireland is likewise strikingly illustrated in the Vita of St. Brigid. Many folklorists have posited that she started out as a pagan goddess, associated with poetry, crafts, and springtime fertility, who was later conflated with the sixth century historical abbess St. Brigid of Kildare. Like Patrick, many of the stories in her Vita (recorded by Cogitosus in the seventh century) likely derive from pre-Christian motifs. She is said to have been the daughter of Dubhtach (the dark one) and fostered to a druid (whom she eventually converted) and her miracles often were associated with hospitality and housewifery. One story tells that, while she was making butter, she was filled with such spiritual joy that the butter miraculously overflowed her creel. As a child, she was often scolded for giving away the goods of the household to the poor. Like many other female Celtic saints, Brigid was much associated with nature. (Other examples include St. Lassair, whose name means fire; St. Thanet, associated with a center of pagan worship; and St. Samthann, who was possibly associated with the old pagan autumn festival of Samhain.)

One of the most attractive stories of St. Brigid tells of the visit made to her by another one of Ireland's saints, St. Brendan the Navigator. When Brigid entered the room, pleased to see Brendan, she casually discarded her cloak by "hanging it upon a sunbeam." The astounded Brendan required five attempts before he could duplicate her feat That same cloak miraculously expanded to cover the entire Curragh of Kildare (Cill Doire—the Church of the Oak Trees) when the chieftain agreed to give her land for her convent, "but only as much as her cloak would cover." It also was used to swaddle the newborn Jesus when miraculously Brigid was called from sleep to be midwife to the Blessed Virgin. In Celtic society the aid-woman and foster-mother were among the highest marks of status a woman could hold; therefore, it is likely the story came about as a means of showing the highest veneration for the saint, as well as emphasizing Christ's kin connections with the Irish. Her lineage from the kings and aes dána was also seen as a necessary part of her sanctity. Interestingly, like St. Patrick, St. Brigid is also connected with fire rituals. Up until the twelfth century it is documented that a perpetual fire was kept burning at her church, guarded by nineteen nuns (the twentieth was said to be Brigid herself). The fire was extinguished in 1220 by order of the bishop of Dublin, but was later rekindled and kept burning until the Dissolution of the Monasteries under Henry VIII.

COLUMCILLE AND THE CELTIC MONASTICISM

The idea of the Celtic church as it has been termed has come to be viewed as old-fashioned and controversial as modern scholars have increasingly moved away from an interpretive position based on Celtic identity. Nonetheless, the distinctive practices and outlooks associated with St. Columcille and his successors belonged to the northern isles and were heavily influenced by the social structures and systems of scholarship of the Irish and Scots, most notably those associated with the old aes dána learned elites. These practices often stood in sharp contradiction to those of the emerging Roman church.

Perhaps the best example of the intermingling between Irish secular and clerical power and tradition can be seen in the life of Ireland's third great saint, St. Columcille (known to the Scots as St. Columba) of Iona. With this sixth century abbot and saint we are on firmer historical ground than with Patrick and Brigid, although his main biographer, Adamnan, certainly included many tales of miraculous and supernatural occurrences associated with Columcille. (For example, the first documentary evidence of the Loch Ness monster comes from the pen of Adamnan. The monster threatened to overturn a small boat containing Columcille and some of his followers. The saint reasoned with the monster and sent it back to the depths of the loch.) The name Columcille (Dove of the Church) was probably taken by the saint at the time of his ordination. His original name was Crimthann (the Fox) and he was born into the highest ranks of the great O'Neill clan of Ulster.

What we know of Columcille's education reflects the tight interconnection between the Irish secular and clerical elites by the sixth century. He attained the rank of master poet, with attributable poems in both Gaelic and Latin, and he vigorously defended the rights of the Irish poets when later as abbot he was summoned to the Council of Drumceatt that threatened to outlaw them. In addition to what must have been years of secular training, Columcille entered the Church and studied with Cruithneachtan in Donegal and later with Finian of Moville. After his ordination Columcille returned to the north of Ireland and his cousin, the O'Neill king, gave him the "oak-covered hill" near the river Foyle. This oak grove (Doire—later Derry) was the site of his first church.

What led Columcille to leave his beloved Derry is not entirely clear. The Irish had a tradition of white martyrdom (leaving behind kin and everything one loved in pursuit of holiness), but there is also a persistent tradition that it was his love of scholarship that got him in trouble and led to his exile. The story goes that Columcille went to visit his former teacher Finian of Moville and was shown a rare and valuable manuscript (possibly the first copy of St. Jerome's Latin translation of the Psalms to be seen in Ireland). Columcille coveted the book and eventually could not resist copying it. Finian was furious when he discovered this and demanded that Columcille give him the copy. He refused. The matter was taken to the high king of Tara (an enemy of Columcille's O'Neill clan) and the ruling was made: "to every cow belongs her calf, and to every book

The Cathach, *Psalter of St. Columcille. The Irish monks' love of scholarship is seen in a preponderance of book shrines—elaborately decorated metal repositories of revered manuscripts. The provenance of the* Cathach *(which translates as "the Battler") can be traced through a line of hereditary "keepers" who guarded it and carried it into battle (hence the name) to ensure the protection of the saint. This practice persisted into the sixteenth century.*

belongs its copy." In consequence, Columcille was exiled from Ireland. This punishment seems a bit drastic for the crime, and there is no precedent for it in the Irish law codes. More plausibly, it may have been Columcille's clandestine involvement at the Battle of Culdrevny (a major loss for King Diarmait of Tara) that led to his exile. In any case, under threat of excommunication he set sail from Ireland in 563.

We do not know much about the spiritual state of Scotland prior to Columcille's arrival, although there is a tradition (probably incorrect) that St. Ninian had established a little stone church in Galloway in the late fourth century and converted some of the southern Picts. By the time of Columcille there had been some stabilization in the kingships of Scotland, with a particularly strong confederation emerging in Argyllshire: the kingdom of Dalriada, with its capital at Dunadd and its kings descending from a branch of the powerful Ulster O'Neills—in other words, Columcille's kin. It is probably no accident that Columcille established his church on the tiny island of Iona, which was under the sway of the Dalriadic kings, and by tradition, the first place from which Columcille could no longer see Ireland. The tiny three-mile-long island would become the center of Christianity in the north.

Although Columcille was middle-aged by the standards of the time (probably in his forties) he was energetic and relentless in pursuing his mission among the pagan Picts. His monks traveled throughout Scotland (documented both by place-names and traditions and by the detailed descriptions in Adamnan's biography) converting the natives wherever they went. The style of Christianity he introduced and the way of life he imposed in his monastery are representative of what has been termed the Celtic church. It should be noted that this was never a monolithic set of rituals or doctrines, but rather more of an attitude toward religious practice. It was an individualistic, austere, deeply ascetic interpretation, slightly tinged by Pelagianism (a heresy emphasizing a greater degree of free will in salvation than was accepted by the Roman church). There is a clear love of nature and a celebration of the virtues associated with the pre-Christian Irish aristocracy (seen in the powers of the warrior and the poet). In the miracles associated with Columcille there are frequent references to prophecies and second sight, an ability to communicate with animals, and at least a hint of toleration for pre-Christian practices.

One of the oddest stories associated with Columcille concerns the building of the original church at Iona. Although it does not appear in Adamnan, it is part of the early local place-name tradition and appears in later recensions of the saint's life. In this story demons assailed the monks building the church, every night destroying the work they had done the previous day. Columcille spoke: "It is good for us that our roots should go beneath the earth to which we've come and whichever holy person of our community agrees to die and be buried in the earth, I will give him the kingdom of God." St. Oran (perhaps a kinsman of Columcille) volunteered. In the sixteenth century redaction of the text, Manus O'Donnell explained: "By the will of God and Columcille, Oran died then and he was buried under the clay of the island. Hence, Reilig Oran [Oran's Graveyard] is the name of the place now." This would seem to be a clear reference to the ancient tradition of foundation sacrifices, but it is startling to see in an otherwise fairly typical saint's vita.

Whether through Oran's sacrifice or not, Columcille's church flourished. He lived to old age (probably around seventy-five), prophesying his own death and preparing his monks to continue the mission. He had many disciples and his supposed first words when he landed on Iona had become fact: "This island shall be mighty." The monks from Iona had succeeded in converting the Highlands, and the first Christian king in Britain (Aidan of Dalriada) became king in 576. Monks from Iona carried with them their austerity but also their love of nature, beauty, and learning. From Scotland their influence spread back to Ireland, to the Continent, and also to the north of England.

In the early seventh century Oswald, king of Northumbria, sought refuge in Iona. When he returned to his kingdom in 634 he asked the monks of Iona to send someone to establish a new monastery for the conversion of the northern British. St. Aidan was sent along with twelve companions and founded another island community, Lindisfarne, also to become renowned for its spirituality and scholarship, particularly under Aidan's successor, the powerful St. Cuthbert.

Also at the beginning of the seventh century, Pope Gregory sent a papal mission to England under St. Augustine of Bec to address the spiritual needs of the British people. Augustine landed in Kent and was well received (Queen Bertha, wife of King Ethelbert, was already Christian) and under Augustine's influence the king and many of his retainers were baptized. Augustine built his first church at Canterbury (he is still regarded as the first bishop of Canterbury) and began to extend his mission into the rest of Britain.

Perhaps it was inevitable that the two powerful but somewhat opposing forces of Celtic-style Christianity and Roman Christianity would collide in Northumbria. Both certainly followed the letter of the law of the early church, agreeing in sacramental observance and following the teachings of the early church fathers and the legal decisions of the popes and church councils. However, there were important differences as well. Complaints from the Romans centered largely on superficial matters such as the Celtic configuration of the tonsure (the Irish tonsure was ear to ear instead of a circle on the back of the head) and the way the insular church calculated the date of Easter (both had good precedents for the way they did it, but essentially it was a matter of authority). The insular church favored decentralization and a high level of authority held by each abbot, whereas the Roman church was evolving toward centralization and an organizational structure focused on papally appointed bishops.

The king of Northumbria, Oswy, took it upon himself to resolve the differences by calling a church council, the Synod of Whitby, which was held in 664. (The double monastery of Whitby, housing both male and female religious, was associated with the royal family, and it was a mark of favor for the council to be held there. It was governed by Hild, a powerful abbess with family ties to Oswy's Kentish-born wife, Eanflaed. After Oswy's death Eanflaed retired to Whitby and later became abbess herself.) Perhaps the king really did intend there to be a compromise, but the decentralized Celtic church representatives failed to achieve the unity needed to win their case, and, according to Bede, the Roman representatives persuaded Oswy (based on the "keys to the kingdom" scripture [Matthew 16:19] that gave St. Peter precedence as the bishop of Rome) that only the Roman pope could ensure his salvation. That may have figured into his decision, but so too did the king's likely awareness that the centralized structure of bishoprics could better serve his purposes in trying to centralize the monarchy than the more capricious, individualistic abbots of the Celtic church. The decision was made. The Roman system would be followed in Britain, with a division of territory into dioceses, each to be presided over by a bishop who was appointed by Rome. Not surprisingly, this edict had little immediate effect in Scotland or Ireland, where the Celtic monasteries continued to have a large impact on the spirituality and culture and where the diocesan system was not fully implemented until the twelfth century. The situation in Wales is obscure. Saint David is credited with establishing a church in Pembrokeshire in the sixth century, but otherwise diocesan organization did not occur there until the Norman expansion of the eleventh and twelfth century.

LEGACIES OF CELTIC MONASTICISM

The lasting impact of Celtic Christianity was twofold. First, the mercurial, individualistic Celtic monks continued their zeal for white martyrdom, carrying their love of nature and scholarship into a European continent that had been left culturally desolated after the collapse of the Roman Empire. The monastic foundations at Bobbio, St. Gall, and Luxeuil, as well as many others, were established by Celtic monks and became the great centers of scholarship on the Continent, where classical texts alongside the writings of scripture and of the church fathers were preserved, copied, and interpreted. The Irish monks were excellent Latinists and tolerable in Greek (For example, the eminent Irish theologian John Scotus Eriugena received his one nickname by coming from Ireland and the other by virtue of his knowing Greek.) Without the knowledge and thirst for learning of these Irish monks, it is all too likely that classical learning might have been lost altogether. In addition to those who had been trained at the original Columban foundations, scholars from the second generation establishments, such as Lindisfarne, Jarrow, and Wearmouth, all made their mark on the Continent. Arguably the greatest scholar of the eighth century and founder of the Carolingian Renaissance was Alcuin, student of Egbert of York, a product of Northumbrian learning and spirituality.

Beehive cell, Skellig Mhicil, Ireland. The early Celtic monks did not live in community but rather in their own huts. Sometimes archaeological remains of these cells can be found in clusters, but often they provide evidence of a solitary monk living in isolation. This practice was seen as providing greater opportunities for asceticism and spiritual growth.

Traditional Irish (Celtic) monasteries of the British Isles. This map shows the location and distribution of some of the most important early Celtic monasteries. They were often situated on rocky coastlines or other remote locations to help further the monks' asceticism and association with nature.

St. Martin's Cross, Iona, Scotland. This is an example of one of the many stone crosses in Ireland and Scotland erected by the early Celtic monasteries to mark a place of worship and to tell religious stories through the pictorial representations carved into the crosses.

At home, the love of beauty and spiritual fervor of the Celtic church was made manifest in the awe-inspiring manuscripts produced in the scriptoria of the Celtic monasteries. The *Book of Kells* (now housed at Trinity College, Dublin) may have been originally written in Iona and was later moved to Kells. *The Lindisfarne Gospels*, although not quite as intricate as the *Book of Kells*, is breathtaking in its own right, and the *Book of Durrow* should be mentioned alongside the other two. All show evidence of influences from earlier Celtic artistry in their capitals and carpet pages, including spirals and whorls that resemble the markings of Newgrange, as well as intricate Celtic knotwork and distinctive human and animal representations that capture personality even in their more abstract renderings. In addition to Scripture and other Latin religious texts, the Celtic monks copied Irish manuscripts. Quite possibly because of the close social and cultural ties between the Church and the secular aes dána, the edict against pagan writing seems to have been little observed in

The Lindisfarne Gospels, *written in Northumbria about 720. These represent the finest work produced by the English monasteries. Top: A portrait of St. Matthew. Bottom left: An ornamental page in the form of a cross. The interlacing curved lines are characteristic of Anglo-Saxon art and may represent a continuation of Celtic style. Bottom right: A table showing where parallel passages can be found in the four gospels. Note the architectural setting and the symbols of the four evangelists at the top of the four columns.*

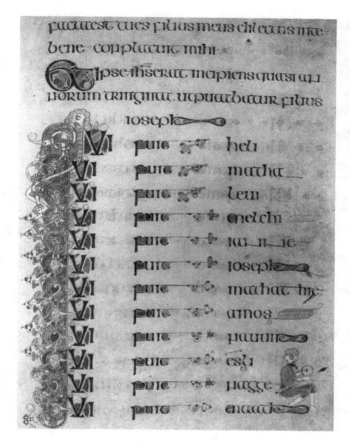

The Book of Kells.
*Shown here is
Christ's genealogy,
from Joseph to
Adam, according
to St. Luke. The*
Book of Kells *may
have been started
on Iona and then
moved to Kells for
safekeeping.*

the Celtic monasteries. Much of what we know concerning the early Irish law codes, as well as the earliest Irish recensions of Irish epics and other vernacular poetry and narrative (such as the *Táin bó Cúailgne* [*The Cattle Raid of Cooley*] and the *Lebor Gabála Erenn* [*The Book of Invasions*]), we owe to the Irish monastic copyists.

In addition to the amazingly beautiful manuscripts, the monasteries also contained works of art in the form of highly decorated altar plate. Most likely these items were the products of the best of secular craftsmen, although it is possible that some of the Celtic monks may have come from hereditary families of craftsmen and been able to craft items themselves. The Ardagh Chalice is probably the most famous example of the breathtaking intricacy of early medieval Celtic metalcraft, and some of its stylistic features have been correlated with those found in such secular art as the Tara brooch. In addition to housing the items belonging to the church, the early Celtic monasteries served as a form of safety deposit box for the wealthy Gaelic elites. Because the churches were made of stone (one early word for church in Gaelic is *clach*, which means rock or stone) in a society largely served by wooden buildings, they were regarded as a safer place to store valuables, in terms of both fire risk and possible clan warfare. The local chieftains, patrons of the churches, made use of this storage feature and also bestowed lavish gifts of cloth and plate. The riches of the Celtic monasteries would prove to be their undoing.

SUGGESTED READING

Bamford, Christopher and William March. *Celtic Christianity: Ecology and Holiness*. Stockbridge, MA: Lindisfarne Press, 1982.

Brown, Peter. *The Rise of Western Christendom: Triumph and Diversity, AD 200–1000*. Oxford: Blackwell, 1997.

Cahill, Thomas. *How the Irish Saved Civilization*. New York: Anchor, 1996.

deBreffny, Brian. *In the Steps of St. Patrick*. London: Thames & Hudson, 1982.

DePaor, Máire, and Liam DePaor. *Early Christian Ireland*. London: Thames & Hudson, 1964.

Donaldson, Gordon. *The Faith of the Scots*. London: Batsford, 1990.

Duckett, Eleanor. *The Wandering Saints of the Early Middle Ages*. New York: Norton, 1959.

James, Simon. *Atlantic Celts: Ancient People or Modern Invention*. Madison, WI: University of Wisconsin Press, 1999.

Mayr-Harting, Henry. *The Coming of Christianity to Anglo-Saxon England*. London: Batsford, 1972.

O'Donnell, Manus. *The Life of Colum Cille*. Edited by Brian Lacey. Dublin: Four Courts Press, 1998.

Patterson, Nerys. *Cattle Lords & Clansmen: The Social Structure of Early Ireland*. Notre Dame, IN: University of Notre Dame Press, 1994.

Rahtz, Philip. *Glastonbury*. London: Batsford, 1993.

Ritchie, Anna. *Iona*. London: Trafalgar Square Publishing, 1997.

Scherman, Katherine. *The Flowering of Ireland: Saints, Scholars and Kings*. Boston: Little Brown, 1981.

Smyth, Alfred P. *Warlords and Holy Men: Scotland, A.D. 80–1000*. London: Edward Arnold, 1984.

Chapter 4

Early Medieval Britain and Ireland and the Impact of the Vikings

As the Church was developing, changes were also taking place politically in the North Atlantic. In the far north, in Scandinavia, a number of rival lordships were emerging and by 800 CE a growing population, possibly affected by changing climatic conditions, had need of expanding resources. This region was in no way a consolidated political state at this point. There were strong tribal and therefore regional identities. The highly elaborate social structure that we have seen with the Celts was not present here, but there was some functional similarity. Society consisted of various specialists: the warrior elites, pagan priests, poets and seers, craftsmen, farmers, and slaves. The areas we now know as Norway, Denmark, and Sweden were not separate entities. Their people shared a common language (Old Norse) and cultural background, worshiping the same pagan gods and loving riddles and poetry that extolled the virtues of a warrior society. Above all, whatever else their role in society, they were seafarers and fearless adventurers, and to satisfy their need for resources, they turned their attention to their neighbors to the south. The ensuing conflicts contributed greatly to the eventual formation of identities in the British Isles.

THE VIKING RAIDS

In 793 the Viking raids on Britain began, shattering the peace of the old Celtic monasteries. They first arrived in Lindisfarne, and writing from Charlemagne's court, a shocked Alcuin, perhaps the foremost scholar and theologian of his day, described the news he had received:

> The pagans desecrated the sanctuaries of God, and poured out the blood of saints around the altar, laid waste the house of our hope, trampled on the bodies of saints in the temple of God like dung in the street. . . . What assurance is there for the churches of Britain, if St. Cuthbert, with so great a number of saints, defends not his own?

The Vikings (a collective term for the Scandinavian raiders) were attracted by the great wealth of the churches. Our knowledge of these raids comes to us through the pens of the clerics of the sacked monasteries, decidedly not

Irish round tower. The round towers that still dot the Irish landscape may have been built as protection from the Vikings, for both the monks and their valuable manuscripts and altar plate.

unbiased source material. The monks emphasized the paganism of the raiders, but it is highly unlikely that the Vikings had any religious—or antireligious—motivation in mind. The monasteries were storehouses of treasure: costly fabric and altar plate, gilded manuscripts, book shrines, bishops' crosiers, and reliquaries—a literal boatload of wealth—in the custody of monks who would not fight back. The lure was irresistible. The monks tried to hide the things they valued the most, either burying them or, primarily in Ireland, securing them in high round towers that were possibly built for that purpose. The location of many of the monasteries on islands or on the coasts made them easy targets for the swift longships. Over and over the Vikings attacked: Iona was sacked in 795, 802, 825, and 986. Each time the surviving monks rebuilt. In 794 Jarrow/Monkwearmouth was attacked and in 795 the Irish raids began: Rathlin, Inishmurray, and Inishboffin. The important episcopal see of Armagh was attacked repeatedly—three times in the single year of 832. The monks (and sometimes nuns as well) fled or suffered martyrdom at the hands of the Vikings, and even when the Vikings attacked secular settlements there was little in the way of coordinated resistance. The raids were too quick and the fighting style was too different for effective counterattack.

The Ardagh Chalice, early eighth century. The most magnificent piece of Irish altar plate that has been found to date, the Ardagh Chalice illustrates the immense wealth of the Irish monasteries, the breathtaking artistry of the Irish metalworkers, and the compelling lure for the Viking raiders. The intricate decorations show influences from both Saxon and Celtic art, reminiscent of the Book of Kells *and* Lindisfarne Gospels. *The Ardagh Chalice was found in a potato field during the nineteenth century, along with two other chalices and four brooches, none of later date than the tenth century. They may have been buried to safeguard them from the Vikings.*

BRITISH POLITICAL STRUCTURES: THE SCOTS, THE ANGLO-SAXONS, AND THE IRISH

Despite the potentially unifying force of Christianity, Britain was still a land of small regional kingships and local authority. Like Scandinavia, Scotland had seen the emergence of several kingships of varying strength and organization in the years between the withdrawal of Rome and the eighth century. On the Borders (the old Tyne-Solway line of demarcation) the kingdom of Strathclyde dominated to the west and the Goddodin, descendents of the Uotadini, to the east, clustered around the area that would become Edinburgh. North of the areas that had seen Roman influence, the expanding kingdom of Dalriada, closely affiliated with its Irish Gaelic-speaking neighbors and kinsmen, held sway in Argyllshire. North of the Forth and east of Dalriada lay the kingdom of the Picts.

Aside from a few monumental inscriptions, the Picts left no written documentation; therefore, our knowledge of this group of people is extremely vague. There are references to the matrilinear organization of Pictish society, but the evidence for this is controversial and shadowy at best. The Romans began using the term *picti* during the third century, a description that has greatly influenced subsequent popular impressions of the "painted people of the north." To the Irish they were the Cruithne and to the Welsh they were known as Prydan. Both terms derive from the same root word as Britain or Briton, and they may in fact have been related to the Britons of the border regions and Wales. By the eighth century, however, their neighbors regarded the Picts as a very different group from the Britons. Bede, in the *Ecclesiastical History of the English People*, remarks that they were two separate people speaking two separate languages; however, it is unclear how much firsthand knowledge he had. Certainly there is nothing in the accounts of Columcille and his followers' interactions with the Picts that suggests an insurmountable language barrier. Modern research suggests that Pictish may in fact have been linguistically related to Welsh/Brythonic and so would have had the same relationship to the language of Dalriada as Welsh to Irish: *P*-Gaelic versus *Q*-Gaelic, but still derivative of a common Goidelic source.

In addition to their conflicts with the Dalriadic Scots (a designation based on terminology that called Ireland "Scotia"—a confusion that still complicates discussion of these peoples), the Picts also appear in documentary evidence as enemies of the Angles in Northumbria. The Anglo-Saxons first appear in the historical record as Germanic raiders and invaders at the end of the period of Roman occupation. When the Roman forts were no longer garrisoned, the Anglo-Saxons came in great numbers, conquering, settling, and eventually establishing lordships or kingships throughout England. By the sixth century their language and culture were dominant in the south, although they were not organized into a centralized state. There may have been as many as twelve of these lordships or kingships at one time, but seven survived. These are referred to as the Heptarchy: three Saxon (Essex, Sussex, and Wessex), three Anglian (East Anglia, Mercia, and Northumbria), and one Jutish (Kent). These kingdoms differed somewhat in customs and laws, but by and large there was much intermingling of the three groups and at least some sense of common identity. Nonetheless, there was certainly rivalry and conflict as well, and during the pre-Viking period in Britain, one or another of the Anglo-Saxon kingdoms would claim the high kingship or overlordship of the others. The high king was called the *bretwalda*.

In the sixth century Kent was dominant, followed by Northumbria in the seventh century and Mercia in the eighth. By the ninth century, the kingdom of Wessex was on the rise, and its king began calling himself king of all England. He could not, however, claim the Scottish territories. The advance of the Anglian kingdom of Northumbria into Scotland had been halted in May 685 at the decisive Battle of Nechtansmere by the Pictish king Bridei. Bede gives a brief description of the battle:

> The very next year [685] . . . king Egfrid, rashly leading his army to ravage the province of the Picts, much against the advice of his friends, and particularly of Cuthbert, of blessed memory, who had lately been ordained his bishop, the enemy made show as if they fled, and the king was drawn into the straits of inaccessible mountains, and slain with the greatest part of his forces.

Although it would be incorrect to think of England and Scotland as distinctive countries at this point, their divergent history, society, languages, and culture were already being established, as was conflict over the border regions.

Across the Irish Sea a similar process of political development was taking place. Here there was no clash of different ethnic or linguistic groups to trigger division, but in politics as in religion, Celtic systems tended to favor decentralization. Political organization was based on the clan or extended family, with strong regional identities and political allegiances based on family politics. The largely independent lordships or kingdoms of Ireland roughly corresponded to the geographical quarters of the island, rather confusingly referred to as the *Four Fifths* (*cúige*) of Ireland: Leinster (southeast), Munster (southwest), Ulster (northeast), Connacht (northwest), and the royal kingdom of Meath (situated around the old strongholds of the Boyne Valley). Each of these regions was dominated by a particular family or families (the O'Neills and O'Donnells of Ulster, the MacMorroughs of Munster, etc.) and political action was determined by an ever-shifting constellation of alliances and feuds. Theoretically, there was a high king or overlord of Ireland, but in reality this was rarely acknowledged. Even the famed Brian Boru, who is sometimes given credit for unifying Ireland, held the title only briefly in 1002.

VIKING EXPANSION AND SETTLEMENT

After the initial series of raids in the ninth century, the impact of the Vikings began to take different forms in the various regions of the British Isles. In Ireland the annals report that in the early 840s the Vikings began to overwinter for the first time, subsequently establishing *longphort* (ship harbors) to use as bases. Their primary base in Ireland was at Dublin. It was used until 902. During this period the Vikings became part of the local landscape, engaging in trade

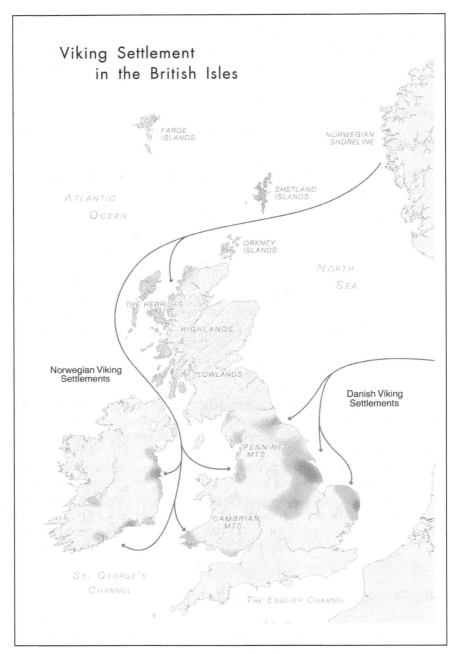

Viking settlement in the British Isles.

and sometimes becoming involved in the intricacies of clan politics. Dublin was well situated as a base for raids into Scottish and English territories. At times the Vikings clashed with other Vikings as the two groups, the *dubhgall* (dark strangers—or Danes) and the *fionngall* (fair strangers—from Norway), struggled for supremacy.

In 902 the Vikings were driven out of Dublin by one of the local Gaelic chieftains, but by 914 they were back in greater numbers than ever, landing and establishing a base at Waterford and later a trading center at Limerick. In addition, Dublin was reclaimed and expanded. Excavations from Viking Dublin show a well-entrenched settlement, not as extensive but in some ways reminiscent of the great Viking trading cities of Hedeby (Germany) and Birka (Sweden). It was a walled town, with wooden streets, shops, and houses, and there is evidence of local manufacturing of goods as well as importing and exporting. In nonurban Ireland, this was a new concept and set Dublin (and to some extent Limerick and Waterford) apart from the pastoral Gaelic lordships. Building alliances among the Gaelic chieftains, the Dublin Vikings hoped to control Waterford and Limerick, the western seaboard of Scotland, and Northumbria as well.

Viking Dublin, showing excavations taking place. Viking Dublin was the foremost Viking town in Ireland. It established the importance of the port city, later to become the capital of Ireland, in commerce and military strategy. Excavations conducted at Wood Quay from 1974 to 1981 yielded much archaeological evidence of the society and material culture of the Viking settlers.

The Hebrides and west Highlands of Scotland served a different purpose for the Vikings. After the initial raiding period, the ports of the west became stepping stones on the sea routes between Scandinavia and Britain. We do not know with certainty when the Vikings first overwintered in the Scottish territories. It is quite possible that they had been doing this for some time in the Shetland and Orkney Islands off the northern coast of Scotland, even before the advent of the raids in the 790s. There is no clear evidence in fact that the Norse colonies in Shetland and Orkney have any connection with raids or conquest. Given the biased nature of our sources, it is sometimes easy to forget that the Norse were highly sophisticated merchants and traders and to some extent the "piracy" of the raids may have been viewed by the Scandinavians as an extension of already established commerce. The Shetlands and Orkneys, located with convenient proximity to Viking shipping lanes, may have been early sites of trade exchange and settlement without any of the trauma of the raiding period. Place-names and personal names from these areas suggest a cultural blending between the Norse and the indigenous population, but in time Old Norse (Norn) came to dominate as the spoken language of these islands and was accompanied by Norse ways of life such as building design, farming methods, and folk beliefs.

In the western isles, Viking settlement was sporadic, sometimes accomplished through conflict and sometimes through assimilation with the Gaelic inhabitants. Modern DNA studies (although currently based on small sample pools) show an extremely high influence of Viking bloodlines in the Hebrides,

Rune stone, Iona, Scotland. The Vikings who settled the Hebrides and western coast of Scotland assimilated with the Gaelic families in these regions to produce a hybrid culture. The galley at the center of the stone vividly depicts Viking influences in this seafaring territory.

with Norse characteristics predominating through the male line and Gaelic more apparent in the female, at least partly corroborating what is suggested in the Irish annals—dynastic marriages between the Norse chieftains and Gaelic heiresses.

There was no establishment of trading centers such as we have seen in Ireland, and in many ways the Hebridean Vikings seem to have become more assimilated in terms of their adaption of the Gaelic language and culture than vice versa. Certainly these tiny islands were of no great value politically, and it may be that they were merely overshadowed by the bigger goals of extending Viking control over Strathclyde and Northumbria. Moreover, by the mid ninth century, there was a new political entity: the kingdom of Alba, presided over by Kenneth MacAlpin. It was essentially an amalgamation of the old kingdom of the Picts and the Dalriadic Scots, and although it was not formed through a popular unification movement as has been envisioned by some modern Scots nationalists, it would eventually form the foundation of the kingdom of Scotland. Significantly, at this time, and for centuries to come, Alba did not include Argyllshire and the Hebrides. The continuing strength and independence of the

Tombstones of the Lords of the Isles, Iona, Scotland. The Lordship of the Isles, centered on the west highlands and islands of Scotland, was a seaborne polity presided over by one branch of the MacDonald Clan. The founder of the Lordship, Somerled of the Isles, was of mixed Gaelic and Norse descent, and the Lordship represented an amalgamation of the two cultures as can be seen in the depictions of swords and armor on the tombstones.

chieftains of the western highlands and Hebrides, themselves descendants of intermarriage between the Norse and the native Gaelic families, resulted in the formation of the powerful Kingship and later Lordship of the Isles. During Kenneth's reign the kingdom of Alba provided stability and some measure of centralization in the Scottish regions. However, when he died in 858, the Viking threat loomed large, from the north, south, and west.

In England after the initial raiding period, the Vikings began extending their influence through settlement and military conquest. They first over-wintered in Canterbury in 850. It is assumed that the Vikings had a growing interest in the continental Carolingian empire and perhaps to that end they increased their attacks in southern England—hitting towns including London, Dorset, and Rochester, perhaps with a view to securing the northern flank of any continental expeditions. In 865 the largest Viking army ever assembled (the logically named Great Army) landed in East Anglia. A truce was concluded with the East Anglians and the Vikings continued their march to the north. The kingdoms of Mercia and Northumbria were devastated. In 866 the Vikings seized the old Roman city of Eboracum and transformed it into a military base and trading center that they named Jorvik (modern-day York).

In 878 a temporary check to their increasing power came from a victory won by Alfred the Great, king of Wessex. Alfred is remembered as perhaps the greatest of the Anglo-Saxon kings, and his victory against the Danes at the Battle of Edington bought the kingdom of Wessex a few years of peace. Alfred negotiated the terms by which the Vikings (identified as Danes in the *Anglo-Saxon Chronicle*) would settle in a defined territory that encompassed East Anglia and parts of Mercia and Northumbria. It was known as the Danelaw because within these boundaries the Danes could manage their own government and observe their own legal codes. The peace lasted for almost a hundred years, and during this period the Vikings truly became settlers. In Northumbria it was reported that "they proceeded to plough and support themselves."

The area of the Danelaw, particularly Northumbria, furnishes us with a great deal of linguistic and archaeological evidence of the Viking settlement. Place-names in that region often contain the suffix -*thorpe* (Bishopthorpe, Towthorpe, etc.), indicating marginal lands, or -*by* (Balby, Selby, etc.) marking the village of . . . with a personal name. The settlements themselves were based on the fortified urban model favored by the Vikings, as can be seen in the foundations of the five boroughs that were established within the Danelaw: Derby, Leicester, Stamford, Nottingham, and Lincoln. The most extensive archaeological evidence comes from York, specifically the Coppergate area (named not for copper but for barrel making), where the unusual conditions of the site preserved an entire wooden street with its shops and furnishings.

A nearby Viking cemetery was preserved, and an ambitious project, funded by the York Archaeological Trust, was undertaken to recreate the street and populate it with animatronic figures wearing the faces and clothing of the Viking inhabitants, painstakingly recreated through forensic archaeology. The result was the Jorvik Viking Center, an interactive museum in which modern visitors could literally walk the streets of Viking York and come face to face with the Viking craftsmen and women who lived there. (The museum has recently been closed due to flooding with no date for reopening.) The images from this project showed the Vikings of Britain in a new light—not just as the ferocious, bloodthirsty raiders that we find in the monastic sources, but also as craftsmen and farmers—men, women, and children going about their daily lives.

Animatronic figure from Jorvik Viking Center, York, England. The Jorvik Viking Center was built near the site of an actual Viking settlement at Coopersgate, York, and modern museum engagement techniques were used in designing the museum to include living history demonstrations and robotic figures depicting life in Viking York. The faces of the animatronic figures are forensic reconstructions of remains found in a Viking cemetery nearby.

With the relative peace established by Alfred, the Anglo-Saxon monarchy was able to coexist and expand even with the continuing Viking presence. Alfred has been the focus of many apocryphal legends, but his claim to greatness is largely undisputed. In addition to his military and diplomatic skills, he was able to codify the "dooms," or legal codes of the various parts of the Heptarchy into a single unified law code. He also tried to establish Anglo-Saxon as a single written language by using it for monastic chronicles (now known to us as the *Anglo-Saxon Chronicle*) and the translation of Bede and other religious works from Latin into Anglo-Saxon. He established a court school (reminiscent of Charlemagne's) to educate the royal family and the nobility, and during his reign his chief advisor, the archbishop of Canterbury, St. Dunstan, began restoring the English monasteries that had been damaged in the Viking raids. Alfred died in 899 and his successors were eventually able to recover the Danelaw (through assimilation of the Danes) and transform the kingdom of Wessex into the kingdom of England.

In the west, Viking chieftains either took over the old Welsh lordships (some of which probably dated to the fourth century shadowy beginnings of the Welsh heroic age) or in some cases created entirely new ones. It is not clear, although it seems very likely, that this process involved dynastic marriages and other political alliances similar to what we have seen in Ireland and Scotland. By the tenth century there was a new dynasty in Gwynedd (that of Rhodri the Great) and Morganwg (the later Glamorgan) was beginning to emerge as a powerful territory. In Dyfed, Hywel Dda became king, briefly taking control of Gwynedd as well. He is associated with the writing of an important set of law codes; their foundation in Celtic rather than Viking law indicates, as in the Hebrides, greater adaption by the Viking settlers of Celtic patterns of society than the reverse.

THE SECOND WAVE OF VIKING INVASIONS AND THE ANGLO-SAXON SUCCESSION

The tenuous peace that had been forged by Alfred was broken in 994 by the simultaneous invasions of Olaf Tryggvason, king of Norway, and Sweyn Forkbeard, king of Denmark. The Danes sacked and burned London and murdered the archbishop of Canterbury. This time there was no King Alfred, but only his great-great-grandson, known to history as Ethelred the Unready (r. 978–1013, 1014–16). His nickname actually came from the Anglo-Saxon word *rede* and meant that he was lacking good counsel, but the other interpretation has stuck because of its obvious appropriateness. Ethelred accepted the Danish demands for tribute payment (called Danegeld) in 991, but in 1002 he ordered a massacre of the Danes in England, which led to an invasion by the Danish King Sweyn in 1003. Ethelred continued to pay tribute but sporadic fighting persisted. In 1013 Sweyn invaded again. Ethelred fled to Normandy, where he was welcomed by his father-in-law, the Duke of Normandy, whose daughter Emma had recently become Ethelred's second wife. In Ethelred's absence, Sweyn seized the kingship of England, reigning until his death in February 1014. On his death a group of English noblemen opened negotiations with Ethelred, willing to support his restoration if he would agree to reforms that they demanded. Ethelred returned to England and again claimed the throne, reigning from 1014 until his death in 1016. He was succeeded by his son, Edmund Ironside, who died the following year.

By Anglo-Saxon custom, succession was normally from father to son, but technically each new king was to be elected (or have his succession upheld) by the *witan*, the king's counselors. In 1016 the witan was faced with the prospect of no adult male heir of the Wessex line. Based on a treaty between Edmund Ironsides and Cnut, son of Sweyn Forkbeard, in which they had agreed to divide the kingdom, it chose to elect Cnut as king.

Cnut ruled from 1016 to 1035, following Anglo-Saxon law and customs in every way. Because Cnut was also ruler of Denmark, Norway, and much of Sweden, his reign brought England into what was essentially an Anglo-Scandinavian empire. Nonetheless, in England, his only deviation from Anglo-Saxon norms was his division of England into four earldoms (Wessex, East Anglia, Mercia, and Northumbria), presumably to assist with the governing of all areas of his realm. He reigned effectively, maintaining control over his kingdom and defeating the Scots on his borders. Cnut was married twice, first to Elfgifu, an Anglo-Saxon heiress, by whom he had one son, Harold Harefoot. When she died, he married Emma, the widow of Ethelred. They had another son, Hardecnut. Although both sons took the throne in sequence, neither proved to be fit for rule. Harold was murdered (possibly on Emma's orders) and Hardecnut died in a fit of drunken apoplexy.

In 1042 the witan was again forced to choose a king and it reverted to the old line of Wessex. Edward, the son of Ethelred and Emma, was now an adult, raised in Normandy and almost entirely ignorant of Anglo-Saxon ways. His nickname was the Confessor because of his strong piety. All reports indicate that he had little interest in becoming king, and when he did become king, he promptly offended the Anglo-Saxon nobility (particularly his chief enemy, Godwin, Earl of Wessex) by relying on his Norman friends and placing them in important offices. He also attempted to appoint a Norman to the archbishopric of Canterbury. The effort failed and Edward was forced to accept the appointment of an Anglo-Saxon, although that appointment was never recognized by the pope. In an effort to improve relations with the Anglo-Saxons, Edward married Godwin's daughter, Edith, but it is quite possible that he remained celibate in his marriage. In any event, the marriage produced no children. Edward's chief accomplishment was the foundation of Westminster Abbey, which was nearly complete when he died in January 1066.

On Edward's death, the two sons of Godwin, Harold, Earl of Mercia, and Tostig, Earl of Northumbria, immediately became claimants for the throne. They based their claims on the fact that they were brothers of the queen and brothers-in-law of Edward, but those were not relationships normally considered in Anglo-Saxon succession. Harold made it clear that he wanted the whole kingdom; Tostig would have agreed to have half, with his brother receiving the other half. A third claimant to the throne had an equally shaky claim, but as events would prove, a better army. This was William, Duke of Normandy, nicknamed the Bastard for literal reasons. He claimed that he was descended from the same line that had produced Emma, queen to both Ethelred and Cnut, but this still in no way connected him to the bloodline of Wessex, and even his own inheritance was somewhat clouded because of his illegitimacy. Moreover, he claimed that he had been promised the throne by Edward, but of course he had no documentary proof. The witan, undoubtedly preferring an Anglo-Saxon to a Norman, named Harold king.

THE SUCCESSION OF 1066

Harold Godwinson was not destined to have a peaceful succession. He was immediately challenged by his brother Tostig, who had concluded an alliance with the king of Norway, Harold Hardrada, who also put forth his claim to the throne based on an earlier treaty between Hardecnut and the king of Denmark. (He also claimed the throne of Denmark.) Tostig and Harold Hardrada assembled a joint army in the north of England. Harold Godwinson marched north and managed to defeat and kill both of them at the Battle of Stamford Bridge, fought on September 25, 1066.

Three days later, Duke William landed on the southeast coast with a large army of Normans. In a panic, Harold marched south again, scarcely stopping for food or rest along the way. The inevitable battle took place at Hastings on October 14, 1066. Harold's troops were exhausted and the Norman fighting style caught them by surprise. The Bayeux tapestry, an amazing account of the battle embroidered on a scroll 270 feet long, shows that it was the Norman arrows (shot high in an arc above their opponents' heads) that were the Anglo-Saxons' downfall. Anglo-Saxon armor did not protect the face, and after the battle it was plain that many of the Anglo-Saxon warriors, possibly Harold among them, had had their eyes pierced by the rain of arrows from the Norman archers. With Harold's death in battle, and the earlier deaths of Tostig and Harold Hardrada, there was no remaining competition. William of Normandy was crowned king of the English on Christmas Day in 1066.

OVERALL IMPACT OF THE VIKINGS: THE CELTIC REGIONS

As we shall see, the Norman Conquest produced far more lasting, fundamental changes in the lives of the people of the British Isles than the Vikings ever did. The Vikings provided a great deal of political disruption, but in most ways did not really change the social structures or cultural outlook of either the Anglo-Saxons or the Celts. Viking customs prevailed in their own towns and territories, but otherwise life went on around them. The great period of manuscript production in the British Isles had ended, but monks on the Continent continued to pursue the expressions of scholarship first founded in the Celtic monasteries.

*The Bayeux Tapestry. The embroidered panels depict events that marked the end of
Anglo-Saxon rule. Top: William's soldiers and horses crossing the English Channel.
Center: The Battle of Hastings. In this early stage of the combat the Norman cavalry
(on the left) is attacking the shield-wall of the Anglo-Saxon soldiers. Bottom: The
death of Harold. Harold is depicted twice, at the center of the illustration, with
an arrow in his eye, and on the right, where he has fallen and is being struck
across the legs.*

The Gaelic-speaking chieftains of both Ireland and the west of Scotland continued to have an enormous influence in both regions, little affected by Viking political structures. The old Gaelic principles of succession remained intact, with the basic organizational feature being the *tuath* (or tribal unit) under the control of a warrior chieftain. By Gaelic law any man of the *derbhfine* (descendants of a common great-grandfather) could inherit, with preference usually given to the old chieftain's brothers before his sons. Because there was no primogeniture, there was no real motivation for chieftains to collect territory merely to pass it along to the next generation. Land was held by hereditary right, because of its strategic use, and because of its mythical connections with the heroes of a family. These rights and remembered laws and genealogies remained the stock in trade of the aristocratic and highly trained aes dána professionals who continued to exercise an important role in Gaelic society until the seventeenth century.

In all of the old Celtic regions (Ireland, Wales, and the Highlands of Scotland), lineage determined status and societal obligations. Much of our understanding of the social structures of these regions comes from the compilations of law codes that delineated expected behaviors and imposed fines for legal violations. These law texts date to the seventh century for Ireland (although extant only in twelfth and thirteenth century manuscripts) and the Welsh laws of Hywel Dda were promulgated in the tenth century. There are no surviving texts specific to the Scottish Gaelic lordships, but there is much evidence that indicates that they adhered to law codes very similar to those of the Gaelic Irish. Every profession and trade was hereditary, and the Gaelic law codes ensured fair treatment for all according to their rank.

Everyone, women as well as men, had an *eiric* (honor price), which was a fine imposed on anyone who committed a crime against them. It was a sliding scale, based on perceived value to society, but all from chieftain to unfree handmaid carried an honor price. Women generally had a smaller eiric than men (in Wales a woman commanded half the *galenas* of her brother and a third the price of her husband). In Ireland, a crime against a woman was viewed as a crime against her guardian (father, husband, brother, son, or chieftain), and he received a percentage of what he would have received if he himself had been injured. Further guarantees of a woman's safety were spelled out in the seventh century Code of Adamnan (Columcille's biographer) that was influenced by canon law and protected the rights of noncombatants.

Both the Irish and Welsh law codes emphasized the importance of marriage in determining status of both men and women (an important point in some of the dynastic marriages concluded between Vikings and Gaelic heiresses). The Gaelic law codes enumerated a startlingly complex number of possible marital arrangements, ranging from concubine to primary wife, designations that seem at least partly dependent on the acceptance of the arrangement by the woman's family. The annals frequently refer to multiple marriages among the Irish elite, but whether these were simultaneous or sequential is somewhat unclear. (An excellent example of the ambiguity can be seen in the nickname of Cathal O'Connor's daughter, Cawlagh Mor, *Port-na-dtrí-namhad* [the meeting place of three enemies] because she was married, probably sequentially, to three men who were feuding.) The frequency of references to multiple marriages for both women and men strongly suggests the importance of dynastic alliances and the reality that, when an alliance no longer was wanted or needed, a new one would be formed. Certainly the law codes make it clear that divorce was acceptable for many different reasons. Some were applicable only to women (such as the husband departing by sea or entering a monastery), but some were applicable to both, such as the freedom for spouses to leave each other temporarily so that a child could be conceived with another partner. Women could also divorce husbands for impotence, homosexuality, or bisexuality; for abuse; or for "revealing the secrets of the marriage bed."

In general, women in Celtic society did not own land (although it should be remembered that land ownership even by men was governed by a different system that emphasized communal rather than individual holdings). A woman was usually accorded rights of maintenance if she was widowed, and her interests were always looked after by her nearest male relative. In some instances a woman might inherit her father's property if he had no sons, and if she was of equal status she sometimes could dissolve a contract made jointly with her husband.

The complex social organization of the Celtic regions based on both inherited status and professional training meant that families maintained monopolies over professions, and sometimes a woman might inherit her father's high-status position. (It is not clear from the annalistic references if this happened only if there were no male heirs or if personal aptitude was considered.) Such references are infrequent, but there was a handful of female high poets (*banfile*) named, and literary sources such as the *Táin bó Cúailgne* refer to female poets (e.g., Fedelm, a prophetic poet from Scotland), as well as the female arms master Scáthach, who taught the hero Cuchulainn his fighting skills. The *Lebor Gabála Erenn* refers to Airmed, the daughter of Diancecht, who was said to be as skilled in the arts of healing as her father.

ANGLO-SAXON SOCIETY AND CULTURE

Anglo-Saxon organizational structures and society largely endured during the Viking period. We do not know much about the organization of the earliest Anglo-Saxon tribal groups, but there are indications that they followed legal precepts similar to those of other Germanic tribes, with honor prices (called *wergeld*), oaths, and ordeals. Although the types of crimes and ranking of worth were somewhat different from those in the Irish law codes, the system of wergeld was functionally similar. When a crime was committed against either the honor or the person, a fine was levied in accordance with that person's value, payable either to the victim or to the victim's family in the case of murder.

The aristocrats, or *eorls*, obviously carried a higher honor price than the *ceorls* (primarily a designation for free farmers). As in Celtic society, even the servants had certain rights and obligations and carried honor prices because their well-being also affected the functioning of the larger kin group. One feature of Anglo-Saxon law that is not paralleled in the Gaelic law codes is the concept of trial by ordeal. This was based on a physical proof of one's innocence or guilt. For example, a man accused of theft or murder would have to carry a red-hot bar of iron a certain number of paces. His hands were bandaged and then inspected in a few days. If they were fiery red (infected), his guilt was proven. If they were healing, he was innocent.

In Anglo-Saxon society women often held high status and were valuable in establishing dynastic marriages. Women had property and maintenance rights and in some cases held property jointly with their husbands. It is interesting to note that some Anglo-Saxon place-names are derived from female names, such as Audley (from Aldgyp) and Edington (from Elfgifu), suggesting that they were held by women in their own right. We also see clear evidence of a woman's ability to exercise political power, at least in the case of highly aristocratic women. For example, Ethelfreda, Alfred's daughter, governed the kingdom of Mercia for seven years during the illness and subsequent death of her husband, the Eorl of Mercia. Alfred's mother, Osburga, was renowned for her nobility and piety and was credited with her positive influences on the character of her son. Anglo-Saxon women also appear to have had a powerful role as abbesses in the church. Perhaps the two best known examples are St. Ethedreda, the founder of Ely in East Anglia, and St. Hild, who founded the double monastery at Whitby in the seventh century.

Politically, Anglo-Saxon society was based around a hereditary monarchy, but it did not follow primogeniture. The importance of the recognition of a successor by the witan imparted a somewhat elective element, although in practice the witan seems usually to have upheld the old king's desires regarding his chosen heir. Territory was divided into counties or shires, each governed by an aristocratic eorl (earl or count) and also served by a shire-reeve (from which derives the office of sheriff) appointed by the king. These administrative units were little affected by the period of Viking settlement. Up until the 1970s the boundaries of many of the medieval shires remained unchanged. The shires were further divided into smaller units called *hundreds* and *ridings*. Although superseded by later organizational units, these terms still appear in some historical ceremonies and documents.

Despite the upheaval of the early medieval period, the Anglo-Saxons produced notable literary and artistic works. In addition to the Latin histories and saints' lives produced in the monasteries by such great scholars as Bede and Adamnan, there was also an emergence of literature, primarily poetry, in the Anglo-Saxon language. Perhaps best known is the epic *Beowulf*. It is possibly the oldest surviving text in Old English and certainly one of the most important ones. The date of composition has been much debated (probably somewhere between 700 and 900). Its Scandinavian setting testifies to its historical context, and the mixture of Christian and pagan elements provides us with a fascinating glimpse into the mental landscape of this period of transition. Almost certainly the poem existed in oral tradition for some time before it was compiled into a written manuscript.

The same mixture of cultures and outlook can be seen in visual terms in the grave goods found in the Sutton Hoo burial. This archaeological site, excavated in 1938, probably dates to the seventh century, close to the proximate date of composition of *Beowulf*. The burial was likely that of Redwald, king of East Anglia, who died in 625. He was buried in a great ship, eighty-six feet long, similar in style to Viking ships of the same era. In addition to complex armor (including a mail coat, spears, sword, and shield), there were also coins and jewelry, most notably buckles and decorations that bear distinctive Anglo-Saxon motifs, reminiscent of the Celtic decorations from Irish gold work and manuscripts, but with specific Anglo-Saxon motifs, such as the "biting beast." The king was also buried with silver goods from the Mediterranean; a Germanic-style lyre (suggesting the importance of recited poetry that we find in the Anglo-Saxon literary tradition); and, oddly, a statue in the form of a fish and a pair of spoons inscribed with the names Saul and Paul. These latter items have been assumed to show Christian influences or to constitute proof that the king had accepted Christianity, although there is nothing intrinsic to the objects to support this claim. Nonetheless, the treasures of Sutton Hoo (now in the collections of the British Museum) demonstrate clearly the dynamic and cosmopolitan culture of the Anglo-Saxons.

The Pitney Brooch. This is an example of Anglo-Saxon metalwork dating to the second half of the eleventh century. It shows the distinctive ribbon beasts (or "biting beasts") that do not appear in Celtic art, but are characteristic of the end of the Anglo-Saxon period.

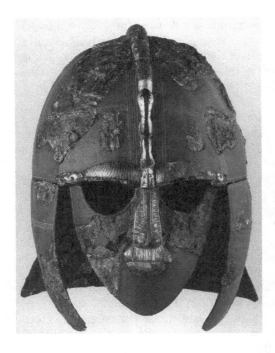

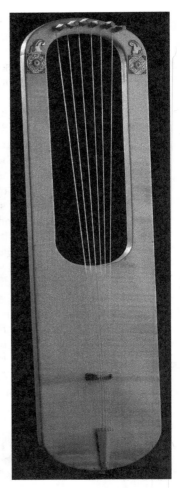

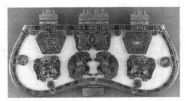

Sutton Hoo Ship burial. East Anglians probably constructed the large wooden ship for the burial of Redwald, a king of East Anglia, who died in 625. The ship was made to convey the king's body symbolically to the afterlife. Top left: The great helmet (partially reconstructed). Top right: The presence of this musical instrument, usually described as a lyre, provides evidence of the importance of music and poetry to the Anglo-Saxon culture as also illustrated by extant literary compositions. Bottom left: A gold clasp, with intricate interlacing lines picked out in blue enamel. Bottom right: The purse lid, ornamented with stylized figures of humans, birds, and dogs.

SUGGESTED READING

Ashe, Geoffrey. *The Discovery of King Arthur*. Garden City, NY: Macmillan 1987.

Bede. *Ecclesiastical History of the English People*. London: Penguin Classics, 1991.

Campbell, James, Eric John, and Patrick Wormald. *The Anglo-Saxons*. Ithaca, NY: Phaidon, 1982.

Campbell, James, *The Anglo-Saxon State*. London: Hambledon and London, 2000.

Davies, Wendy. *Wales in the Early Middle Ages*. Leicester: Leicester University Press, 1982.

Duncan, A. A. M. *Scotland: The Making of the Kingdom*. Vol. 1 of *The Edinburgh History of Scotland*. Edinburgh: Oliver & Boyd, 1975.

Evans, Angela Care. *The Sutton Hoo Ship Burial*. London: British Museum Press, 1986.

Fell, Christine, Cecily Clark, and Elizabeth Williams. *Women in Anglo-Saxon England*. London: British Museum Publications, 1984.

Fitzhugh, William F., and Elisabeth Ward, eds. *Vikings: The North Atlantic Saga*. Washington, DC: Smithsonian Books, 2000.

Laing, Lloyd, and Jennifer Laing, *The Picts and the Scots*. Gloucestershire: Sutton Publishing, 1993.

Loyn, H. R. *Anglo-Saxon England and the Norman Conquest*, 2nd ed. London: Routledge, 1991.

Marsden, John. *The Fury of the Northmen: Saints, Shrines and Sea-Raiders in the Viking Age*. London: Kyle Cathie, 1993.

Newman, Roger Chatterton. *Brian Boru, King of Ireland*. Cork: Mercier Press,1983.

ÓCorrain, Donncha. *Ireland Before the Normans*. Cork: Mercier Press, 1972.

Swanton, Michael, ed. and trans. *The Anglo-Saxon Chronicle*. London: Phoenix, 1996.

Sykes, Bryan. *Saxons, Vikings, and Celts: The Genetic Roots of Britain and Ireland*. New York: Norton, 2006.

Valante, Mary. The *Vikings in Ireland: Settlement, Trade and Urbanization*. Dublin: Four Courts Press, 2008.

Wilson, David M. *The Archaeology of Anglo-Saxon England*. Cambridge: Methuen Young Books, 1976.

———. *The Bayeux Tapestry*. New York: Knopf, 1985.

Chapter 5

Norman Britain

The arrival of the Normans following their victory at Hastings in 1066 was one of the most significant events in British history. Unlike the Vikings, the new Norman ruling dynasty changed everything from political administration to social organization, religion, language, and culture. Arguably, it was the impact of the Normans that led to the creation of both the identities and the conflicts between the eventual four kingdoms of the British Isles: England, Ireland, Scotland, and Wales.

WHO WERE THE NORMANS?

Although with hindsight historians identify the Normans as a specific group of people, their background and identity would not have been as clear in the eleventh century. William, now nicknamed the Conqueror, and his retainers came from the Duchy of Normandy across the English Channel. The name of the territory came from earlier Viking settlement that had resulted in the region being called the land of the Northmen. By William's time there was little remaining of Viking influences in either the land or its inhabitants, except perhaps for a strong inclination and skill in the art of warfare. Normandy was a rich province, well served by natural resources and trade. France was still centuries away from a strong centralized monarchy, and much of the power and wealth of what had once been the Frankish kingdom was concentrated in the hands of the powerful regional noblemen. The political system that had evolved here was very different from that of the Anglo-Saxon kings or Gaelic chieftains.

In Normandy and in the areas where Norman influence held sway, the chief nexus of power was land, not family: therefore, control of the land was tightly regimented through feudal relationships. Even the greatest of lords did not technically own their estates, but held them at the pleasure of the king or overlord. Because the acquisition of land was so essential to Norman politics and society, inheritance was based on primogeniture, in which the eldest son inherited all the lands and titles, thus theoretically keeping the lands intact and resulting in upward mobility from generation to generation as the landholdings of a specific lord were expanded through conquest or marriage.

The pure textbook model of feudalism as a political and military system probably never existed. There were myriad variations and exceptions, but generalizations can be made regarding the overall organizing principle. In the wake of the tenth century invasions throughout Europe (not only by Vikings, but also by Magyars and Saracens or Muslims), collective defense was of utmost importance. Under the feudal system a lord pledged fealty to another (usually stronger) lord and exchanged his military service for protection and maintenance. The stronger lord usually offered a gift of land (retaining the actual ownership of it) that would provide revenue to support the vassal. In return, the vassal guaranteed to provide knightly military service as required by the lord.

The system was rigidly hierarchical—only a nobleman could give or receive the oath of fealty. Contrary to Hollywood images, peasants could not become knights. Of course noblemen varied greatly in wealth and obtaining and maintaining the arms, armor, and extremely expensive war horses needed for combat entailed huge expenses, as did maintaining a fortified dwelling and entertaining large visiting retinues. The more land one had (with its revenue) the better. This often led to a knight swearing multiple oaths of fealty to various lords (sometimes problematic if he ended up serving two lords who were at war with one another) and also to the practice of subinfeudation whereby a knight essentially subcontracted portions of his land and service. Marriages could also either support or complicate feudal relationships. A noblewoman could not

A ceremony of homage and fealty as depicted in a medieval English manuscript. The ceremony constituted a symbol-laden ritual in which a vassal pledged loyalty and service to a lord.

swear fealty herself (because she could not provide military service directly), but she often was deeply involved in feudal politics through her relationships with male relatives.

With the Norman arrival in Britain, the political system of feudalism and its accompanying economic system of manorialism were introduced into regions that were previously organized primarily by kinship ties and communal land use. Although there were certainly differences in social status in both Anglo-Saxon and Celtic society, these took the form of a fine gradation of status ranging from the elites to the unfree servants whereas the Norman view (which became emblematic of the High Middle Ages across most of Europe) was based on a simple tripartite division of social orders or estates: the first estate, "those who prayed" (the clergy); the second estate, "those who fought" (the nobility); and the third estate, "those who worked" (the peasants). Those who worked constituted about 98 percent of European society.

In Europe, and in parts of England after the Norman Conquest, manorialism helped to support and expand the power of the feudal nobility. In manorialism, those who worked labored on the land. They too exchanged service for protection, but in their case, the service was agricultural and the protection was very literal, with the farmed *desmesne* lands often adjacent to the fortified dwelling (or castle) or sometimes within its walls. Although a peasant's rank never changed, there were different degrees of wealth and status even among the third estate, with a freeholder (usually holding a long-term lease) having higher status than a yearly renter. In classic manorialism there was a third rank of peasant (unfree serfs who were bound to the land). In England, estates tended to be smaller than on the Continent, and the practice of using serfs was more limited. Contrary to the picture of Norman and Anglo-Saxon relationships that we see in Walter Scott's *Ivanhoe*, there is no real evidence that the Anglo-Saxons as a group were bound to serfdom to further the political aims of the Normans.

THE NORMANIZATION OF BRITAIN

The Norman arrival was a shock nonetheless. Given the Norman perspective on landholding, after the conclusion of the Battle of Hastings in 1066, William considered that he now literally owned all of England. He immediately began handing out parcels of land to his loyal retainers in exchange for knightly service. They flocked across the channel, especially younger sons who had no chance of inheriting French estates. To the Normans, this was not a hostile conquest but rather the successful completion of William's legitimate (in their eyes) claim to the throne. This point is made very strongly in the (Norman-made) Bayeux tapestry with its panels showing the granting of the right of succession to William by Edward the Confessor. The *Anglo-Saxon Chronicle*, however, paints a very different picture of the Norman takeover.

Although William obtained the submissions of some of the powerful Anglo-Saxon lords in the weeks following the battle, clearly he did not trust them. He immediately began building castles: Montfichet, Baynard's Castle, and the foundations of what would become the White Tower (of London). He built a strategically important new castle at Norwich, which he gave to his friend William Fitz Osbern, whom he soon named Earl of Hereford and lord of the Isle of Wight. While William was celebrating his victory in Normandy in March of 1067, a rising in the west was launched by Edric the Wild in alliance with the Welsh princes. This was only the first of many rebellions. When William returned to England in December 1067, the city of Exeter had declared against him. He laid siege to the city, eventually bringing about its submission. He then erected a castle on the site and moved on to campaigns in Cornwall.

A very serious threat soon came from the north. The English lords Edwin and Morcar, who had previously given their submission, fled to Northumbria where they gained support against the king. At the same time the *aethling* Edgar (the last male of the House of Wessex, grandson of Edmund Ironside, and heir to the English throne) took his mother and sisters and fled to Scotland under the protection of the Scottish King Malcolm. William obtained an oath of fealty from the Scottish king, but the peace was short lived. William built castles at Warwick, Nottingham, York, Lincoln, Huntingdon, and Cambridge. In spite of this fortification, more risings occurred in the north, along with a spate of resistance in the south—from Cornwall to Devon to Somerset. In the winter of 1069 Edgar and the Northumbrians were joined by Sweyn Estrithson, who had set sail up the Humber in command of a large Danish fleet. (Sweyn also had a tenuous claim to the English throne, although he did not advance it during the events of 1066.) Furious, William arrived in York with all of his court and regalia (to make his sovereignty clear) and then, as Orderic Vitalis, Benedictine monk and chronicler, tells us: "In his anger he commanded that all crops and herds, chattels, and food of every kind should be brought together and burned to ashes with consuming fire, so that the whole region north of Humber might be stripped of all means of sustenance." This perhaps was the real conquest.

Even with the horrific devastation of Northumbria, William's hold on England was not secure. There were two more major uprisings in 1070 and 1072, highlighting both internal and external dissension. The first, an odd affair, centered around a charismatic leader named Hereward the Wake. The rising started in the fenlands around Ely, a territorial holdout of members of the old Anglo-Saxon ruling party. It is not altogether clear how Hereward came to lead the rebellion. Although his story has the quality of a folktale (he may have been the original Robin Hood), Hereward was a real historical figure. Hugo Candidus in his history of the Abbey of Peterborough tells us that Hereward "held land of the Abbey" and he appears in the Domesday survey as holding land in Warwickshire. The stories called him an outlaw (outlaw in the formal sense of being outside the law) even before the rising against William, and the *Anglo-Saxon Chronicle* mentioned his first appearance in the events of the rising as the arrival of "Hereward and his gang," indicating that he had an already established reputation.

The rebellion started in Peterborough when the fenland rebels joined a Danish expeditionary fleet and sacked the abbey. The Anglo-Saxon version of the story explained that this was done to save the relics that were in the custody of a Norman bishop who had been installed by William. After the raid, the Danes sailed away and the rebel force under Hereward moved on to Ely. They were joined (or accompanied) by the Earls Siward and Morcar. The stories tell of many deeds of valor and derring-do as the rebels made essentially the last stand against the Normans. William laid siege to the island, and whatever the truth of the stories, it is an incontrovertible fact that Hereward and the rest held out against the Normans for nearly a year. Depending on which account one consults, at the end they were overcome either by William's superior military strategy or by the treachery of the monks who handed over the monastery to William. In any case, Earl Morcar was captured and imprisoned by William for the rest of his life (Edwin had already died in Scotland by this time). All accounts agree that Hereward was nowhere to be found. In the best outlaw hero tradition he had made his escape, and so he became the folk hero who stood up to the conquerors and almost won.

If Hereward's rebellion reminds us that there were still internal pockets of resistance, William's other chief challenge provides evidence of external threat. The Scottish monarchy was growing in power and in 1072 was ruled by a strong king with an interesting agenda. Malcolm III, known to later generations as Canmore (*Ceann Mór* or "big head," in a political rather than a physical sense), had already harbored English rebels during the Northumbrian campaign, and although he had sworn lukewarm fealty to William, his interests plainly favored an anti-Norman stance. The Scottish kingdom by this time had evolved to incorporate most of the old kingdom of Strathclyde and the central uplands, but Malcolm still had challenges from the territory of Moray to the north and from the west, which retained strong Norse influences. (At that time, the Hebrides and the Isle of Man were under Norse rule.) It was not to Malcolm's benefit to have a strong Norman neighbor to his south. Moreover, he was now married to the atheling Edgar's sister Margaret.

Malcolm seems to have had no interest in entering the fray for the English kingship, but he did have strong reasons for wanting to secure his southern flank. The area south of Strathclyde had uncertain boundaries—by the time one reached the Humber it was English, but the territories in between could theoretically belong to either the Scots or the English king. It was this region that Malcolm sought to control. William objected and brought his armies north again, arguably in an even greater display of strategy than Hastings. William swept through Lothian to Stirling, crossed the ford there, and moved on to the Tay, where he was met by the Norman navy. Astounded and overwhelmed, Malcolm submitted at the fort of Abernethy in September 1072. The terms of his fealty were unclear, probably at the time and certainly to those who came after. Was he submitting to William's sovereignty as lord of Cumbria and Lothian (which titles he held) or as king of the Scots? Most likely it was the former because those were the debatable territories technically outside the kingdom of Scotland and thus subject to William's authority, but it could be seen as the surrender of Scotland to her neighbor to the south. The issue was further clouded by the granting of Malcolm's eldest son, Duncan, to William as a hostage. This point about the precise terms of the feudal relationship between the king of the English and the king of the Scots would continue to haunt Anglo-Scottish relations from that point forward.

NORMAN INFLUENCES IN SCOTLAND

Although this campaign was a military defeat for the Scots, the actual process of normanization in Scotland probably came not from the king's oath of fealty, but rather from the queen's taste for civility and culture. Although she was of the House of Wessex, Queen Margaret had been exposed to the Norman lifestyle and had developed a fondness for the beautiful buildings, tapestries, and books that went with the Norman way of life. She had a Hungarian mother and had been brought up in Hungary; therefore, she had little personal knowledge of the old Anglo-Saxon outlook. The image of Margaret that comes from her biographer Turgot (her confessor and the Saxon bishop of St. Andrews) is that of a determined, pious woman, intent on securing the interests of her sons and probably somewhat intimidating to her rough northern husband. Turgot recounted one story of the saintly Margaret kneeling to wash the feet of a beggar. When Malcolm saw her doing this, he knelt beside her to help. She was literate and Turgot tells us that Malcolm kissed her books of devotion and quietly removed them from her chamber so that he could have them bound with gold and jewels.

Although Margaret was known for loving beauty, she encouraged pious austerity. She favored the Benedictine order and had a church built at Dunfermline (the town in which she and Malcolm married). She is also remembered for involving herself in calling church synods to reconcile the differences in observance that still existed between continental practice and the remnants of the old Celtic church. (For example, Lent began five days later in Scotland than elsewhere in Christendom, and it was a common belief in Scotland that ordinary people should not receive the Eucharist because they were too sinful.) Margaret had scholars from Canterbury come to debate the matter, and Turgot tells us that she herself took part in the debates, aided by her husband, who acted as interpreter, "both to say and do whatever she might direct." The result was a smoothing out of the points of dissension and the emergence of a stronger, more welcoming church. As part of her personal patronage, Margaret encouraged Anglo-Normans to settle in Scotland, and Malcolm upheld her preferences for the Norman language and customs.

It may have been Margaret's advice that inadvertently led to her devoted husband's death. After the death of William, Malcolm agreed, perhaps at Margaret's request, to meet with William Rufus at Gloucester to renew his oath of fealty. When the time for the meeting came, William Rufus refused to meet with the Scots king. In a fury, Malcolm rode north, mustered an army and led it back into Northumbria. At Alnwick, he was caught in an ambush and he and his son Edward were killed. Another son, Edgar, came to Margaret to tell her of the death of his father and brother. Edgar found her already grievously ill. When she was told, Turgot tells us that the queen did not weep, but gave thanks that her grief had purified her soul in its last moments. She died three days later and was buried in her church at Dunfermline. She was canonized in 1250.

In the short term, it appeared that the stabilization of the Scottish monarchy that had come under Malcolm and Margaret was about to be lost. Donald Bane, the brother of Malcolm Canmore, appeared with a great number of supporters, mostly anti-Norman Scottish lords who opposed the introduction of Norman feudal estates and the anglicization of the church. Although Malcolm and Margaret had five more surviving sons, Donald seized the throne, claiming the Celtic right of lateral succession. Donald and his supporters drove out the settlers, and Malcolm's sons (with the exception of Edmund) fled to the south. Malcolm's son by his first marriage, Duncan, who had been held hostage since the Treaty of Abernethy twenty years before, was already at the court of William Rufus. Not surprisingly, by this time Duncan was thoroughly normanized, and after giving his oath of fealty to William Rufus, he received the endorsement of the English king, went north "accompanied with what aid he could get of English and French," and deposed his uncle. He was promptly murdered (probably at the behest of his half-brother Edmund) and Donald Bane returned to the throne. Although elderly by the standards of the time (he was over sixty), Donald joined an insurrection in Northumbria; in his absence he was again deposed, this time by Edgar, second son of Malcolm and Margaret.

Truly his mother's son, Edgar was calmly confident of the future. While encamped near Durham he had seen a vision of St. Cuthbert, who promised him guidance and protection. Edgar held the throne, and the succession passed to his brothers Alexander and David in turn. Both were essentially Anglo-Norman in outlook, David having spent much of his youth in the Norman court where his sister Edith/Matilda, married to Henry I, was queen. Both furthered their mother's patronage of the church and realized that at least to some extent they owed their inheritance to the Norman king to their south.

During the reigns of the three sons of Malcolm, especially that of David I (1124–53), the Scottish monarchy regained its stability and the process of normanization was rapidly extended. The abbeys and monasteries were filled with Norman bishops, land ownership based on the feudal model was implemented through much of the kingdom with written charters and laws guaranteeing inheritance through primogeniture, and Norman settlers (often friends made by the brothers during their times of exile) came north and built castles and estates after the Norman feudal model. In the royal court, French language, music, and cuisine was favored, and within less than fifty years the ruling elites of Scotland included the FitzAlans, de Bruses, de Balliols, and others whose names show their Norman heritage.

It should be emphasized, however, that Scotland was by no means fully unified at this time, nor was normanization universally the pattern in all regions. Moray, still being governed by descendants of the old Celtic mormaer earls— who highly valued their independence against the throne, remained a problematic area for the Scottish Canmore kings. Also, in the west (the Hebrides and parts of Argyllshire) essentially another kingdom was emerging. This was the Kingdom of the Isles (later known as the Lordship of the Isles), a powerful seaborne confederation that by this time was almost a perfect blend of Norse and Gaelic cultures. Somerled, the first recognized Lord of the Isles, reigned from 1130 to 1164 and was as impressive a leader in his own right as his contemporary, David, the son of Malcolm III.

THE NORMANIZATION OF IRELAND

One could say that normanization in Scotland began with a woman; this too was the case in Ireland, although in a very different way. During the time of the Conqueror, the Normans sought to secure England and to extend their control over Scotland and Wales, but really gave no thought to Ireland. Aside from lingering trade from the old Viking port towns, Ireland had no particular attraction. There was no nascent centralized monarchy and no rich estates to govern. Mostly there were warring Gaelic chieftains, and it was a fight between two of them over a woman that brought the Normans to Ireland, changing Irish politics and society forever.

The two rival kings, Dermot MacMurrough of Leinster and Tiernan O'Rourke of Breffny, were part of a larger feud revolving around the bitter power struggle between the lords of Ulster and the lords of Connacht. There had been battles, burnings of monasteries, pillaging, and ravaging going on for years. At the heart of the issue lay O'Rourke's humiliation resulting from his wife's abduction by MacMurrough. Her name was Derbforgaill (usually translated as Dervorgilla), daughter of the king of Munster, and both Gaelic and Norman sources agree that she was the one who arranged the abduction. Geoffrey Keating, a seventeenth century scholar of the Irish annals, makes this clear:

As to Dermot, when this message reached him he went quickly to meet the lady, accompanied by a detachment of mounted men, and when they reached where she was, he ordered that she be placed on horseback behind a rider, and upon this the woman wept and screamed in pretence as if Dermot were carrying her off by force; and bringing her with him in this fashion, he returned to Leinster.

(Lest one have the wrong sort of image in mind, it should be noted that MacMurrough was forty-two at the time and Dervorgilla was forty-four.)

O'Rourke recovered her a year later, but the two men's antipathy was unabated. The feud continued for ten years, but by 1166 MacMurrough had lost most of his allies. O'Rourke had cornered him, and he was about to be attacked by the Norse of Wexford, along with various chieftains from North Ulster. In anger and despair, MacMurrough fled, taking his grievances across the Irish Sea to Henry II, king of England, but also lord of Normandy. Focused on his efforts to build his cross-channel power, Henry had already been thinking about Ireland and most likely (although some historians still debate it) already had a bull, "Laudabiliter," from Pope Adrian (still the only English pope), authorizing him to invade Ireland in the name of religious reform. Henry accepted Dermot's oath of fealty and sent an open letter inviting his subjects to come to Dermot's assistance. The response was lukewarm at best, and Dermot himself began recruiting among the Welsh Normans. One of the greatest of these was Richard de Clare (known as Strongbow). To further his own political aspirations, Strongbow agreed to lead an army to Ireland to restore Dermot's lost lands on the condition that Dermot give him his eldest daughter, Aoife, and with her the right of succession to the kingdom of Leinster.

The Normans arrived in Ireland in May 1169, among them Fitzhenrys, Fitzgeralds, Barrys, Prendergasts, Roches, and Carews, a roll call of the Norman lords who would come to control Ireland. They were attacked by the Norse of Wexford, whom they sent scrambling in retreat. Strongbow himself arrived a bit later, accompanied by more Norman knights. They captured the city of Waterford, and the marriage between Strongbow and Aoife took place as had been arranged, emblematic of the joining together of Gaelic and Norman lordships. The Normans then marched on Dublin. They were trapped and besieged by Rory O'Connor, king of Connacht, but the Gaels were unfamiliar with siege warfare and, after about two months with no provisions, the Normans decided to try

Effigy of Richard de Clare, "Strongbow," in Christ Church Cathedral, Dublin. Strongbow married Aoife MacMurrough and their union can be seen as emblematic of the process of normanization in Ireland. This effigy is a replacement for the supposed original that was crushed in a roof collapse in the sixteenth century and likely depicts another knight. However, the identification of the monument with Strongbow indicates his continuing symbolic importance.

Ruins of Hugh de Lacy's Castle, Trim, Ireland. This castle is one of the best examples of the Norman-style ramparts and other fortifications that were incorporated into the castles erected by Norman lords to protect from encroachments by the Gaelic Irish.

breaking out. Rory's forces were not at guard as they should have been, and he himself was bathing in the Liffey. In the sortie most of the Irish were killed. Rory himself barely escaped, and the siege was lifted. In less than a year the Normans had conquered all of Ireland, securing victories against the Norse and the Gaelic chieftains. In October 1171 Henry arrived, taking credit for the victories and demanding submission of the Irish lords. Rory was among those who acknowledged Henry as overlord, as did the bishops of Ireland, convened under Laurence O'Toole, the reforming archbishop of Dublin.

The military conquest of Ireland by the Normans was now complete, followed by the usual phase of castle building and feudalization of the territories occupied by the Norman lords. The style of castle favored in Ireland was the motte-and-bailey, quickly built even in hostile territory and defensible with a small number of retainers. Many of these strongholds have now been excavated, providing insights into Norman military organization and agricultural methods. Although the process of normalization in Ireland was dramatic, it did not destroy the underlying structures of society or the culture of the Gaels. What resulted was an oddly hybridized society, consisting of both Gaelic and Anglo-Norman ways of life. The customs of the Normans prevailed in their own fiefs, but not all of Ireland was part of the feudal network. Moreover, in time, the Normans appropriated the Gaelic language and culture, becoming as the famous phrase would have it, "more Irish than the Irish themselves."

THE NORMANS IN WALES

When William arrived in England in 1066, Wales was a confusing patchwork of principalities and chieftaincies. There was no nascent kingdom or national identity and to a large degree the initial introduction of Norman fiefs and lords was not perceived by the Welsh as having any great impact. William, however, was eager to secure the west and encouraged the usual settlement and castle building along the frontiers by his loyal retainers. He did not wish to annex Wales, treating it similarly to the way he had treated Scotland—as an independent realm whose acknowledgement of overlordship was to be sought. His knights were not ordered to conquer Welsh lands, but they were not forbidden to do so if they wished. There was no real center of power or organized resistance, but William recognized the power of Rhys ap Tewdwr as the ruler of Deheubarth. Although the land was not invaded, it appears that during William's visit to Wales in 1081, he probably secured Rhys's oath of fealty. In any event, the *Domesday Book* records in 1086 that Rhys was paying a tribute of £40 per year to the English king.

In 1087 William died, and the carefully orchestrated strategies and agreements that he had maintained began to fall apart. Rhys had been an important linchpin in Welsh policy, but in 1088 his kingdom was attacked by Bernard of Neufmarché. In the aftermath Rhys was killed. Without him, Welsh resistance exploded and what had seemed like an easy, casual conquest suddenly turned violent and militant. Under both William II and Henry I, the English Crown, unwilling to commit the resources needed to completely conquer Wales, was nevertheless unwilling to allow it to be ceded to the rule of the Welsh lords. The result was an ongoing state of war for the next two hundred years, with Norman efforts concentrated on maintaining a buffer zone of castles along the Welsh Marches.

Interestingly, Rhys's daughter, Nest, figures prominently in Welsh-Norman relations. She had a spectacular lineage, descending from the great Rhodri Mawr (the first Welsh ruler to be called the Great as a result of his resistance to the Vikings and consolidation of the kingdoms of Gwynedd and Powys) as well as the illustrious law giver Hywyl Dwa. She was the only legitimate daughter of Rhys and his wife, Gwladys ferch Rhiwallon of Powys, and so she had immense status as a dynastic pawn. She caught the eye of William's youngest son, Henry I, and bore him several illegitimate children. She was married twice, first to Gerald Fitzwalter (by whom she had several children, including the ancestor of the Fitzgeralds of Ireland) and secondly to Stephen, the constable of Cardigan (by whom she had at least one son, Robert FitzStephen, another one of the Norman conquerors of Ireland). Nest has been called "the queen-bee of the Cambro-Norman swarm" and the list of her descendants is staggering. Besides the two sons mentioned above, she was the grandmother of Giraldus Cambrensis (Gerald of Wales), chronicler of English, Irish, and Welsh affairs during the twelfth century, and at least theoretically, she was the ancestress of Henry Tudor. Giraldus made an interesting statement that reflected his ancestry and the ambiguous state of affairs between the Normans and the Welsh, saying that he was too much of a Norman for the Welsh and too much of a Welshman for the Normans.

CONSOLIDATION OF NORMAN POWER IN ENGLAND

In England, the Norman Conquest was secured by 1071. Given the Norman zeal for the acquisition of land, it is no surprise that one of the great monuments of William's reign was his compiled documentation of the lands and revenues of England, called the *Domesday Book*. In it were listed manors, lords, revenues, taxes, number of peasants, and even the number and kinds of livestock. Each estate was measured in "hides" (which varied from 40 to 120 acres) and the tenants were not named. Nonetheless, the data contained in this document provide a wealth of information for historians. One of the most dramatic points illustrated by the data is that, by 1087 (the year of William's death and the completion of the *Domesday Book*), only about 5 percent of the land remained in the hands of the pre-Conquest Anglo-Saxon families. About 50 percent was held by Norman settlers, 25 percent by the Church, and 17 percent by the king and queen outright. It also appears from the document that agricultural life in Britain was being reorganized along the lines of manorialism, but that impression may have come more from the scribes, who were recording notes in terms they knew, rather than from the actual reorganization of the land.

When William died in 1087, he left behind not only his legacy in the British Isles, but also his Duchy of Normandy and three sons (a fourth predeceased him). His oldest son, Robert Curthose, was to inherit the Duchy of Normandy; the second son, William Rufus, was to rule England; and the youngest, Henry, was paid a sum of money to renounce his claims. A daughter, Adela, had been married to the Count of Blois. William Rufus became king of England as

The Domesday Book. *This was a detailed survey of the population, land ownership, and income in England, undertaken at the behest of William the Conqueror.*

William II, neither as popular nor as effective as his father. He soon had the Duchy of Normandy to contend with as well. Robert, having decided to join the First Crusade, had mortgaged the duchy to his brother William to provide revenue. Although William Rufus reigned until 1100, there was little to distinguish his reign. He never married, evidently preferring the company of concubines, and his death in a hunting accident may not have been altogether accidental. (There were those who suggested that his ambitious younger brother Henry might have had a hand in it.)

In any case, Henry took the throne in 1100 and was unpleasantly surprised when his older brother Robert returned from the Crusade, everyone having long since concluded that he was dead. In light of Henry's official renunciation of his claims, Robert believed, correctly, that he should have inherited the English throne. He invaded England, but withdrew before going to battle. In Normandy, his vassals were so incensed by the years of ineffective rule that they invited Henry to invade Normandy. He did, securing a victory at the battle of Tinchebrai. Robert spent his remaining years in prison, and once more all the lands of William the Conqueror belonged to one man. Henry was by far the best of the three sons in terms of administrative ability. He was nicknamed Beauclerc for his interest in the law. He did much to tighten royal administration and extended the control of the church by the English monarchs.

Henry married and had a son, William, but the succession that had looked secure became a crisis when William died in 1120. (He drowned when his ship sank in the English Channel. Chroniclers tell us that he was drunk at the time.) Henry had no shortage of illegitimate children (having fathered at least twenty), but his only legitimate heir was his daughter Matilda. She had been married twice, first to the Holy Roman emperor and then to the great Norman lord Geoffrey of Anjou. Henry sought to provide for her succession, but the Norman lords refused to accept a woman as their monarch. Instead, when Henry died in 1135, they installed Stephen, son of Henry's sister Adela and her husband, the Count of Blois, on the English throne. Matilda invaded England in 1139 and a turbulent period of civil war followed. David of Scotland, Matilda's uncle, also took advantage of the unrest to lay claim to territories in northern England. Finally, in 1153 a compromise was reached with the Treaty of Wallingford. It provided for the uncontested rule of Stephen for the rest of his life, but the succession of Matilda's son Henry, upon his death. Because Stephen's son had already died, this arrangement was agreeable to all parties. When Stephen died in 1154, Henry II took the throne, giving the country one of the most dynamic and influential kings that England has known.

SUGGESTED READING

Barlow, Frank. *The English Church, 1066–1154*. London: Addison-Wesley Longman, 1979.

———. *The Feudal Kingdom of England, 1042–1216*, 3rd ed. London: Longman, 1979.

———. *William Rufus*. Berkeley, CA: University of California Press, 1983.

Barrow, G. W. S. *Kingship and Unity: Scotland, 1000–1306*. Edinburgh: Edinburgh University Press, 1981.

Brown, R. Allen. *The Normans*. New York: St. Martin's Press, 1984.

Chibnall, Marjorie. *Anglo-Norman England, 1066–1166*. New York: Blackwell, 1986.

———. *The Debate on the Norman Conquest*. Manchester: Manchester University Press, 1999.

Davies, John. *A History of Wales*. Middlesex, UK: Allen Lane, 1990.

Davies, R. R. *The Age of Conquest: Wales, 1063–1415*. Oxford: Oxford University Press, 2000.

Davis, R. H. C. *The Normans and Their Myth*. London: Thames and Hudson, 1976.

Dolley, Michael. *Anglo-Norman Ireland*. Dublin: Gill and Macmillan, 1972.

Flanagan, Marie Therese. *Irish Society, Anglo-Norman Settlers, Angevin Kingship: Interactions in Ireland in the Late Twelfth Century*. Oxford: Oxford University Press, 1990.

Head, Victor. *Hereward*. Gloucestershire, UK: Sutton, 1995.

Loyn, H. R. *The Norman Conquest*, 3rd ed. London: Hutchinson Educational, 1982.

Lydon, James, ed. *The English in Medieval Ireland*. Dublin: Royal Irish Academy, 1984.

MacPhee, Kathleen. *Somerled: Hammer of the Norse*. Glasgow: Neil Wilson, 2004.

Moody, T. W. and F. X. Martin (Eds.). *The Course of Irish History*, revised edition. Niwot, CO: Roberts Rinehart, 1994.

Prebble, John. *The Lion in the North: One Thousand Years of Scotland's History*. Middlesex, UK: Penguin, 1971.

Wormald, Jenny, ed. *Scotland: A History*. Oxford: Oxford University Press, 2005.

Chapter 6

Britain in the High Middle Ages

The accession of Henry II in 1154 began a new dynasty in English history, that of the Plantagenets, named for the emblem of the dyer's broom (*plante genet*) that appeared on the arms of the counts of Anjou. The dynasty is also known as the Angevins, another reference to Henry's descent from the counts of Anjou. In addition to the changes coming with the dynasty, all of Europe was entering a time of transformation, collectively called the Twelfth Century Renaissance. During this period many themes emerged: the evolution of feudal monarchies, the changed relationship between monarchs and popes, a new emphasis on religious orders, the growth of urbanization, the newly emergent styles of art and architecture known as the Gothic, and the new system of philosophy and scholarship called scholasticism. In this increasingly complex and interconnected European community the role of Britain was yet to be defined.

In many ways the twelfth century was an almost magical time in Europe, one of those golden ages in which conditions and personalities came together to produce huge transformations in society. Even to nonspecialists, the twelfth century is recognizable as the most medieval of the medieval centuries. With its castles and cathedrals, crusaders, and scholars, it is the era most often depicted in Hollywood medievalism. Although many of the processes of transformation had already begun in the eleventh century, several factors contributed to the dramatic changes of the twelfth century, both in Britain and on the Continent.

THE AGRICULTURAL REVOLUTION

Aside from a few remnants of Roman settlements and Viking trading centers, Europe began the Middle Ages as an almost entirely rural society. Particularly in England, the basic organizing unit was the village; by the Norman period it was often attached to the stronghold of the feudal lord who governed. Crop yields were low, risks from bad weather were high, warfare between rival lords complicated agricultural life, and the whole society lived in a precarious subsistence economy. For the freeholding peasant farmer, the equation was grim. One grain planted yielded three grains harvested if one were lucky. The freeholder usually owed the equivalent of one grain as rent to the lord, one grain to be paid to the Church as a tithe, and one grain to be held back for next year's crop. All too often, the choice was to starve now or starve later. In theory, the lord was supposed to look after his tenants and serfs, but this did not always happen.

In the late eleventh century, several changes took place in agricultural life that began to improve the situation. On paper, they sound minor, but in practice they began having a great impact on the medieval economy. Perhaps the most significant agricultural change was the implementation of the three-field system in which plantings rotated seasonally from wheat to legumes to lying fallow. Wheat depletes the nitrogen in soil, and if only wheat is grown the field will eventually stop producing. Introducing legumes restores nitrogen to the soil. Allowing the field to lie fallow for one season lets it recover so that it will again produce a full yield of wheat. (Three-field rotation was not always possible in rugged terrain such as that of Scotland and Wales. In those mountainous areas barley or oats were the only cereal crops that would grow and seaweed sometimes replaced the legumes to help replenish the soil.)

Other changes were also underway. In areas where it was possible, fields were arranged in long narrow strips, all under cultivation by different peasants. One might have a strip here, another two miles away, and another five miles away. By the end of the eleventh century efforts were being made to consolidate the fields and to take better advantage of two technological breakthroughs: the padded horse collar and the heavy-wheeled plow. The classical world had used a light scratch plow, which only drew a line on top of the soil. It worked fine in the light dry soils of the Mediterranean, but very poorly in the heavy wet fields of northern Europe. By the end of the eleventh century a new type of plow was being developed with a moldboard that cut into the soil and turned it over, allowing a more effective means of planting. In addition, for areas that used horses as draft animals, the new padded horse collar, unlike the neck traces that had been used by the Romans, enabled the horses to pull with the full strength of their shoulders. (In many areas oxen continued to be the draft animals of choice. They were slower but cheaper to feed. In the rugged mountainous regions of Britain, it was impossible to use draft animals and so the foot plow continued to be used well into the early modern period.)

The combination of the new technologies with the new techniques in farming resulted in increased crop yields, and for the first time, there was enough of a surplus that not everyone needed to be farming. This led to the emergence of true towns, which existed primarily for trade, but quickly became governmental and ecclesiastical centers as well.

THE URBAN REVOLUTION

Britain followed the continental pattern of the growth of urban development during the twelfth century, although the charters often came first and the actual town building lagged behind. As early as the reign of Henry I, royal charters were being given to towns. Henry I authorized 17, Henry II granted 75, and during their reigns Richard and John granted more than 250 charters. Of

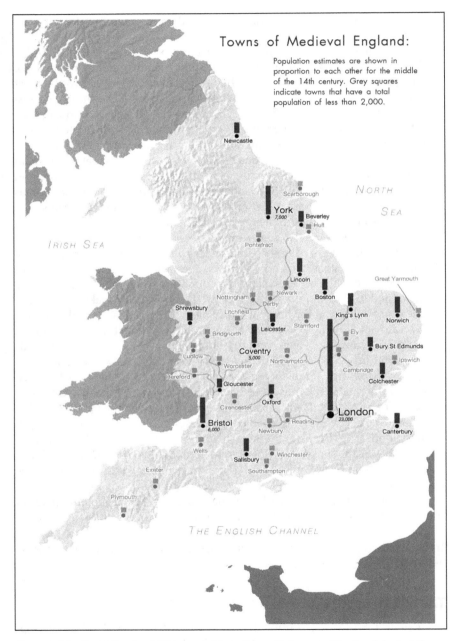

Towns of Medieval England:

Population estimates are shown in proportion to each other for the middle of the 14th century. Grey squares indicate towns that have a total population of less than 2,000.

Newcastle

NORTH

Scarborough

York
7,000

Beverley

Hull

SEA

IRISH SEA

Pontefract

Lincoln

Great Yarmouth

Nottingham   Newark   Boston

Shrewsbury   Derby

Litchfield   King's Lynn   Norwich

Bridgnorth   Stamford

Leicester   Ely

Coventry   Bury St Edmunds

5,000   Northampton   Ipswich

Ludlow   Worcester   Cambridge

Hereford   Gloucester   Colchester

Cirencester   Oxford

Bristol   London

6,000   Reading   *23,000*

Newbury   Canterbury

Wells

Salisbury   Winchester

Southampton

Exeter

Plymouth

THE ENGLISH CHANNEL

Towns of medieval England. This map shows the main towns of England during the High Middle Ages. Population estimates are difficult to ascertain for this period, but the map shows how small, by our standards, the towns were at that time. London, at twenty-three thousand, was by far the largest, and that was small in comparison to the towns of the Continent.

course, a charter did not necessarily mean that a town would actually be established. One of the best examples of a planned town that did not work was Edward I's Nova Villa, located at Poole Bay in Dorset. It was given a charter in 1286, the site was established, and town planners were appointed by the king. Nothing happened. No one wanted to move there. People went instead to the growing town of Poole, four miles away across the bay. It had been started forty years earlier by the Earl of Salisbury, and perhaps he simply had gained the initial advantage. More likely the successful site had local commercial advantages that the king and town planners did not understand. On the Continent planned cities boomed during the twelfth and thirteenth centuries (a quick glance at a map reveals numerous Newtons [New Towns], Newburghs, and so forth). In Britain, town growth tended to be more circumstantial, often taking place on the sites of old Roman settlements or forts, near churches with their saints' day market fairs, or at clear entrepôt locations such as ports or rivers.

Of course, London was the most notable example of a medieval British town, but other towns such as Bristol and York were of regional significance. It is important to note that these towns were exceedingly small by modern standards. The original walls of the City of London were slightly more than two miles long and enclosed a space of only about one square mile. Technically the difference between a medieval village and town was the existence of a wall in the case of a town. Villages could certainly be places of manufacture and commerce, but they lacked the fortification of a wall and often the commercial regulation associated with town charters.

In Scotland, the distinction between village and town was especially nebulous. Glasgow plainly functioned as a town well before its formal charter (the cathedral was founded in 1136, but the charter was not given until 1175). In the intervening years there is clear evidence of the existence of a weekly market. Incidentally, the name *Glas ghu* (the dear green place) reminds us of its rural roots, a far cry from the post-industrial images of the city on the Clyde. Similarly, Aberdeen was an important center of the North Atlantic fishing trade well before its charter was given. Some towns such as St. Andrews never possessed royal charters and were never really market towns, but were rather associated with ecclesiastical centers.

Nonetheless, whatever the specific nature of urban development, the foundation and growing emphasis on town life during the twelfth century helped propel many of the other changes associated with that century. With the new organization of society along more commercial lines came more emphasis on regulation and governmental controls. At the same time there was more opportunity to choose one's occupation, and even the old tripartite division of society into clergy, nobility, and peasants began to be challenged with the emergence of a new category: tradesman or merchant. In other words, there were now individuals who worked, but not on the land, and whose relationship with the other social orders was ill defined. As a group these tradesmen and merchants were very concerned with their rights and *freedoms*, a word and a concept that did not even exist in the classical world.

The transformation in society meant that sons did not necessarily do only what their fathers had done before. Theoretically they could learn something new (there was a new emphasis on education) and could rise in status, never breaching the abyss between peasant and noble, but still becoming a successful wealthy merchant and rising in the world. From today's perspective, social mobility was limited, and the new professions had their own hierarchies, but comparatively, this new world of the twelfth century offered far more opportunities than before. Rising in the professions was strictly regulated and took a long time, but it was possible.

The guild system (also an innovation of the twelfth century) provided the opportunity for a young boy to be apprenticed to a master tradesman when he was about seven years old. This was a contractual arrangement and required that the boy's father be able to pay a certain sum of money for his maintenance. In return, the tradesman received the labor of the apprentice and agreed to teach him the trade. (This is a modification of the service for protection model of earlier years, now with a commercial focus.) After about seven years, the apprentice would be elevated to the status of journeyman (the word comes from the French *journée* or daily laborer). He now knew enough to perform the trade under the direction of the master. After seven more years, he could present himself for recognition as a master. For this he needed to have enough money to purchase his own set of tools and to produce an acceptable "masterpiece," which was submitted for approval by the masters of the guild. Once he was approved, he could set up his own shop and take his own apprentices. (The use of the male pronoun is deliberate. Not until very late in the middle ages were females allowed to participate in the guild system.)

Similar hierarchical forms of training were used by both the nobility and the Church. The young son of a nobleman could expect to serve as a page for about seven years, learning the ways of warfare and the court before becoming a squire who accompanied his master (the knight) on campaign and then finally aspiring to knighthood (master craftsman) with his own weapons and retainers. In the Church, a young man would serve as an acolyte and then deacon before becoming a priest. These different stages were accompanied by increasingly strict vows. The rise of universities in the twelfth century (under the auspices of the Church) meant that scholars were usually clerics and followed the same path as the novitiate. We still observe this tradition in the form of our higher degrees of education in which a scholar first earns the bachelor's degree, then the master's degree, and finally the professional degree of the doctorate.

TWELFTH CENTURY RELIGIOUS LIFE

Not surprisingly, many of the dramatic changes associated with the twelfth century were connected with the rise of the Church during this period. By this time, and particularly because of the Norman connection, religious life in the British Isles was increasingly affected by the politics and issues of all of Western

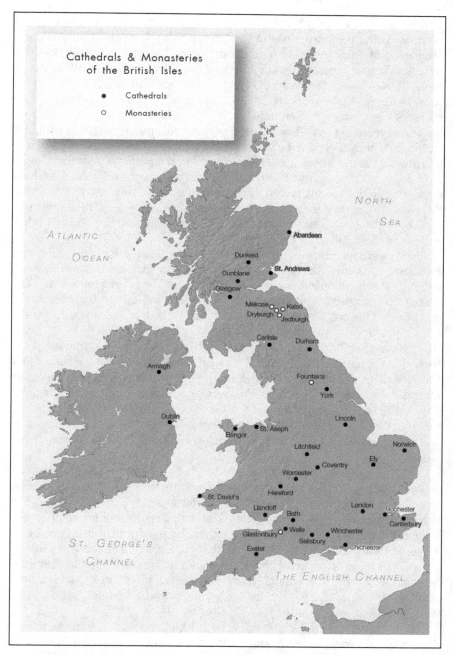

Cathedrals and monasteries of the British Isles. This map shows the episcopal sees of Britain during the High Middle Ages along with the important Scottish Border abbeys, Fountains in Yorkshire, and Glastonbury in the south of England.

Christendom. The Church had suffered badly in terms of power, status, and revenue during the disruptions of the tenth century invasions of the Vikings, Magyars, and Saracens, but by the end of the eleventh century, it too was rebuilding and expanding. Arguably the worst pope ever was the tenth century's John XII. He was eighteen years old and took his pick of the pilgrim women who came to Rome. The sources are unclear as to specifics (he either died of sexual excess or was murdered by an irate husband), but he died in his bed and not on his knees, revealing to us how low the papacy had sunk. Likewise, the monks, particularly of the Benedictine houses, had developed a taste for luxury and secularism, and even bishops openly participated in the profits of feudalism, often keeping great estates stocked with luxury items and mistresses. Of course there were also religious idealists who were appalled by all of this, and by the end of the eleventh century the call for reform was gaining fervor. There were two aspects of the reform movement, one within the monasteries and the other within the papacy itself.

The monastic reforms began in France in the late tenth century and were associated with the Abbey of Cluny (hence, the Cluniac Reforms), which although it was a Benedictine house, spearheaded the reform movement. The Cluniac Reform movement was aimed at improving overall spiritual observance and involved the creation of a number of daughter houses that would follow the same reforms, each with an abbot who would be appointed directly by the pope. (Of course, this idea would work only with a serious, reform-minded pope; therefore, the monastic reformers also called for reforms within the papacy.) By the eleventh century the monastic reforms had taken hold and reformers increasingly demanded the removal of secular authority from Church matters. This was known as the Doctrine of the Two Swords and derived from the scriptural reference "render unto Caesar that which is Caesar's and render unto God that which is God's." The call for a reform-minded pope was soon to be answered.

In 1046 there were three claimants to the papal throne. The Holy Roman emperor, Henry III, who was himself very interested in clerical reform, called a church synod, the Synod of Sutrei; refused to support the claims of any of the three; and appointed his own candidate. This man died within a few months, but it appeared that a precedent had been set for the appointment of a pope by an emperor. Henry died ten years later and his son, Henry IV, succeeded as a minor. In 1073 two events occurred that essentially set the scene for the definition of papal authority: the young Henry IV reached his majority, and a fiery reformer, in many ways the architect of papal monarchy, was elected pope. This was Hildebrand, who took the name of Gregory VII.

During the years of Henry's minority Hildebrand was active in the reform movement. He was a decisive, impatient man, always wanting reform to move faster than it did. He had many new ideas that he was eager to implement. Specifically, he wanted to guarantee the freedoms of the Church (very much in keeping with the emerging societal emphasis on freedom and liberty) and the ability to create something new. In his words, he wanted "to create right order in the world" and he wanted to transform the whole world, both lay society and clerical. He saw the way to accomplish this as being the creation of a monarchical government of the Church with the pope as sole leader. In 1075 he issued a formal document stating his position and containing three key points: (1) subjects could be absolved from fealty to bad rulers, (2) the pope could depose emperors (in other words, he meant to have a role in secular affairs), and (3) the pope could be judged by no authority on earth and could depose and reinstate bishops on his own authority. Not surprisingly, the Holy Roman emperor, a dynamic, ambitious young man in his own right, objected vehemently.

For a time the conflict between the two men took the form of a war of words (each using careful etiquette to insult the other), but in 1076 it came to a spectacular head, referred to as the Investiture Controversy. On the surface, it was about the right to appoint bishops, but in fact it was a symbol of the much larger question of the power struggle between kings and popes. Losing all patience, Henry called the pope a usurper. The pope retaliated by excommunicating him and declaring him deposed as emperor. The nobles of the Holy Roman empire quickly took the opportunity to rebel. Henry had to do something. Taking advantage of the fact that priests were obliged to receive penitents, Henry forced Gregory VII to see him. The pope kept the emperor waiting on his knees for three days in the snow outside the papal fortress of Canossa before finally receiving him and formally absolving him. Neither side could claim victory, but in the short run the emperor got his kingdom back and he had appeared to be more of a victim than an antagonist. In the long run, Gregory had forced the issue of papal monarchy and for at least the next three centuries the relationship between popes and kings would remain tense and problematical as both secular and clerical power grew in strength.

THE REIGN OF HENRY II

As these sweeping changes were taking place on the Continent, England was embroiled in her own problems during the turmoil of the successive reigns of the sons of the Conqueror and the contested rule of Stephen and Matilda. When Henry II took the throne in 1154, he intended to bring about his own changes in authority and governance. He was a young man when he became king, having already inherited Anjou and Normandy. Moreover, he had married the richest heiress in France, Eleanor, who brought as her dowry the unimaginably rich duchies of the Aquitaine and Gascony.

Eleanor also brought some political liabilities. She had been the wife of Louis VII of France, who divorced her in 1152. Eight weeks later she married Henry, thus giving rise to speculation as to the cause of the divorce. Several possibilities were suggested: She had been on crusade with her husband in the Holy Land and perhaps had had an affair with her uncle, Raymond of Antioch; perhaps she and Henry had already started an affair while she was still married to the French king; or perhaps the king simply wanted to pursue a life of celibacy and so put her aside (although it should be noted that he later remarried and

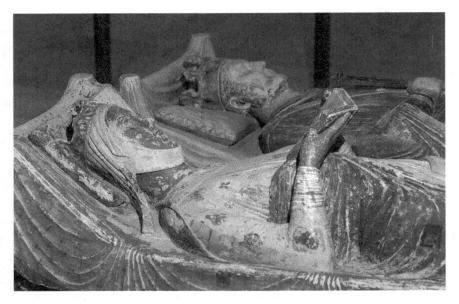

Effigies of Henry II and Eleanor of Aquitaine, Fontevrault Abbey, France. The effigies show the couple much more at peace than they were in their actual domestic life. Through both their inheritances and force of personality they had a lasting influence on the evolution of the English monarchy. Eleanor's love of literature and the arts is vividly shown by the book depicted in her hand.

had sons, whereas his marriage with Eleanor had produced only daughters). In any case, she was a vibrant, educated, and intelligent woman, and as the years would show, extremely capable in political matters. She had benefitted from her father's indulgence and the lack of a male heir to inherit the lands of the Aquitaine in her own right, guaranteed by the terms of her father's will.

Louis VII seems to have harbored no ill feelings for Henry, but to his son and successor, Philip Augustus, relations with the English king would become a major focus of politics. This tension was exacerbated by the fact that Henry was by far the greatest landholder in France whereas the French kings at this time essentially possessed only the Ile de France. It has been argued that for Henry his English inheritance was almost an afterthought. His French lands were the most important in terms of revenue and power, but the British Isles were an important part of his strategy and so he set about consolidating his authority.

Perhaps partly because of the extent of his holdings and the difficulties of administration across the Channel, Henry was especially interested in creating effective institutions of government focused on clearly defined laws and a well-trained bureaucracy. The old Anglo-Saxon monarchy had developed a good system of local government with its shires and shire-reeves who collected taxes and administered justice, but William had not wanted a local power base (presumably for the obvious political reasons) and so had superimposed the feudal structure. The result was the creation of a new set of ruling elites (the barons) who spoke a different language and were of a different background from their subjects. The barons had the right to hold their own courts, in both meanings of the word. They could dispense justice and in practice they could hold more real authority than a king. Henry I had attempted to address the situation with the addition of circuit judges appointed by the king and with the creation of the Office of the Exchequer for financial affairs, but neither was very effective. (The Exchequer was particularly unwieldy, still working with tally sticks and Roman numerals.)

Henry II, who by all accounts had a real talent for administration and a deep interest in the workings of government, began expanding and fine tuning centralized authority. He made major innovations in both criminal justice and civil law. In the area of criminal justice he implemented the idea of a grand jury of twelve freemen who would act as an indicting jury for felony offenses. (This was not a trial jury. Innocence or guilt could still be established by ordeal.) Sheriffs were required to report all cases of murder, arson, theft, and other criminal offenses to circuit judges (formalized by Henry II into the justices of Assize) with the clear expectation that the king's law would be upheld. In the area of civil law he introduced a completely new practice of giving royal control over citizens' lawsuits. This was gradually incorporated into the institution of the King's Court, in which all subjects would be entitled to the same procedures and be governed by the same laws (which had certainly not been the case in many of the baronial courts). One of the most common causes of dispute was the dispossession of land, and in 1166 Henry instituted the Assize of Novel Disseisin, which allowed those dispossessed the guarantee of a writ and jury. With all of these legal innovations the judges sought some means of ensuring consistency and common law began evolving based on customary practices and precedents in addition to the formal statutes of the realm.

In his zeal to promote legal reforms, almost inevitably Henry was destined to cross swords with the Church. Partly as a result of the Hildebrandine reforms aimed at limiting secular meddling in the Church, any cleric accused of a crime was guaranteed the right to be tried in a Church court, governed by canon law, not civil law. Punishments in these courts were rarely severe, at worst often consisting of fasting, doing penance, and occasionally undertaking a judicial pilgrimage. Clerics were rarely deprived of their titles and holdings, and there was no real incentive to adhere to the king's law. Moreover, in England, even if a cleric were found guilty of a crime, he could appeal his case to Rome. Henry tried to overturn this (in his opinion) abuse of the law by issuing the Constitutions of Clarendon in 1164. This allowed clerics to be tried in Church courts, but required sentencing to be done in the royal courts. This innovation was violently objected to by Henry's archbishop of Canterbury, Thomas Becket, not because he wished to promote criminality, but because it violated the established doctrine of the Two Swords.

Thomas Becket was a complex man, as was Henry, and it is extremely difficult to sort through all the layers of opinion that have accumulated around the history of their great clash. Becket was an Englishman, of Norman stock, born in London around the year 1118. His father was a successful merchant and because Thomas showed an aptitude for scholarship he was sent to study with the archbishop of Canterbury. The archbishop recognized his abilities and sent him to study canon law at Bologna and Auxerre. Eventually the archbishop appointed Becket to be archdeacon of Canterbury. At about the same time Becket's considerable skill in law and administration came to the attention of Henry II. The two men became friends and Henry appointed him royal chancellor. It was not unusual at this time to have an educated man who was connected to both church and state, and Henry probably did not think anything of the matter except that he was glad to have a friend in a key administrative position.

In 1162 Becket was appointed archbishop of Canterbury. He resigned the chancellorship, warning Henry that there would almost certainly be a conflict of interest, and two years later he was proven right with the issuance of the Constitutions of Clarendon. Henry was furious at the challenge to his authority by

Thomas Becket. Probably a depiction of the saint in a later medieval stained glass window of Canterbury Cathedral, this panel escaped destruction by the iconoclasts of the sixteenth century.

a former friend, and in 1164 Becket fled into exile in France. The French king, still Louis VII at this point, tried to use diplomacy to mend the relationship, but more conflict arose over the issue of authority when Henry violated both precedent and precedence by asking the archbishop of York (instead of the archbishop of Canterbury) to crown his son as heir in 1170. Becket responded by obtaining from the pope the suspension from office of the archbishop of York and the excommunication of the bishops of London and Salisbury, who had assisted in the ritual. The archbishop and the bishops served an appeal to the king. With the king's permission Becket had returned to England and Henry was celebrating Christmas in Normandy. The story goes that, upon receiving the appeal, Henry shouted and cursed his cowardly court, saying "Will no one rid me of this troublesome priest!" Four knights, hearing these words, took them as an order and crossed the Channel to take action. Historians do not agree on Henry's actual involvement in the affair. In any event, at midnight as Becket prayed at the altar, the four knights rushed in, striking him with their swords so violently that one of the swords broke. The archbishop lay dead at the altar.

Almost immediately reports of miracles at the cathedral began circulating. Instead of destroying the power of the archbishop, Henry had created a martyr, with far more power than a mortal king could ever have. In 1173, three short years after his assassination, Becket was canonized. The following year Henry did penance at his tomb, walking barefoot and wearing sackcloth. He received five strokes of a rod from each bishop present and three from each of the monks present. In this particular dispute, the Church had won. Becket's shrine at Canterbury became one of the primary pilgrimage sites in medieval Europe.

Although Henry lost this key conflict and his later years were clouded by his disputes with his sons and his poor treatment of Eleanor (she was imprisoned from 1173 until his death in 1189 for siding with his sons against him), he is still reckoned as one of England's greatest, most transformative kings.

PLANTAGENET RULE IN BRITAIN: THE SONS OF HENRY II

With all his great abilities, the one thing that Henry could not do was to replicate them in his sons. Ironically, having gambled everything and precipitated the Becket crisis over the coronation of his son, it all came to nothing with the death of young Henry in 1183. This left Richard, Geoffrey, and John all struggling for control and egged on by both the new French king, Philip Augustus, and their mother, Eleanor. The film *The Lion in Winter* vividly portrays the turmoil and sadness of Henry's final years. In the film the young and ambitious Philip says to the aging Henry, "But I will win. I have time on my side." Although there is no historical evidence of Philip having said these words, the concept rings true. Henry died in 1189, and his well-ordered kingdom quickly dissolved into chaos during the reigns of his two sons, Richard and John. (Geoffrey died in 1186 leaving no heirs and Henry's posthumous son, Arthur, died in prison after challenging John.)

Although the Robin Hood legends portray him as Good King Richard, for his English subjects Richard Coeur de Lion was largely a cipher. He spent only six months out of his ten-year reign in England, and his heart was in crusading, not in administration. It is a testimony to Henry's legacy that with Eleanor acting as regent the kingdom essentially ran itself during these years, but with increasing tensions over issues of law and revenue. When Richard was captured by the Muslims in 1198 and a king's ransom (100,000 marks) was demanded for his safe release, all his subjects in both the British Isles and on the Continent suffered. In Richard's absence, Philip Augustus had made good his ambitions, gradually eroding the power of the great French landholders and incorporating their lands into the jurisdiction of the French monarchy. Richard had scarcely been released and returned to England when he was called to battle again in France. He died besieging the castle of Chalus in 1199.

Richard was succeeded by his brother, Bad King John as the legends call him. Historians are more divided in their opinion. Although he certainly does not rank as one of England's great kings, he may not have been as bad as popular belief would indicate. He was not politically astute and had more than his share of bad luck, but in a lot of ways the cards were already stacked against him by the time he inherited the throne. His other nickname, John Lackland, says it all: his French holdings had been absorbed by the very able Philip Augustus and his English inheritance had been squandered by Richard's crusades.

Unobservant as always, John had failed to learn the lessons of the Investiture Controversy or of Henry's conflict with Becket. When the monks of Canterbury elected their own archbishop (in violation of the king's right), John appointed his own nominee. Both candidates set off to Rome to have their appointments confirmed by the pope. The reigning pope was Innocent III, arguably the most powerful of the medieval popes and a strong proponent of papal monarchy. He was thoroughly offended by John's failure to keep his realm in order and appointed his own candidate, Stephen Langton, an Englishman with impeccable credentials. With his characteristic bull-headedness and lack of political awareness, John refused to accept the appointment, barring Langton from entering England. The Pope excommunicated John and placed England under interdict in 1208 (meaning that none of the king's subjects had access to the sacraments). The pope indicated that he would use more force if necessary, calling on the king's subjects to depose him (a right held from the time of Hildebrand's reforms). John finally realized the hopelessness of the situation and accepted the appointment of Langton in 1213, but in the process he was forced to accept the premise that England was a fief of the papacy. This had never been accepted by William the Conqueror or his heirs, and so in agreeing, John lost a great amount of status and power. Additionally, he was forced to pay the pope an annual tribute of 1,000 marks, which he did not possess.

Langton remained one of John's greatest enemies and he undoubtedly helped to organize the barons in opposing the king. They were angered by the power John had ceded to the Church, by his disastrous (and expensive) military campaigns in France, and above all by what they considered the mismanagement of the kingdom. If Henry II is an example of feudal monarchy at its best, John is an example of its worst. By this time, feudal relationships had become so tangled through the process of subinfeudation that the lines of revenue and authority were impossible to sort out.

When John introduced a new tax on movable goods to support a new campaign in France (which culminated in the Battle of Bouvines in 1214— a decisive victory for the French king), the barons had had enough. They met in 1215, first demanding that he affirm the Coronation Charter of Henry I (a fairly innocuous agreement, but one that limited the king's rights of scutage, a tax levied in place of a knight's military service to the king) and other forms of taxation. John refused and asked for more time. The barons then drew up a longer document, the Magna Carta (the Great Charter), which set out their demands in more specific form. This time John had no choice. On June 15, 1215, in the meadow called Runnymede outside Windsor Castle, he reluctantly signed the document. The Magna Carta was not the great document of freedom that some think it to be. It primarily concerned the rights of the barons, with some extension to freemen, but in no way pertained to serfs. Essentially it simply spelled out the conditions of feudal rights as they existed or had existed in previous times. In no way a progressive or innovative document, it does, however, reveal changes in mindset that had taken place by the early thirteenth century. Among other points, the king was to refrain from using foreign mercenaries in his wars; the Church was to be independent (this was articulated in very vague terms); no extortionate taxation could be implemented (such as Richard's ransom); and perhaps most significantly, no scutage could be levied except with the permission of the Great Council. It is this last point that gives the document the reputation as laying the foundation for parliamentary government.

John died in 1216, shortly after accepting the barons' terms. His nine-year-old son, Henry III, succeeded him. Although Henry reigned for more than fifty years, he produced little of lasting importance. In the early years of his reign administration ran smoothly under Henry's steward, the brave and chivalrous William Marshall, but after Marshall's retirement, affairs floundered. In defiance of the king's authority, in 1265 Simon de Montfort (Henry's brother-in-law) summoned his own Parliament to discuss matters of the realm. There is evidence that parliaments had been convened periodically in the intervening years and that such assemblies were beginning to be viewed as a permanent institution. However, prior to 1265 they had been attended only by the Great Council. Simon's Parliament is often regarded as the first true Parliament because it included burgesses as well as barons, knights, and clerics.

Simon was killed in battle against the king in 1265 and Henry III reasserted his personal authority, but he was in bad health and increasingly relied on his son Edward. This young man, who became king under the title of Edward I in 1272, was a worthy successor to the Conqueror and to Henry II. His goal was to extend the power of Britain itself, independent of the continental holdings, and his strategy was to fully incorporate and exploit the resources of all four kingdoms of the British Isles: England, Ireland, Scotland, and Wales.

SUGGESTED READING

Barlow, Frank. *Thomas Becket*. London: Littlehampton Book Services, 1986.
Barraclough, Geoffrey. *The Medieval Papacy*. New York: Norton, 1968.
Bartlett, Robin. *England under the Norman and Angevin Kings, 1075–1225*. Oxford: Oxford University Press, 2000.
Bradbury, Jim. *Philip Augustus: King of France, 1180–1283*. New York: Routledge, 1997.
Butler, John. *The Quest for Becket's Bones*. New Haven, CT: Yale University Press, 1995.
Duby, Georges. *William Marshall: The Flower of Chivalry*. New York: Pantheon Books, 1985.
Gillingham, John, *Richard I*, 2nd ed. New Haven, CT: Yale University Press, 1999.
Hoskins, W. G. *The Making of the English Landscape*. Middlesex, England: Hodder and Stoughton, 1955.
Lopez, Robert S. *The Commercial Revolution of the Middle Ages, 950–1350*. Englewood Cliffs, NJ: Prentice-Hall, 1971.
Morris, Colin. *The Papal Monarchy: The Western Church from 1050 to 1250*. Oxford: Clarendon Press, 1989.
Platt, Colin. *Medieval England*. London: Scribner, 1978.
Poole, A. L. *From Domesday Book to Magna Carta, 1087–1216*. Oxford: Clarendon Press, 1955.
Postan, M. M. *The Medieval Economy and Society: An Economic History of Britain, 1100–1500*. Berkeley, CA: University of California Press, 1973.
Warren, W. L. *The Governance of Norman and Angevin England, 1086–1272*. Stanford, CA: Stanford University Press, 1987.
———. *Henry II*. Berkeley, CA: University of California Press, 1973.
Weir, Alison. *Eleanor of Aquitaine*. Middlesex, UK: Ballantine Books, 2001.
Whyte, Ian D. *Scotland before the Industrial Revolution: An Economic and Social History, 1050–1750*. Essex, UK: Longman, 1995.

Chapter 7

Identity Formation in the Four Kingdoms

The period of the later Middle Ages in Britain was characterized by war, disease, famine, religious upheaval, and political turmoil. Some historians refer to these years as the calamitous centuries, and certainly much that had been built up during the High Middle Ages in terms of societal structure and political development was broken down and reconfigured as the result of one crisis after another. Some were caused by deliberate choices on the part of the governing elites, but many were perceived as acts of God, unanticipated, difficult to fathom, and often impossible to address.

NATIONAL MONARCHY

When Edward took the throne in 1272, England had been weakened by the combined ineffective reigns of Richard, John, and Henry III. Edward was a dynamic, ambitious young man, and his reign represents what is often viewed as a new style of monarchy: an emerging *national monarchy* as opposed to the older *feudal monarchy*, perhaps best exemplified by Henry II. This distinction is undoubtedly more obvious to historians in hindsight than it would have been at the time, but it does illustrate changing patterns of authority and different outlooks that emerged during the course of the Middle Ages.

One of the central themes that had been established by Edward's time was the recognition that Parliament was there to stay and that a successful monarch must learn how to deal with it. Unlike that of his grandfather, John, Edward's strategy was to try to work with Parliament and to avoid direct confrontation. Perhaps partly following the innovations of Simon de Montfort's Parliament (see chapter 6), Edward made sure that representatives from both the burgesses and the Church were included along with the barons in the meetings he regularly called. (This also partly reflects the growing importance of towns and town government in addition to the old county-based officials.) At this time Parliament, as suggested by its derivation from the French word *parler* (to speak), was primarily a meeting intended to expedite discussion and debate between the king and the most important governing elites. It did, however, continue to have a role in judicial proceedings at least through the thirteenth century; even today, the House of Lords sometimes plays a role similar to the American Supreme Court in judicial decisions. The modern legislative function of Parliament developed fairly slowly, although under Edward I, Parliament began ratifying taxation and providing the structures through which royal statutes were enacted. It was not until the fourteenth century that Parliament began promulgating its own laws.

The best example of the changes taking place in Parliament during Edward's reign was the so-called Model Parliament of 1295. It received this nickname because its membership largely consisted of those who would later come to be seen as the main representatives of Parliament. In his quest for taxation to support his wars, Edward called together those whom he thought might contribute: seven earls, forty-one barons, all the bishops and archbishops of England, seventy heads of religious houses, two knights from each shire, two representatives from each borough, and representatives of the lower clergy. (This last group did not continue to be a part of Parliament in later years but met independently in its own convocation.) All of these representatives were given the power to make decisions for the group they represented, thus providing the basic foundation of representational government in Parliament.

Edward's wars, the cause for calling the Model Parliament, constitute the other main theme of the shift toward national monarchy during the thirteenth and fourteenth centuries. With the loss of many French holdings during the reign of John, the English monarchs' best chance for territorial expansion

Edward I in Parliament. This is a later drawing by an artist of the Tudor period. Alexander, the king of Scotland, is shown on Edward's right; Llywelyn, Prince of Wales, is on his left. Both are known to have attended an English Parliament, but not at the same time. Judges (with wigs) sit on the "woolsacks" in the center of the floor. Bishops may be recognized by their mitres (pointed hats) and noblemen by the bars of ermine fur on their gloves.

seemed to be the kingdoms to the north and west: Scotland, Ireland, and Wales. In many ways, Edward's wars with these kingdoms helped forge a sense of national identity for both the conquerors and those who were subject to conquest. The tangled relationship among the four kingdoms of Britain that has affected so much of British history has its main roots in the later Middle Ages, starting with Edward's Wars of Expansion.

WARS OF EXPANSION: WALES

As we have seen, the Norman kings had encouraged the expansion of Norman lords into the Welsh territories, building castles and maintaining feudal retinues to secure the frontier. It was not a full-scale operation of conquest, but both military campaigns and intermarriages had interconnected the Normans and the Welsh, with increasing tension between the two. The Welsh considered the Normans to be interlopers, and the Normans increasingly viewed the Welsh as inferior, with their tribal organization and incomprehensible language and culture. Because the Welsh were not organized into any kind of centralized polity, resistance to the Normans was difficult and usually tended to be localized.

Only rarely did a leader emerge who would try to unite the different families. One such man was Llywelyn ap Iorwerth, usually called Llywelyn the Great. A contemporary of King John, he in many ways represented the Welsh version of feudal monarchy. He did not seek the title of king, but he strove mightily to increase his control of land and to bring other Welsh lords under his overlordship. At Aberdyfi (chosen because it was the site where the sovereignty of Maelgyn Fawr, effectively the first king of Wales, was recognized six hundred years earlier), Llywelyn presided over a meeting of the lords of Wales at which the lesser lords proclaimed their fealty and allegiance to him. He also used the idea of dynastic politics, intending to further his aims. However, his decision to marry King John's daughter Joan did not necessarily serve him well. John tried to extend his own authority into Wales, and with his usual ability to anger and offend, precipitated a Welsh revolt. In the political turmoil that ensued, many of the lesser lords who had been reluctant to support Llywelyn now turned to his leadership. With John excommunicated for the Stephen Langton affair (chapter 6) and his subjects placed under interdict, the ever politically astute French king, Philip Augustus, probably acting on a suggestion of Pope Innocent III, wrote to Llywelyn asking for an alliance. His letter is not extant, but Llywelyn's reply survives, written in a tone of bemused honor that he would be approached by so illustrious a prince. Meanwhile Innocent III had given papal approval to the Welsh Revolt and released the Welsh from the terms of interdict. Needless to say, John was furious with his son-in-law Llywelyn. The Welsh Revolt slowed down John's war with Philip, and the rising of the barons made it impossible for him to militarily subdue the Welsh. Llywelyn emerged from the episode stronger than ever.

Llywelyn the Great and his sons, Gruffydd and Dafydd. The manuscript illustration shows the last native Prince of Wales on his deathbed along with his two sons.

The Magna Carta contained only three references to Wales, the most significant being the effective establishment of two different categories of lords, those of Wales itself and those of the Border or Marcher lands. This constituted legal recognition of what already had evolved as a de facto line of demarcation between native Welsh and Cambro-Normans. In the succeeding years, the Marcher lords stood as a sort of buffer state, at least nominally owing allegiance to the English kings, but often proving untrustworthy and ruthlessly pursuing their own alliances and ambitions. Henry III was content to let this stand, but when his son Edward took the throne, he was determined to impose his own will on Wales. It was Llywelyn the Great's grandson, Llywelyn ap Gruffydd, who became his chief nemesis.

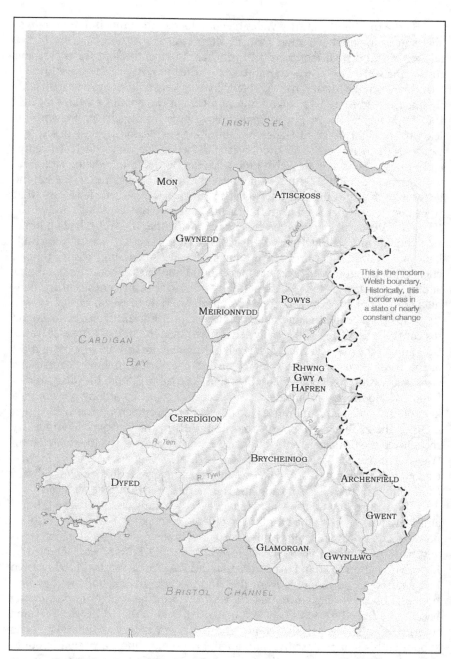

This is the modern Welsh boundary. Historically, this border was in a state of nearly constant change

Medieval Welsh principalities, circa 1100. This map shows the principal regions and lordships of Wales during the High Middle Ages. The Border was often in flux, and after the conquest of Wales by Edward I a new distinction was introduced between the Welsh lords and the Marcher lords of the frontier zone.

By the thirteenth century Wales had developed into a much more progressive and cosmopolitan region than is often realized. Although many of the ancient cultural traditions were still in place, such as the love for poetry and music, the Welsh had also been influenced by the innovations of the twelfth century. Increasingly, social rank was determined by land holdings rather than family lineage, and there were increasing numbers of the populace who were neither lords nor peasants. For example, tax records from Meirionnydd show at least thirty-eight different trades including eight goldsmiths, four poets, and twenty-six shoemakers. The twenty-six parishes of Meirionnydd had twenty-eight priests. Sons of both Welsh lords and Marcher lords were being educated, with attendance high at both continental and English universities. Although the geography of Wales did not lend itself to urban development, it is clear that trade had greatly increased from the twelfth century when Giraldus Cambrensis (Gerald of Wales) dismissed the whole issue, saying that the Welsh had no interest in buying and selling. Henry III had allowed unrestricted trade between England and Wales, and the main products of Wales, including cattle, timber, cheese, horses, hounds, hawks, and wax, found markets on both the Continent and in England. With the growth of fulling mills in the thirteenth century, flannel became a major export, second in importance only to Welsh cattle.

With both economic and political motivations, Edward I sought to extend his control over Wales. In 1258 Llywelyn II assumed the title of Prince of Wales. Building on the political gains of Llywelyn the Great, he had the support of most of the Welsh lords and even some of the Marcher lords. In 1265 negotiations were successfully concluded for Llywelyn to marry Elinor, the daughter of Simon de Montfort. Her lineage was impeccable, counting among her uncles a king of England, a king of France, and a Holy Roman emperor. In 1267 Llywelyn attained the zenith of his power when Henry III in the Treaty of Montgomery recognized the principality of Wales and Llywelyn's right to the title of Prince of Wales. A proxy marriage took place in 1275 and Elinor sailed from France. Undoubtedly viewing the marriage as another dangerous alliance plot, Edward (now king) captured her ship and had the heiress imprisoned at Windsor.

This kidnapping was only part of a quickly escalating crisis between Edward and Llywelyn. Llywelyn had a number of legal complaints against the English government (including failure to enforce treaty laws with the Marcher lands and harboring of enemies of Wales in England), and Edward was offended by Llywelyn's failure to attend his coronation in 1174. Worse yet, by 1176 Llywelyn had ignored six summonses from the king to come to England and pay him homage. Llywelyn explained that he was not refusing, but only postponing because he feared for his safety at a court that had harbored his enemies and imprisoned his wife. He also communicated his grievances to the pope, who supported his suit against the king for imprisoning Elinor. Llywelyn wrote to Edward, offering to resolve their differences through the arbitration of the French king. Needless to say, Edward refused.

Finally losing all patience (of which he never had much in the first place), Edward declared Llywelyn an outlaw and invaded Wales in August 1177 with an army of eight hundred knights and fifteen thousand infantry, many of whom had been recruited in Wales. (This was a characteristic of Edward's Wars of Expansion. He understood the need for using local tactics wherever possible, and there is evidence that he or his advisors must have consulted the works of Giraldus Cambrensis [Gerald of Wales] in drawing up their battle plans.) The English king seized the grain harvests so that the Welsh would have no food during the upcoming winter, and Llywelyn was forced to submit at the Treaty of Aberconwy on November 9, 1277.

For a time, Llywelyn seemed to follow the king's demands, officially granting homage, marrying Elinor in the king's presence, and dutifully paying all the fines required of him by the Treaty of Aberconwy. However, a combination of events in 1282 led to another outright rebellion by Llywelyn. The English were seizing territory with no regard for Welsh law, another revolt by one of his rivals was drawing support from Llywelyn, and Elinor died giving birth to their only child. Probably all of these things contributed to his decision to go to war against Edward one more time.

This war is often regarded as the last stand of the Welsh against English encroachment, although there were further revolts in 1294 and in the mid fourteenth and early fifteenth centuries. It was a fierce campaign, hard fought on both sides. Llywelyn's territories were confiscated and he was killed in battle later in 1282. In a show of English power Llywelyn's brother was executed and his daughter was sent to a convent. All of the symbols of Welsh princely power were captured or destroyed, and Edward celebrated his victory with a formal "progress" through Wales, militarily securing Wales by erecting some of the most formidable castles ever built—Caerphilly, Harlech, Conwy, and Caernarfon. In 1284 Edward enacted the Statutes of Wales, under which the

Caernarfon Castle, Wales. This castle is an excellent example of the heavily fortified castles that Edward and his retainers built in Wales to try to maintain control over the native Welsh lords.

Welsh would be governed up to the modern era. English law was introduced, English customs were encouraged, English colonization was invited, and Edward's son was given the title Prince of Wales, a title held by the eldest son of the reigning English monarch up to today. Wales was divided into the Principality of Wales, governed directly by the English Crown, and the Marcher lordships.

WARS OF EXPANSION: SCOTLAND

To the Scots, the wars fought with England between 1296 and 1342 are the Wars of Independence, and to a large extent one could say that the political identity of Scotland as a nation was forged at this time. Certainly, there had been a long-standing kingdom of the Scots, but because it was at first essentially a confederation under the Dalriadic kings and then a regional monarchy under the Canmore line, the idea of a truly unified polity had never been achieved. The Highlands were not fully integrated (and it could be argued, never would be because of differences in language and culture), and the Lordship of the Isles retained its fierce independence from royal authority through all the years of its existence. Nonetheless, the wars against Edward provided a common enemy and helped unify the Scots. It has even been argued that the vision of Edward's enemies was greater than that: the creation of a pan-Celtic state that would have included Scotland, Ireland, and Wales. This is difficult to assess because it never came to fruition, but there are hints of it in the Scots' alliance with Llywelyn II and in the campaigns of the Bruces in Ireland.

The strength of the Canmore line held through the twelfth and up to the late thirteenth century. This period saw the expansion of royal power over more areas of Scotland. Even through the period of normanization, the independence of the Scottish kingdom was recognized and the English and Scottish royal houses regularly intermarried, building dynastic relationships between the two. Malcolm's son David married the Conqueror's grandniece, William the Lion married the great-granddaughter of Henry I, Alexander II married John's daughter Joan, and Alexander III married the daughter of Henry III. However, not everything went smoothly. William the Lion gave two of his daughters to John with the understanding that they would be married to English princes. It never happened, and the Scots for many years attempted to pursue a breach of contract suit at the papal court. The tangled Anglo-Scottish relations occasionally erupted into border skirmishes, and the key issue of the matter of homage had not been resolved. It was still unclear if Malcolm Canmore's original act of fealty had involved only a portion of lands on the border or the whole of the kingdom of Scotland. The Scots, with good reason, interpreted it one way and the English the other way. The issue became even cloudier with the Treaty of Falaise in 1174 (in which the Scottish king acknowledged fealty to Henry II), or more specifically, with its cancellation by Richard I in return for payment. The Scots argued that this act relieved them of any homage owed to the English king. The point of contention again came to a head in 1286 upon the death of Alexander III of Scotland.

Alexander married Henry III's daughter Margaret. He had a long reign (thirty-five years) and was a popular and well-liked king. The succession seemed secure, with two sons and a daughter, Margaret, who married the king of Norway, Eric II. Then disaster struck. Within two years, his younger son died; his wife, Margaret, died in childbirth; and his older son fell victim to disease, dying on his twentieth birthday in 1284. It is unclear what exactly his illness was, but it is said to have unhinged his mind. In his final moments he uttered a prophecy: The sun of Scotland would set on the morrow, and his uncle (Edward) would fight three great battles: "Twice will he conquer, in the third he will be overthrown."

Left effectively heirless, Alexander called a council of the lords of the realm, seeking their approval for the succession of his infant granddaughter in the event that he would have no other heirs, and he hastily remarried in 1285. There were no more heirs. Hurrying home to his bride a few months later on a stormy night, Alexander ignored the advice of his councilors to wait until the next day to travel. He set out at night and, outpacing his companions, fell from his horse in the darkness and was killed. The throne of Scotland was in the hands of a three-year-old girl, the Maid of Norway.

A Council of Guardians, chosen by the Scots, was appointed to rule on behalf of the little Maid. The Council of Guardians was a somewhat motley crew, consisting of Bishop William Fraser of St. Andrews; Duncan MacDuff, Earl of Fife; Alexander Comyn, Earl of Buchan; Bishop Robert Wishart of Glasgow; James the high steward; and Black John the Wolf, lord of Badenoch. The council excluded two of the most ambitious families in Scotland: the Balliols and the Bruces, both of which had claims to the throne. Scotland's precarious political situation was not lost on Edward. He immediately began negotiations to marry his son Edward (II) to the Maid (another Margaret). Probably fearing for his daughter's safety, Eric of Norway asked for Edward's protection. She set sail for Scotland in September 1290 but died on the voyage before being in sight of Scotland. Political chaos erupted.

The ongoing feud between the Bruces and Balliols escalated to a civil war as both families fought for control of Scotland. In 1291 the Scots asked Edward to adjudicate the competing claims to the Scottish throne. Both Robert Bruce and John Balliol signed documents acknowledging Edward's overlordship. Balliol went one step farther, making it clear that he regarded himself a vassal of the English king. Although Edward selected him and he was coronated in 1292, it was clear that Edward intended for him to be a puppet king. Edward brought Balliol to court, confiscated three of his castles, and demanded other humiliating proofs of his acceptance of Edward's overlordship. Although Balliol complied, he proved to be not quite the puppet that Edward expected. When Edward demanded troops from the Scots for a campaign in France in 1294, Balliol refused. In 1295 he formed an alliance with France, which would become known as the Auld Alliance and which provided the linchpin of Scottish politics for the next three hundred years.

Enraged, Edward invaded Scotland in 1296, deposing Balliol and stripping from him his rings and the coat of arms from his cloak. This is likely the source of Balliol's contemporary nickname, Toom Tabard (empty jacket), although it is often assumed to be a comment on his spinelessness. As Edward crossed the border, he massacred the inhabitants of Berwick and went on to defeat the Scots army at Dunbar. He forced two thousand of the greatest lords to swear fealty and acknowledge his feudal overlordship, and perhaps most important symbolically, he captured the Stone of Scone upon which Scottish kings were crowned and took it back with him to Westminster, where it became part of the English coronation chair. (The saga of the Stone of Destiny, as it is called, figures prominently in the history of Scottish nationalism. It was recaptured by the Scots in 1950 and then it [or perhaps a copy] was reclaimed by the English before being returned to Scotland in 1996, shortly before devolution gave Scotland its own modern Parliament. An arrangement was made to transport it to London whenever required for coronation ceremonies.)

After his thorough defeat of the Scots, Edward went on to his French campaign. In his absence Scottish resistance intensified, this time under the leadership of William Wallace, a supporter of the Balliols. Wallace has been portrayed as a common man standing against the forces of royal oppression, but in fact he was of noble blood, although not much else is known about him. Blind Harry's great poem, "The Wallace," depicting his life and victories was written generations later. What is clear is that he was a charismatic leader, and through joining with the strategic skills of Andrew Murray, Wallace and his men soundly defeated Edward's forces at the Battle of Stirling Bridge in 1297. Edward came

The English coronation chair, Westminster Abbey. The illustration shows the Coronation Chair with the Stone of Scone (coronation stone of the Scottish Kings) before the stone was returned to Scotland in 1996 as part of the Scottish devolution settlement.

north himself a year later and defeated Wallace and his army at the Battle of Falkirk. (Murray was killed at Stirling and this may have contributed to the loss at Falkirk.)

Wallace escaped and eluded capture until 1305, when he was betrayed by one of his soldiers and handed over to the English. Edward's vengeance was fierce. Wallace was accused of treason for having violated his oath of fealty (an oath he never took) and a great show was made of his execution. He was hanged, cut down while still alive, castrated, drawn, and quartered. It was meant to be a clear message of Edward's wrath, similar to what he had exacted upon Llywelyn's brother in Wales, but for once, he had miscalculated. Wallace became a martyr to the cause of Scottish independence. The resistance to Edward and the hatred of the English grew even stronger.

After Wallace's defeat, the guardianship of Scotland devolved upon a volatile triad: William Lamberton of St. Andrews; young Robert Bruce of Carrick (grandson of the Bruce who had claimed the throne in 1291); and John Comyn the Red, lord of Badenoch, who was a kinsman of John Balliol. The ongoing feud between the Bruces and Balliols had culminated in the bitter rivalry between Robert Bruce and Red Comyn. In 1306 there was a meeting between Bruce and Comyn at Greyfriars Church in Dumfries. Historians are still debating exactly what happened, but the story goes that Bruce came out a few minutes later and said "I believe I have killed Red Comyn." One of Bruce's followers said, "Believe? Then I'll go in and make sure!" The fourteenth century poet John Barbour summarized it with the immortal lines, "However the quarrel fell, he died thereby, I know full well." It was probably murder, it was definitely sacrilege, and it forced Bruce's coronation without the support of many of the Scottish elites.

Edward recognized the potential threat and attempted a new war against the Scots. By this time he was old and ill, and the account of his last campaign is emblematic of his life. He came north one last time, seeking to do battle himself against the Scots and vowing that he would not rest until "God has given me victory over the crowned traitor (Bruce) and perjured nation." Before he reached the border, it was clear that he could not stay on his horse. He was carried to the nearby Lanercost Priory by the monks and remained there for nine months. Although seriously ill, he still was in command. He was delighted to hear that Bruce's brothers had been taken captive. He ordered their executions in similar manner to that of Wallace, and he had Bruce's queen imprisoned and his young daughter sent to a nunnery. As a final barbarous touch, he ordered that Bruce's sister Mary, along with Isabel of Buchan (who had crowned Bruce as representative of the MacDuff clan, which held the traditional right of crowning Scottish monarchs) be imprisoned in lattice cages on the walls of Berwick Castle, exposed to the elements and subjected to the jeers and debasement of passersby. When he heard that Bruce had come out of hiding and was once again preparing for battle, Edward asked to be carried on a litter at the head of his army. He made it only as far as Burgh-on-Sands. He died there, three miles from the Scottish border, with his eyes turned toward his old enemy. He asked that his bones be carried into Scotland and his heart taken to the Holy Land. His son did neither.

Edward II was no more successful on the battlefield than he was on the throne. It took him seven years to return to the Scottish campaign, seven years in which Robert Bruce consolidated his power, waged guerilla warfare against English garrisons and forces while avoiding pitched battle, and trained his army.

The Declaration of Arbroath. The declaration of Scottish independence addressed to the pope in 1320, probably written in the Abbey of Arbroath. Signed by eight earls and thirty-one barons, it contains an eloquent plea for Scottish sovereignty: "as long as but a hundred of us remain alive, we will never on any conditions be brought under English rule." It has become a strong symbol of the modern Scottish nationalist movement.

Edward II finally marched in 1314, at the head of an enormous army of over twenty thousand men to relieve Stirling Castle, under siege from the Scots. Despite the numbers, the superiority (and leadership) of the Scots army soon told the tale. The Battle of Bannockburn (June 24, 1314), one of the most significant battles of the Middle Ages, was won by the Scots. It secured Bruce's position on the throne, and at least for the time, Scottish independence. In 1320 the Scottish lords wrote an eloquent letter to the pope asserting their independence and nationhood. In this document, the Declaration of Arbroath, the Scots made clear their position:

> As long as but a hundred of us remain alive, never will we under any conditions be brought under English rule. It is in truth not for glory, nor riches, nor honor that we are fighting, but for freedom—for that alone, which no honest man gives up but with life itself.

It was a new era and Scotland was, in a sense, a new nation. In 1328, weakened by the murder of Edward II and the minority of Edward III, the English renounced all claims to jurisdiction in Scotland.

WARS OF EXPANSION: IRELAND

In Ireland the process of English expansion was more piecemeal and unfocused, but every bit as significant. One Irish historian noted that the tragedy of the Norman invasion of Ireland was not the conquest because that never actually happened, but rather the "half-conquest" that left Ireland caught between two polities and two cultures.

In the years following Henry's II's annexation of Ireland in 1169, the expansion of English control centered on two areas: the Church and the English (or Anglo-Norman) lordships. The process of diocesan organization in Ireland predated Henry's arrival, having begun in earnest under Archbishop Malachy of Armagh. The arrival of the Cistercian Order in the twelfth century also served to connect Ireland more strongly with universal Christendom. The great Cistercian abbeys of Mellifont, Holy Cross, and Trim became important centers of religious life, not just for the monks, but also for the lay population. Holy Cross, with its relic of the True Cross, was an important pilgrimage site. The records of the miracles associated with Holy Cross afford us a fascinating glimpse into popular religious beliefs and practices of medieval Ireland. Trim likewise was associated with a wonder-working relic.

The Irish annals also provide abundant testimony to the role of the Cistercian houses in everyday religious observance. The chieftains and the other elites of Ireland were great patrons of the religious houses, often giving rich gifts of altar plate during their lifetimes and leaving donations for perpetual prayers after their deaths. Interestingly, the annals additionally provide us with a glimpse into a darker side of the role of churches in Irish society. As was true elsewhere in Christendom, according to canon law, churches were considered places of sanctuary where someone running from the law or from an enemy would be protected. All too often, as we have seen with the dispute between Robert Bruce and Red Comyn, a fight would be carried into a church, resulting in injury or murder on sacred ground.

Under the Normans preference was usually given to English bishops, but no official stance on the issue was taken until 1217 when, during Henry III's minority, the king's steward, William Marshall, gave orders that no Irishman was to hold an episcopal see. This act seems to have been based more on colonial control than on religiosity, and the pope, Honorius III, objected. Nonetheless, the process was generally observed, with occasional exceptions when an Irish candidate was considered harmless or politically desirable. With the strong control of the Gaelic lords in the north, Armagh remained largely in Irish hands until 1306. At that time, the archiepiscopal see of Armagh was split into the *ecclesia inter Anglicos* (the Church among the English) and the *ecclesia inter Hibernicos* (the Church among the Irish), a de facto division that aptly summarizes the duality in political and cultural identities during the Middle Ages in Ireland.

By the end of the thirteenth century the expansion of the Anglo-Norman lordships and way of life had reached their greatest extent. By this time the agricultural methods of the English, such as the three-field system, had been introduced into Ireland, but the innovative and important heavy-wheeled plow saw limited use in either the boggy soil of central Ireland or the rocky soil of the perimeter. In those regions Gaelic farming methods continued to be used, including the practice of plowing by the tail, in which a light plow was attached to the horses' tails. The English found this practice particularly barbarous, although some modern historians have argued that it was both an effective and humane method because it meant that both the horse and plowman would stop quickly when the horse encountered any obstruction, thus protecting both from injury.

Town life in Ireland was situated in the old Viking trading centers that included Waterford, Wexford, and Limerick, and new towns were also growing up near the new Norman castles and new religious houses. These settlements were very similar to those in England, having areas designated for certain trades and laws concerning market days, weights, measures, and guild regulations. These towns were primarily settled by English speakers, but it is clear from the annals and other sources that everyday intermingling of the two populations was not uncommon. After about 1220, English colonization began to spread into the west: Clare, Galway, Sligo, and north to Derry. Here the Gaelic lords were more firmly established and although the names of landowners appear in the documentation as Anglo-Norman, they soon became hybridized, adapting to the Gaelic culture and way of life rather than the opposite. Moreover, by midcentury the annals show that there was beginning to be a growing political resistance to Anglo-Norman rule on the part of the Gaelic lords.

King John had held the title of lord of Ireland, and in 1254 Henry III gave his son Edward (I) a huge estate including Ireland, the Channel Islands, and Gascony. The grant included the language that it was made "provided that the land of Ireland shall never be separated from the crown of England, and no one but Edward and his heirs, kings of England, shall ever claim or have any right in that land." Thus, the destinies of the two lands were tied together, although by no means was all of Ireland under the control of either Edward or the English colonial government. On the face of it, Edward was not particularly interested in Ireland, aside from its resources and revenues, and given the half-conquest there were plenty of Irish lords eager to rise against an absentee monarch. Edward was not willing to invest his resources in Ireland, and the English colony contracted as lawlessness (and gaelicization) spread. In 1297 the English Parliament banned those of English descent in Ireland from wearing Irish clothing or hairstyles (a clear indication that the English settlers were doing just that).

With the death of Edward I in 1307 and the accession of his much weaker son, Edward II, the situation in Ireland became increasingly unstable. In 1315, the year after the Battle of Bannockburn, Edward Bruce, the only surviving brother of Robert Bruce, set sail with an army of Scots soldiers and landed in Antrim. His motivations are unclear. He may have been seeking his own fortune, he may have been under his brother's orders with an intent to expand the Scottish kingdom, he may have been seeking simple revenge for the execution of his three brothers nine years previously by Edward I, or he may have been part of an alliance of lords who were seeking to implement a pan-Celtic kingdom/empire that would straddle the Irish Sea and eventually include Wales as well. In any case, Edward Bruce took the title of king of Ireland and was supported by some very powerful Gaelic lords including the O'Neill chieftain. Unfortunately, given the clan politics of the Gaelic lordships, the support of O'Neill meant the alienation of those who were opposed to O'Neill. The fragile new kingship languished and collapsed when Edward was killed by a group of Anglo-Irish colonists at the Battle of Fochart in 1318.

The demise of Bruce and his kingship, however, did nothing to strengthen English colonial government in Ireland. It was increasingly recognized that the ecclesiastical division was echoed in the political realities. Ireland was in fact two nations, consisting of the old Gaelic lordships and the lands controlled by the English monarchs and the descendants of the Anglo-Norman colony. These settlers were becoming increasingly gaelicized and were involving themselves in clan politics. By the later Middle Ages the English Crown controlled less and less of Ireland.

Although Edward II reigned until 1327, the remaining years of his kingship produced little of lasting importance. He failed to advance his father's efforts toward internal expansion and instead saw the growth of increasingly distinctive and powerful identities and polities in both Scotland and Ireland. Moreover, Edward lost control of his French inheritance. He married a French princess, Isabella, the daughter of King Philip the Fair of France, and although they had children it was not a happy marriage. Unhappy with Edward's preference for his male companions (most notably Piers Gaveston), Isabella connived with Roger Mortimer (an Englishman at the French court). They became lovers and together demanded Edward's abdication. With no supporters, he accepted their demands and abdicated in favor of his teenage son, Edward III. He was imprisoned in Berkeley Castle in 1327 and was murdered that year, most likely on the orders of Isabella and Mortimer. Subsequent years would see the rise of a new type of monarchy and new challenges during what has been termed the Calamitous Fourteenth Century.

SUGGESTED READING

Barrow, G.W. S. *The Kingdom of the Scots: Government, Church, and Society from the Eleventh to the Fourteenth Century*. Edinburgh: Edinburgh University Press, 2003.

Cosgove, Art, ed. *A New History of Ireland*. Vol. 2, *Medieval Ireland, 1169–1534*. Oxford: Clarendon Press, 1987.

Cowan, Ian B. *The Medieval Church in Scotland*. Edinburgh: Scottish Academic Press, 1995.

Davies, John. *A History of Wales*. Harmondsworth, UK: Penguin Books, 1993.

Gwynn, Aubrey. *The Irish Church in the 11th and 12th Centuries*, rev. ed. Edited by Gerard O'Brien. Dublin: Four Courts Press, 1992.

Jenkins, Geraint H. *A Concise History of Wales*. Cambridge: Cambridge University Press, 2007.

Lydon, James. *The English in Medieval Ireland*. Dublin: Royal Irish Academy, 1984.

Lynch, Michael. *Scotland: A New History*. London: Century, 1991.

McDonald, R. A. *The Kingdom of the Isles: Scotland Western Seaboard, c. 1100–1336*. East Linton, UK: Tuckwell Press, 1997.

Nicholls, Kenneth. *Gaelic and Gaelicized Ireland in the Middle Ages*. Dublin: Gill, 1972.

Richter, Michael. *Medieval Ireland: the Enduring Tradition*. New York: Macmillan, 1988.

Chapter 8

Britain in the Later Middle Ages

Edward II's son, Edward III, reigned for fifty years and his reign saw an astounding series of crises—political, religious, and social. The later Middle Ages was a time of great turmoil, referred to by historians as the Calamitous Fourteenth Century, or the Age of Adversity. Like the rest of Europe, Britain was shaken by the Babylonian Captivity (1305–78) and subsequent Great Schism of the Church (1378–1415), the Hundred Years War (1337–1453), and the advent of the Black Death (beginning in 1348). The scourges of the fourteenth century left few institutions intact and society was forever changed.

THE CRISES OF THE FOURTEENTH CENTURY: RELIGION, WAR, AND PLAGUE

The so-called Babylonian Captivity (when the papacy was essentially annexed to the French Crown) came about partly as the result of the growth of national monarchy in France. The building of France began under Philip Augustus (one historian has called him "the King who put France together" in reference to his expansion of Crown lands). When he took the throne in 1180, the kings of France controlled only the environs of Paris, with the largest percentage of French land in the hands of the Norman/Plantagenet kings of England. Through careful strategy and aided by the bad luck of King John, Philip had managed to consolidate most of the duchies of France under royal authority. Over the next hundred years or so without an institution like Parliament as a counterbalance, the French monarchy had grown very rich and powerful. The French nobles always had to be kept in check by the monarchy, and the only other threat to power was the Church.

As we have seen, the power of the popes was also on the ascendant through most of the Middle Ages, and, perhaps not surprisingly, a major clash came between the French King Philip the Fair (1285–1314) and perhaps the most extravagant interpreter of the doctrines of papal monarchy ever to sit on the papal throne, Boniface VIII (1294–1303). The immediate issues of the conflict are familiar: taxation of the clergy and the trials of clergymen, specifically the legality of appeals to Rome, the same issue that caused the dispute between Henry II and Becket. Boniface claimed absolute authority over these matters and sent an angry public letter to Philip, warning him that, if a ruler was wicked, the pope could intervene in any secular matters within the king's realm (this was based on the old reforms of Gregory VII). With great sarcasm, Philip replied by letter, addressing the pope as "Your Fatuousness." Boniface countered by issuing a bull proclaiming that it was necessary for salvation for all humans to be subjects of the pope.

Philip had had enough. He sent in a gang of ruffians to kidnap the pope. They burst into the papal palace and threatened him. It is not altogether clear if they harmed him physically, but he died soon after. (He was eighty years old and had not been well.) Philip immediately secured the election of a French pope (who never went to Rome) and set up the new Avignonese papacy, with a pope resident in France under the control of the French kings—hence, the nickname Babylonian Captivity.

Far from being just a French crisis, the conflict between Philip the Fair and Pope Boniface rocked all of Europe. Establishing the papacy as essentially a puppet institution under the control of the French monarchy had repercussions for all of France's allies and enemies, not the least those in the British Isles.

To put it in modern terms, England and France were the two great superpowers of Europe during the fourteenth century. Their monarchies were interconnected through years of intermarriages and feudal relationships, and as both expanded and consolidated their power, a collision of interests was probably unavoidable. The clash came over the Aquitaine. From the English perspective this rich duchy was part of their feudal inheritance, brought to the Plantagenets through the dowry of Eleanor, Henry II's queen. From the French point of view, the land was a French duchy and therefore under the control of the kings of France. Both wanted control over the same piece of land, and both had good reasons to believe they were right.

The war started in 1337, an incredibly complicated, great sprawling war that involved several imbedded dynastic crises, and it went on for 116 years through times of famine and pestilence. It marked the definition of a deep-seated enmity between the French and the English that lasted until World War I, and it divided Europe into supporters of one camp or the other. In addition to the conflict over control of the Aquitaine, Edward III asserted his claim to the French throne. (He actually had a fairly good case. The direct Capetian line failed in 1328, and Edward probably had as good a claim as Philip the Fair, both sharing a great-grandfather who had been king of France.) Edward knew better than to try to seize the French crown, but he used his claim as a threat and to try to increase doubts concerning the rights of the French king.

In the early phase of the war, the English had several notable military victories, including a defeat of the French navy off the coast of Sluys. Psychologically the English victory of Crecy in 1346 and the capture of the French king were of immense importance. The English longbowmen won the day, badly defeating the French, who had chosen to use the newer crossbow with disastrous results. Also in 1346 the English won a victory over the Scottish allies of the French at Neville's Cross. The Scottish king, David II, was captured. In 1347 the French port of Calais fell to the English. It would remain in English hands until 1558, longer than any other French territory.

Effigy of Edward III, Westminster Abbey. Edward III reigned for fifty years and helped transform England into one of the greatest powers in Europe. His avowed claim to the French crown started the Hundred Years War.

The focus on military affairs was shattered in 1348 with the arrival of a new calamity. In that year the Black Death arrived in Italy and began making its way northward. Although we know that the disease had been endemic in Asia, the Europeans of the time seem to have been unacquainted with it. Certainly it was very different from the previous Great Plague of Justinian, and the Yellow Plague of early Ireland. (We do not know the pathology of these plagues, but the symptoms described were very different from those of the Black Death.)

For many years historians have confidently reported that the Black Death was bubonic plague, spread by the black rat population of Europe, but the most recent biohistorical research has raised many questions and suggested that it may not be as simple as that. Certainly medieval hygiene was such that humans and rats lived in proximity, and we know that the bubonic plague bacillus is transmitted through contact with rodent fleas that harbor the germ. However, there are no reports in the documentation of any great rat mortality in the Middle Ages, which one would expect based on modern incidences in which entire prairie dog communities are wiped out by the disease. Also, we have an abundance of detailed accounts of the symptoms of Black Death victims, and not all of them fit the pathology of the bubonic plague. It may be that the pneumonic plague (in which the disease manifested chiefly in the respiratory system) and the septicemic plague (in which it entered the bloodstream) were in fact the result of different pathogens.

Whatever the specifics of the disease may have been, it killed between a third and a half of the European population and left devastation of every description in its wake. Whole villages were decimated, and everywhere the plague struck people viewed it as a judgment of God on their sinfulness. Because the causes of the disease were not understood, it was attributed to everything from Jews poisoning the wells to God's taking sides in the battles of the day. At first, until it crossed the Channel, the English thought it was a visitation upon the French. Similarly, a chronicler reports that the Scots, fighting on the Borders, took great pleasure "hearing of the cruel plague amongst the English [they] attributed it to the avenging hand of God . . . [but] a fierce pestilence arose, and blew a sudden and monstrous death upon the Scots, and some 5000 of them died in a short time." Those who were able fled north, bringing the disease with them. Across the Irish Sea, the Irish at first thought they were safe. (The disease moved more slowly into the cold and more sparsely populated regions of the north.) However, it eventually arrived there too in 1349.

A Franciscan friar from Kilkenny, John Clyn, gives us one of the most chilling firsthand accounts:

> There is hardly a house in which only one has died, but as a rule man and wife with their children and all the family went the common way of death. . . . Among the dead expecting death's coming, I have set [this] down in writing. . . . Lest the writing should perish with the writer and the work fail with the worker, I leave parchment to carry on the work, if perchance any man survives, or any of the race of Adam may be able to escape this pestilence and continue the work I have begun.

The chronicle stops suddenly and another hand has written "It appears the author died here."

The overall impact of the Black Death is nearly impossible to conceive. In addition to the psychological horror, the ramifications of a population loss by one-third to one-half, depending on location, were myriad. In many places no one was left to harvest or to plant the fields; what serfs remained on estates often fled, terror-stricken by the advance of the disease and often with no steward or lord left to stop them. In the towns, production and commerce often came to a standstill. The lengthy training required by the guild system could not provide for the rapid advancement of the craftsmen who were left, and often it was impossible to obtain resources because of difficulties in transportation or manufacture.

Of course the markets declined as well. In some instances entire settlements disappeared. In other aspects of life the impact was equally powerful. Lawlessness was rife, with the greatly reduced ranks of law enforcers and courts. In the Church, access to the sacraments was often difficult because of the large percentage of priests who had died in the plague. (The mortality rate of that section of society was particularly high due to the attendance of priests upon the sick and dying.)

Despite the devastation of the plague, after only a brief interruption, the Hundred Years War continued, as did the Avignonese papacy. In 1377–78 several events occurred that produced even more political and social dislocation. Edward III died, and the English succession quickly became problematic. Almost exactly at the same time, the Church became even more divided with the election of a Roman pope in addition to the French pope. One holy Catholic and Apostolic church was now split in two with loyalties divided across Europe. Those who supported France (including Scotland) sided with the Avignonese papacy, whereas the enemies of France (most notably the English) sided with Rome.

THE ENGLISH SUCCESSION

The English succession problems were not the result of too few heirs but rather too many. Edward III and his queen, Philippa of Hainault, had twelve children. Five of these were daughters and two died in infancy, but five sons survived to maturity, and the rival branches of the family would continue fighting amongst themselves for the next century. The eldest son, another Edward (known as the Black Prince because of his black armor) was very popular and was one of the heroes of the Hundred Years War. Had he become king, all might have been well, but he died in 1376, a few months before his father. By the English laws of primogeniture, when Edward III died, the crown passed to the Black Prince's son, who took the throne as Richard II, only ten years old and no match for his powerful uncles, the Dukes of Lancaster and York.

During Richard's minority, England was increasingly under the influence of his uncle, the powerful John of Gaunt, Duke of Lancaster. Richard's first real political action was as a teenager when he successfully ended Wat Tyler's Peasant Revolt of 1381 by proclaiming himself the king of the common people. It was a fine act of bravery, and perhaps he really meant it, but subsequent events do not cast him in that character. He loved luxury, he showed no real concern for the problems of the poor, and he was a poor mediator between different factions. In 1399 he took an army to Ireland to try to enforce English rule. It proved a costly error of judgment. In his absence, Henry of Lancaster (son of John of Gaunt, who had just died) returned to England from his exile in France and began rallying support against Richard. When Richard returned from Ireland, Henry had already seized the throne. With the cooperation of Parliament, Richard was forced to abdicate. He was imprisoned in Pontefract Castle and died in February 1400, probably murdered. The Lancastrians ruled from 1399 to 1461, but the factionalism continued under the Yorkists, descended from the third and sixth sons of Edward III.

Shakespeare gave us wonderful images of both Henry IV and Henry V, but of course they were idealized to suit the politics of Shakespeare's time rather than those of the fifteenth century. Nonetheless, Henry V will always be remembered as the hero of Agincourt (1415), perhaps the most significant battle of the Hundred Years War, then into its seventy-eighth year. Shakespeare put the

Effigies of Henry IV and his queen, Joan of Navarre. Son of John of Gaunt, Henry IV was idealized by Shakespeare as the fun-loving "Prince Hal," whose reign as king was challenged by rebellions from the Welsh and the powerful Percy family. Joan was his second wife.

glorious "Upon St. Crispin's Day" soliloquy in the mouth of Henry V, and although the words were Shakespeare's, the sentiment probably captured contemporary attitudes. In what has been called one of the most stirring expressions of English nationalism, Henry said,

> From this day to the ending of the world, but we in it shall be remember'd; we few, we happy few, we band of brothers, for he today that sheds his blood with me, shall be my brother. . . . And gentlemen in England now a-bed shall think themselves accursed they were not here, and hold their manhoods cheap whiles any speaks that fought with us upon Saint Crispins Day.

Although Agincourt looked like a lost cause with the French army hugely outnumbering the English, Henry rallied his troops and perhaps against all odds his archers won the day, establishing a new and lasting image of victorious England. Agincourt was the last hurrah of the mounted knight, and with the victory of the bowmen, a new era in both warfare and politics began.

By the Treaty of Troyes in 1420, Henry V married Catherine, daughter of the French king, and was recognized as the heir to the French throne. By 1422 Henry controlled all of northern France including Paris and it looked as if the English were about to emerge victorious from the Hundred Years War. However, to the great shock of the English, their young and popular king died that year, leaving only a young child, Henry VI, as king of both England and France. As fate would have it, the French king, the intermittently mad Charles VI, also died, leaving his young son, Charles VII, to fight to regain the crown of France. Oddly enough, the English Duke of Bedford was named regent for both minors.

English archers at Agincourt. This contemporary manuscript illustration shows the dramatic change in battle-field techniques that had taken place by the Battle of Agincourt in 1415. Although mounted knights were still present, the English victory was attributed to the "stout yeoman" with their long-bows.

The last phase of the Hundred Years War centered on the eventual crowning of Charles, the French dauphin, by Joan of Arc, the Maid of Orleans. She assisted with his victories and saw him established on the throne in 1429. In 1430 she was captured and put to trial as a heretic, although ultimately her offense was political not religious. Her execution was ordered by the English Duke of Bedford, acting as an agent to the French faction of Burgundians. Even with her death, or perhaps partly because of it, the young French king suddenly found his nerve and began driving the English out of France. By 1453 the French had regained all of the land that had been lost during the Hundred Years War (with the exception of Calais) and the English were much worse off than when they started. Additionally, in 1455 a new civil war began in England, the so-called Wars of the Roses, which was named by later historians for the armorial insignias of the rival factions—the red rose of Lancaster and the white rose of York.

Henry V, the hero of Agincourt, is usually considered to be one of England's great kings. He reclaimed much of the territory that had earlier been taken by the French in the Hundred Years War, but died when only thirty-six, leaving behind an infant son as heir to the thrones of both England and France.

THE FIFTEENTH CENTURY: A TIME OF TRANSFORMATION

For the common people the fifteenth century was a time of both continuing turmoil and rebuilding as society struggled to come to terms with the calamities that had befallen them during the fourteenth century. By the time the population (still kept in check by the frequent revisitations of the plague and by other diseases such as smallpox, malaria, and typhus) began the slow road to recovery in the fifteenth century, the basic institutions of medieval Europe had changed. Feudalism was rapidly disappearing, partly due to the breakdown of the complex political network during the worst of the plague years and partly due to the new style of warfare that centered around the stout yeomen of Agincourt rather than the wealthy (and increasingly obsolescent) mounted knights.

Although written at the end of the fourteenth century, Chaucer's great work, *The Canterbury Tales*, provides us with a literary glimpse into the changes taking place within society. Chaucer himself was a product of the turbulent fourteenth century, born circa 1343 and serving successively under Edward III, John of Gaunt, and Henry IV. He was captured during the Hundred Years War, served as a messenger, and perhaps traveled to Santiago as a pilgrim himself. He was closely connected to the court, having married the sister of John of Gaunt's mistress. Throughout his life, Chaucer was an astute observer of humanity and of changing social conditions, and these are reflected in *The Canterbury Tales*, written in 1390. The emphasis on self-directed religiosity, changing social structures, shared popular culture, and a blend between the old and the new is evident in his text. Significantly, his use of Middle English also reflects the transition to a new era.

It has been argued that this period began the rise of the middle class, although it must be noted that this is such a vexed question of premodern history that it perhaps has little real meaning. Sometime between the twelfth and the sixteenth centuries the structures of society shifted to create a middling order, but the exact causes and manifestations of the shift are much debated. Certainly we can begin to see increasing political involvement by the yeomen or burghers, and a society increasingly focused on urban rather than rural life began to emerge. The guild system, a legacy of the High Middle Ages, continued to function in terms of licensing and trade regulations, but the rigid and slow ascent through the ranks was often modified. With new types of trades and commerce (including weaponry, different styles of fashion, new metalworking, the beginning of clock making, and different techniques of textile production) the old guild categories were reconfigured.

A new feature of this late medieval period was the creation of female guilds. Often these were connected with women's work (for example, the Fripperer's Guild, composed of women who decorated clothing with lace and fripperies). Women's guilds tended not to have the status or wealth of the male trades; nonetheless the access of women to guild protection was a major social change. In general, the years following the Black Death were good for female earning power. Because of the overall reduction in population, women were allowed to do work they could not do in the High Middle Ages and for some of these jobs they received wages nearly equal to those of men. (A good example would be female stonecutters and carriers. Women had been strictly forbidden to engage in such work by the powerful Mason's Guild of the High Middle Ages. After the Black Death, labor was so badly needed to rebuild the destroyed towns that women were employed in these jobs, earning on average 95 percent of the wages of male laborers.) Although there was a gradual increase in literacy for both men and women during the late Middle Ages, access to university educations and the professions (law, medicine, theology, and philosophy) was still strictly regulated and effectively only accessible to males of the higher social orders.

In terms of religious life, the effects of the Black Death and the other social dislocations of the late Middle Ages cannot be emphasized too strongly. During the peak of the Black Death it is clear from the sources that reactions usually took one of two extremes: profound secularism ("eat, drink, and be merry for tomorrow we die") or a sort of militant spiritualism, probably best exemplified by the wandering bands of flagellants who passed through continental and British towns scourging each other and calling for all people to leave aside their sins. By the fifteenth century, with otherwise something of a return to normalcy in daily life and the rebuilding of the towns, spiritual dislocation was still everywhere evident. The combination of the terrors of the plague and the simultaneous breakdown of the institutional church during the Great Schism led to great uncertainty and profound changes in religious life.

Although officially the Great Schism ended in 1415 with the appointment of Martin V, and technically everyone in the British Isles was Roman Catholic again (in one of many waves of anti-Semitism, the Jews residing in England were expelled by Edward I in 1290), society was far from a return to normalcy. Trust in the institutional church had weakened (as evidenced by the rise of proto-Protestant sects in the late fourteenth century) and there was an increasing emphasis on private devotion. Even among clerics and third-order laity (those who took vows in a religious order while technically retaining their lay status) this trend can be seen. In particular, there were increasing numbers of lay confraternities (a form of religious guild connected with a religious order) and in the growth of the orders of friars—the Franciscans and Dominicans, founded in the thirteenth century—who were rigorously ascetic and focused their energies on itinerant preaching rather than communal monastic life.

Although the seven sacraments (baptism, confirmation, marriage, holy orders, communion, penance, and the last rites [now usually referred to as the anointing of the sick]) administered by the institutional church were still the centerpiece of late medieval Christian observance, "do-it-yourself" sacramentals, such as pilgrimages, the reciting of the rosary, and private shrines, seem to have been on the rise as popular devotional practices. Sacramental observance had long been associated with regional customs, and by the late Middle Ages, religiosity and popular beliefs often intersected.

Religious observances would probably seem shocking to our modern sensibilities if we could see into a late medieval church. There were usually no pews and everyone milled around in the nave, sometimes conducting business, sometimes accompanied by livestock. Often there were multiple Masses being said (one at the main altar and others at the various side altars consecrated to the Blessed Virgin and to various saints). Because there was a strong belief that witnessing the elevation of the Host at Mass protected one from death on the day of the Mass, occasionally there were stampedes as people rushed from one altar to another, trying to see the elevation as many times as possible. The sick were often carried into churches, hoping for miracles at the shrines.

Although frequent attendance at Mass seems to have been common, frequent communion was not. Most people probably received the Eucharist only at Christmas and Easter. It is debated how much ordinary people understood of the Mass, which was conducted in Latin. They certainly knew the responses and could recite the prayers, but we simply cannot know how much they actually comprehended. Contemporary descriptions of church services indicate that people were often more intent on their private prayers and were not particularly engaged in any communal ritual.

However, the communal component of religious life was certainly present in the rite of penance. Closed confessionals did not exist at this time and sins were confessed in church or to the wandering friars with neighbors within earshot awaiting their turns. In many ways, though, this was viewed as appropriate. Sin hurt the community and was a matter of grave importance to all its members. Absolution was also communal. Penances were known and everyone was engaged in making sure they were carried out.

In daily life, personal connections with the saints provided the focal point of religious observance. One historian has argued that the saints replicated kinship relationships and were seen as approachable intermediaries who would lobby on the behalf of the petitioner, just as earthly patrons assisted in times of need. Saints were specialists, and one sought their expertise as needed. For example, St. Anne was the patroness of childbirth and St. Roch defended against plague. Every guild had its patron saint: St. Barbara for breadmakers and St. Joseph for carpenters. Some saints were associated with agriculture (St. Ignatius protected from locusts) and some with daily mishaps (St. Anthony was known as the saint of lost objects). In battle, men prayed to their local warrior saint—St. George for the English, St. David for the Welsh, and St. Andrew for the Scots—and everyone prayed to St. Michael the Archangel to defend them from evil. The cult of the saints permeated all human activities and was little changed by the growing distrust of the hierarchies of the institutional church. Likewise, the religious customs that governed daily life such as the church calendar, days of fasting and abstinence, and family prayers continued to be observed and perhaps even gained in popularity during the late Middle Ages. (As an example, the number of fast days per week reached its peak in the fifteenth century, with most people fasting three days a week on Wednesdays, Fridays, and Saturdays.)

One interesting testimony to the late medieval religious outlook comes from iconography and the depiction of Jesus on the cross. In the High Middle Ages, Jesus was usually depicted as Christ triumphant, but in the spiritual turmoil of the late medieval period, he was usually depicted as suffering, often bloody and broken. There was even a new form of private devotion that focused on the meditation of the Five Wounds. This is also the same time period that produced representations of the dance of death and the cadaver tomb, a time that the great historian of the era, Johan Huizinga, simply called macabre.

The religious tensions of the late medieval period also gave rise to a number of heretical movements, which many historians now understand as the beginning of the Reformation, although it much predates Martin Luther. On the Continent the best known of the late medieval heresies were those of the Albigensians and the Waldensians. The heresy of the Albigensians (or Cathars) was a belief in dualism or Manichaeism, in which everything was either bad (including the body and marriage) or good (pure spirit). The movement was very radical and anticlerical, as was the Waldensian heresy, which greatly threatened the established order of both church and state. The Waldensians believed in complete egalitarianism (including the right of women to preach) and they rejected the sacraments and the authority of the church hierarchy. There were other groups as well, including the Brethren of the Free Spirit (who advocated egalitarianism and free sex) and the Adamites (who rejected clothing and raised their children in common, believing all were conceived by the Holy Spirit). In Bohemia the Hussites called for religious reform and increased social justice.

Woodcut illustration from Hans Holbein's Dance of Death. *Although Holbein's series of woodcuts showing the encounter with death of different members of society from all ranks and professions was not published until 1538, the pictures vividly capture the feeling of horror and the macabre that characterized the period of the Black Death.*

In England, the most important reform movement was that of John Wycliffe. His followers were called Lollards, a derogatory term for their incomprehensible speaking in tongues. Wycliffe challenged the pope and other aspects of the sacramental church such as the saints and the sacraments. Although he was a theologian, educated at Oxford, he finally admitted that he did not believe

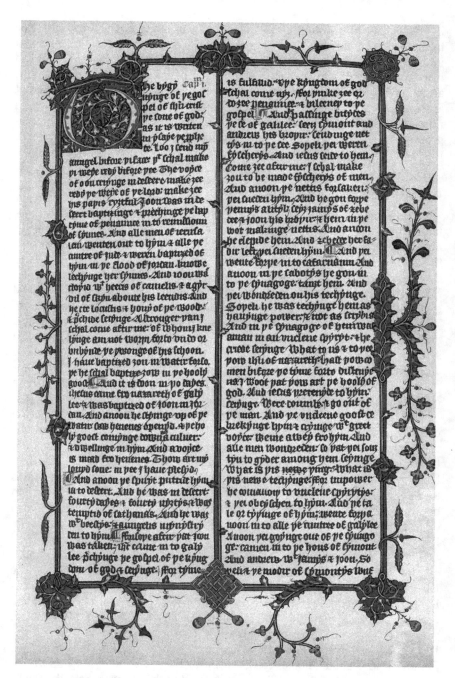

Page from Wycliffe's Bible. This fourteenth century translation of the Bible was the work of the Lollards, a group whose ideas of Church governance and an emphasis on the scriptures prefigure the later Reformation movement.

in the doctrine of transubstantiation (the transformation of the bread and wine to the body and blood of Christ in the Eucharist). He also argued for personal interpretation of the scriptures (arguably a clear bridge to the Reformation) and in connection with this was involved in an English translation of the Bible, although his personal contributions are unclear because the translation did not appear until after his death. The pope condemned Wycliffe's teaching and a number of his followers were burned for heresy. The movement went underground in the early fifteenth century, but many of the arguments resurfaced in the Protestant rhetoric of the sixteenth century.

THE LATE MIDDLE AGES IN IRELAND

The religious malaise of much of late medieval Europe seems to have largely bypassed the Irish. There is no evidence here of heresy or heterodoxy, but rather intense personal piety coexisting with a firm respect for the institutional church. The process of gaelicization, which had begun in the fourteenth century, continued apace into the fifteenth century. Descendants of the Anglo-Norman lords were becoming increasingly integrated into Gaelic political and social life and in some cases becoming indistinguishable from the native Irish. The Statutes of Kilkenny, passed in 1366, sought to address the problem, ordering that the two nations of Ireland must live separately, follow separate legal systems, and even worship separately. The statutes expressed concern about the degeneracy of the English colonists, who were ordered not to adopt the language, clothing, or culture of the natives. Although the Statutes of Kilkenny are often cited as a triumph of English authority, they actually reveal only the frustration of the English government. Gaelic culture was on the ascendant and could not be stopped. Recognizing the futility of preventing cultural exchange, the English sought to maintain their control over Irish land. However, here too their influence was rapidly shrinking. By 1465 it was recognized that the English controlled only the counties of Meath, Louth, Dublin, and Kildare. In this area any Gaelic Irish were "to take English surnames, to go as English, and to be sworn lieges within a year." An act of 1494 provided for the construction of a ditch around Dublin to try to prevent cattle raids by the neighboring Gaelic lords. This was the origin of the Dublin Pale—a stockaded enclosure that served as a forlorn reminder to the English of the limit of royal authority in Ireland.

Regardless of politics, trade flourished in the port towns of Ireland. By the late Middle Ages, Irish trade routes extended to such far-flung locations as Lubeck, Lisbon, and Florence. Irish exports included hides, timber, wool, and grain, as well as linen, butter, herring, and some gold ornaments (although gold working was declining as technologies from other suppliers outstripped the Irish). Import items included the usual luxury goods of silks and spices (still important in the late Middle Ages), but by far the most important import was wine from France and Spain, which was favored in the courts of both the Gaelic and the gaelicized lords. (Gaelic poetry of this period provides numerous references to chieftains drinking "the ruby-red wine of Spain.")

Irish Families & Lordships
(c. 1500 CE)

Irish families and lordships. This map illustrates the regions associated with the
Gaelic families and lords who retained regional power up to the early modern period.
In some cases different branches of a family occupied different territory (as in the case
of the Fitzgeralds of Kildare and the Fitzgeralds of Desmond [Munster]).

There are no sources that let us draw accurate conclusions concerning the population of Ireland during the late Middle Ages. Certainly there was a decline in population during the worst years of the Black Death, although perhaps overall it was less than in England due to the sparse and more rural settlement of Ireland. The Irish annals, trade records, legal documents, and other sources do, however, provide a good indication of the overall demographics of Ireland. Not surprisingly, the vast majority of names in the Gaelic lordships are Gaelic family names and patronymics (the "O'es and Macs" referred to by one early modern writer), but those in the towns are of rather startling mixed origin. They include the expected Norse, Norman, and Gaelic names, but they also show the presence of continental settlers: Flemish merchants, French traders, and even Italian bankers.

Daily life in the towns of Ireland was not much different than it was anywhere else. Walls served as a defense against possible attack, but also often contained fire and disease to the detriment of the inhabitants. As in all medieval towns, there was no provision for sewage and no guarantee of fresh water. One report of Dublin in 1489 commented that "dung-heaps, swine, hog-sties and other nuisances in the streets, lanes, and suburbs of Dublin infect the air and produce mortality, fevers, and pestilence." Most roads were simply dirt paths, and movement across rivers and streams was more often by ford than by bridge. One need only think of the wet climate of Ireland to imagine the impact on travel.

On the other hand, towns offered goods unobtainable elsewhere. Among the guilds represented in Irish towns were the usual medieval trades of blacksmiths, carpenters, coopers, weavers, tailors, cobblers, and masons. Theoretically the Gaelic Irish were forbidden from being admitted to guilds, but the presence of Gaelic names in guild registers indicates that this rule was not enforced.

We have few pictorial representations of Irish townspeople until the sixteenth and seventeenth centuries, by which time the English government had already made the ideological division between the "tame Irish" of the towns and the "wild Irish" of the Gaelic lordships. Early modern representations clearly show that the town Irish dressed modestly and reasonably fashionably; they were very similar in appearance to the English. The wild Irish on the other hand were represented as savages, dressed in animal skins and the shaggy Irish rugs that were another export item. There is no doubt that these images have much more to do with political ideology than with contemporary fashion, but it is quite plausible that the town Irish would have had more access to imported clothing and so may in fact have more closely resembled the English than those who lived in the more geographically isolated Gaelic lordships.

In contrast to the diversity of the Irish town populations, the Gaelic lordships for the most part retained their traditional way of life and ordering of society. The chieftain or lord (whether Gaelic or gaelicized) occupied the highest position in society, supported by his aristocratic retainers, who were often

The Gentleman of Ireland   The Gentlewoman of Ireland

The Civill Irish Woman   The Civill Irish man

The Wilde Irish man   The Wilde Irish Woman

Speed's Map of Ireland (1610), detail showing the dress of the "tame" town Irish and the "wild" Gaelic Irish. The division of the groups, recognizable by their civility or savagery in dress and manners, reminds one of similar images associated with later colonialism.

related to him by blood or marriage. A novelty of the medieval period was the addition of hired mercenaries to bolster a chieftain's army when necessary. They were called *gallowglasses* and often came from the Hebrides of Scotland. They had their own social niche and were often highly transitory, moving between armies as opportunity offered. The aes dána or poet elites continued to have a great influence on Irish society, intensifying as the Gaelic resurgence took place. This is the period of the great *bibliotheques* or compilations of chronicles that provide us with so much information about the social history of Ireland. Although some of the texts undoubtedly come from earlier sources, it is the recensions of this period—including the *Book of Ulster*, the *Book of Connaught*, the *Book of Lecan*, and the *Book of the Dun Cow*—that are most remembered. They provide us with a wealth of details about medieval clan life. Although the entries were often recorded in a rather laconic tone, they provide us with a glimpse into births, deaths, marriages, wars, tournaments, pilgrimages, religious debates, banquets, and other aspects of the daily life of the Gaelic courts. Moreover, from this period we have an abundance of both religious and secular poetry, including the praise poems and battle incitements that were the stock in trade of the chieftains' poets. In all these sources we see evidence of a society that revered bravery and honor, hospitality, and piety.

SCOTLAND

In late medieval Scotland a somewhat similar situation prevailed in which life in the Lowland burgh towns was increasingly divergent from life in the traditional chieftaincies of the Highlands. In this case, the division centered on language, social organization, economics, and customary practices. In Scotland, town life had always been more of a social aberration than it was in England, where Roman towns and Viking settlements had been established in ancient times. Depending on one's specific definition of a town (either as a commercial settlement or as an urban center that held a formal charter from the king), most Scottish towns date from somewhere between the twelfth and the fourteenth centuries. By the thirteenth century many towns possessed royal mints, including Berwick, Carlisle, Edinburgh, Roxburgh, Ayr, Dumfries, Forfar, Glasgow, Inverness, Kinghorn, Lanark, Montrose, Stirling, St. Andrews, and Renfrew. This lengthy list suggests a flourishing Scottish economy and also illustrates the absence of Highland towns. One historian has argued that it is possible that Scotland was richer than England during the thirteenth and fourteenth centuries. To modern minds accustomed to thinking about the relative poverty of Scotland in later years, this seems unlikely. However, given the specific conditions of those centuries, it could have been true. For reasons not altogether understood, the Black Death does not seem to have had as great an impact on the Scottish population as on the English. Scotland was also extremely well suited to the pasturage of sheep and gained a niche in the export of raw wool as opposed to the more hotly competitive trade in finished wool.

As it did elsewhere, life in the Scottish burghs centered on guild production and commerce. Wool and woolens were the primary exports, but leather skins and fish (salmon, cod, and herring) were also exported. The fishing industry in the North Sea helped promote the growth of the Scottish eastern seaboard towns, including Aberdeen, St. Andrews, and Dundee. Import items included the usual luxury goods, such as fine fabrics and spices. As in Ireland, wine was an important import item.

For the inhabitants of the Scottish burghs, a stable monarchy was essential. By the fifteenth century the majority of Scottish burghs were baronial (founded by nobles), but towns still existed that were founded by royal charters as well as ecclesiastical towns. New political power had been brought to the merchants through their role in raising the ransom for David II in 1357, and most burghs continued to have a strong loyalty to the Scottish monarchs. Defense was an important part of burgh life, and we have a dramatic example of the perceptions of a widening gulf between the Lowlands and the Highlands as the "brave burgesses of Aberdeen" stood in defense of their town when it was invaded by the army of Donald MacDonald, Lord of the Isles, in 1411. The incident is recorded in a near-contemporaneous Scots-language ballad called "The Red Harlaw," which celebrates the victory of the Aberdeen burgesses.

The linguistic division of the Scottish-speaking Lowlands from the Gaelic-speaking Highland lordships was both sign and substance of the changes taking place in Scotland during the later Middle Ages. As the Lowlands became more thoroughly identified with the Scottish monarchs, with the Norman-style epis-copal and parochial organization of the church, with English and European trade, and with anglicized social and legal organization, the Highland regions became more culturally isolated, more politically disenfranchised, and increas-ingly dependent on their ties with neighboring Gaelic Ireland. The fifteenth century was a time of cultural richness for both regions of Scotland, but not as part of a unified national movement. The great fifteenth century Scottish poets Henryson and Dunbar were not the products of the ancient Celtic tradition but rather the voices of a new Anglo-Scottish society.

Despite their increasing isolation from Lowland society, the Highland chieftaincies continued to flourish into the fifteenth century. Although our internal sources are sparse, it seem evident that Gaelic-speaking Scotland shared most of, if not all of, the Gaelic institutions that we have seen in place for the Gaelic lordships of Ireland. In Scotland the clan system was well estab-lished, with the same patterns of hereditary chieftains, supported by the gentle-men of their clan (called *duine uasals* or literally the gentle or high-born men). The learned elites (parallel to the aes dána of Ireland) seem to have been in con-trol of the professions, as we see examples of doctors, jurists, professors, and poets from Scotland named in the Irish annals and also represented by their descendants in the early modern period. Unless forced to take action, the High-land chieftains generally seemed to prefer ignoring the Scottish monarchy rather than confronting it. As was the case in Ireland, Gaelic law accorded the

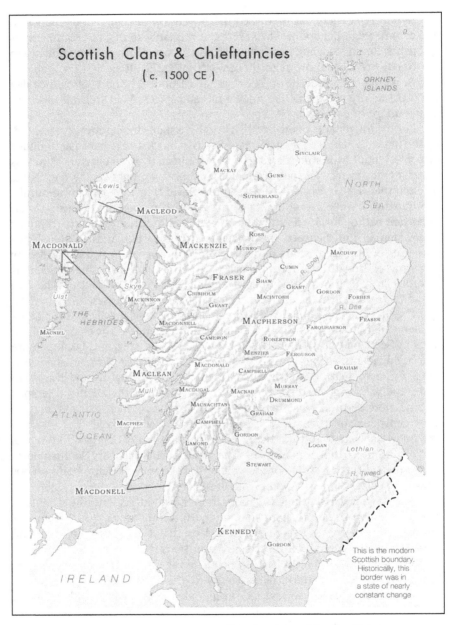

Scottish Clans & Chieftaincies
(c. 1500 CE)

ORKNEY
ISLANDS

SINCLAIR

MACKAY

GUNN

SUTHERLAND

NORTH
SEA

Lewis

MACLEOD

ROSS

MACDONALD

MACKENZIE

MUNRO

MACDUFF

CUMIN

R. Spey

Skye

FRASER

SHAW

GRANT

GORDON

FORBES

Uist

MACKINNON

CHISHOLM

MACINTOSH

R. Dee

GRANT

THE
HEBRIDES

MACDONNELL

MACPHERSON

FRASER

FARQUHARSON

MACNIEL

CAMERON

ROBERTSON

MENZIES

FERGUSON

MACDONALD

CAMPBELL

GRAHAM

MACLEAN

Mull

MACDUGAL

MACNAB

MURRAY

MACNACHTAN

DRUMMOND

MACPHEE

CAMPBELL

GRAHAM

ATLANTIC

OCEAN

LAMOND

GORDON

LOGAN

Lothian

R. Clyde

STEWART

R. Tweed

MACDONELL

KENNEDY

GORDON

This is the modern
Scottish boundary.
Historically, this
border was in
a state of nearly
constant change

IRELAND

Scottish clans and chieftaincies. In the Highland regions of Scotland land was
often held communally under the governance of the hereditary chieftain of the clan.
Clan feuds were often territorial and often involved alliances and strategic marriages
among families who sought to counter the expansion of a rival clan. This map shows
the regional distribution of some of the most powerful clans who continued to hold
power up to the eighteenth century.

right of land usage to the clan rather than to the individual, and most frequently clan feuds started over the encroachment of one clan into the traditional territory of another.

The land in the Highlands was rocky and difficult to farm. Most of the innovations that had improved agriculture in the Lowland regions were useless in this rugged terrain, and the Highland economy remained centered on the cattle trade (as it had been in Celtic times). Often, the main contact of the Highlanders with the Lowland towns was when they brought their black cattle over the drove roads down to southern markets. The difficulties in agriculture gave Highland society part of its distinctive unsettled quality (by Lowland standards). The Highlanders, with little or no market economy, built no towns, and the chieftains, uninfluenced by feudalism, built few great fortified castles. Rather, they had a number of small strongholds, and the entire clan moved from its winter dwelling place to summer shielings (temporary shelters) so that the cattle would have access to the best pasturage. This aspect of Highland society was not understood by the Lowland burghers or often the Scottish monarchs, who attributed the lack of settled life to Highland lawlessness and laziness.

WALES

Despite the political annexation of Wales under Edward I, economically the region was flourishing by the late Middle Ages. The spread of the fulling mill made textile finishing the main industry, and the coastal towns of Wales enjoyed a lively trade with both England and the Continent as commerce revived during the fifteenth century. The social institutions of Wales were changing; gradually the old Welsh lordships eroded as the English took firmer control of the region. Surprisingly, the Welsh language continued to be used, and the late Middle Ages saw a flowering of Welsh poetry, both secular and religious.

The shifting identities of the Welsh under colonial rule can be seen strongly in the last major rebellion by the native Welsh against English occupation. It exploded in 1400 under the leadership of Owain Glyn Dwr. He is something of a mysterious figure. He was descended on his father's side from the royal house of Powys and on his mother's side from the royal house of Deheubarth. He played the role of a traditional chieftain, and his virtues were extolled by the Welsh poets and by his own personal seer, Crach Ffinnant. Although he had served in the English army at one point and was a cosmopolitan diplomat and strategist, for many he exemplified the spirit of the Welsh past, and the rebellion that centered around him rocked the English monarchy and almost resulted in independence for Wales. Shakespeare portrayed him as a sort of wild-eyed magician, and certainly to the English the ardent support of his followers must have seemed beyond ordinary comprehension. However, it seems likely that the rebellion simply happened to have the right man at its helm at the right time.

The story goes that Welsh students studying at Oxford dropped their books and rushed home to take part in the rebellion. The earlier humiliation of the

Statue of Owain Glyn Dwr, Corwen, Wales. This statue depicts Owain as a Welsh patriot. The rebellion he led was the last resurgence of native Welsh power. His defeat by the English led to the annexation of Wales.

Welsh provided strong motivation, and Glyn Dwr's style of guerilla warfare suited his troops and baffled the English. He fought with small, highly mobile troops, emerging from his mountain strongholds for quick attacks on the English. He achieved many victories, but by 1405 English tactics changed and Glyn Dwr's lack of artillery and navy shifted the war in favor of the English. The Anglo-French truce of November 1407 meant the end of Welsh hopes for French assistance. Glyn Dwr's wife, two of his daughters, and his grandchildren were captured and taken to the tower, and a last major campaign targeting the Shropshire border was a dismal failure. By 1410 the rebellion had been suppressed, although some insurgents continued fighting until 1415. We do not know when Glyn Dwr died, but his rebellion marks the last serious rising by the Welsh against the English.

What is most noteworthy about the changing social patterns of Wales during this period was the persistence of traditional forms of culture under the new Anglo-Welsh ruling elites. The old Celtic systems of clan landholding were in decay, but the new ruling lords on their landed estates provided patronage for poets and musicians, who in turn began composing new genres based on traditional forms, but aimed at the tastes of their new patrons. In this way, Welsh language and literature were seen as part of the assimilation process, not as subversive, as was the case in Gaelic Ireland and Highland Scotland.

Other changes in Welsh society point to the relative prosperity and stability of Wales in the later Middle Ages. It has in fact been argued that the collapse of the old Welsh lordships improved the lives of Welsh peasants. Certainly the revival of the Welsh cattle trade in the fifteenth century did much to promote economic growth in the Welsh agricultural regions. It seems clear that the church in Wales was also enjoying increased prosperity by the late Middle Ages. Although Welsh revenues remained substantially below those of the English, benefices provided an adequate living to their incumbents. Interestingly, many of the churches built or rebuilt in Wales after 1450 incorporated the new perpendicular style that had become fashionable in England—another sign of the increasing influence of English customs and styles in the region.

THE END OF THE MIDDLE AGES

As with all chronology it is exceedingly difficult to point to the beginning or end of an era. The Black Death certainly provides a strong line of demarcation between medieval and early modern in terms of social and political organization, religious outlooks, and economic patterns. The feudal system along with manorialism did not survive the plague years, and subsequent structural changes in governing institutions evidence a new era by the sixteenth century. In Britain, the event that brackets and highlights this transformation is known as the Wars of the Roses.

SUGGESTED READING

Beresford, M. W., and J. K. St. Joseph. *Medieval England: An Aerial Study*, 2nd ed. Cambridge: Cambridge University Press, 1979.

Collins, M. E. *Ireland, 1478–1610*. Dublin: The Educational Company, 1980.

Cowrie, Leonard. *The Black Death and the Peasants' Revolt*. London: Wayland, 1972.

Dyer, Christopher. *Standards of Living in the Later Middle Ages*. Cambridge: Cambridge University Press, 1989.

Fawcett, Richard. *Scottish Medieval Churches*. London: Her Majesty's Stationery Office (Historic Buildings and Monuments), 1995.

Grant, I. F., and Hugh Cheape. *Periods in Highland History*. London: Shepeard-Walwyn, 1987.

Hanawalt, Barbara. *The Ties That Bound: Peasant Families in Medieval England*. Oxford: Oxford University Press, 1986.

Hatcher, John. *Plague, Population, and the English Economy*, 2nd ed. London: Palgrave, 1977.

Jillings, Karen. *Scotland's Black Death*. Stroud, UK: Tempus, 2003.

Keen, Maurice. *English Society in the Later Middle Ages, 1348–1500*. London: Penguin, 1990.

Knowles, David. *The Religious Orders in England*, 3 vols. Cambridge: Cambridge University Press, 1956–59.

Labarge, Margaret W. *Women in Medieval Life*. London: Hamilton, 1986.

Lerner, Robert. *The Age of Adversity: The Fourteenth Century*. New York: Cornell University Press, 1968.

Platt, Colin. *The English Medieval Town*. London: McKay, 1976.

Poston, M. M. *The Medieval Economy and Society*. Harmondsworth, UK: Penguin Press, 1972.

Reeves, Compton. *Pleasures and Pasttimes in Medieval England*. Oxford: Oxford University Press, 1998.

Seward, Desmond. *The Hundred Years War: The English in France, 1337–1453*. New York: Atheneum, 1982.

Whyte, Ian D. *Scotland before the Industrial Revolution: An Economic and Social History*. London: Longman, 1995.

Chapter 9

The British Renaissance

The title of this chapter is meant to be provocative. There is currently not much consensus among historians as to what constitutes the Renaissance or a renaissance or who had one or when. Traditionally, of course, the term meant the Florentine classical revival of the fourteenth century, studded with the names of famous artists and scholars, such as Fra Angelico, Raphael, da Vinci, Petrarch, and Pico. However, many historians now agree that the term should be interpreted in a broader sense, referring to an overall change in intellectual and cultural patterns that distinguish the late fifteenth and early sixteenth centuries across all of Europe. For more traditional scholars, the term British renaissance was largely meaningless, but a new generation of cultural historians has focused on the intellectual exchanges taking place between Britain and the Continent during this period. The result is a new view that, in fact, the British were very much part of this new age of cultural expansion and transformation.

THE WARS OF THE ROSES AND THE SHIFTING SUCCESSION

Part of what has obscured the cultural changes in Britain during this time was the tendency of traditional historians to focus on the political turmoil associated with the Wars of the Roses (1455–85). Most certainly this reality was present, but it did not preclude cultural change, nor did it greatly affect the regions of the British Isles outside of England. The Scots and the Irish had their own political problems during this period, but in both locations this was also a time of great cultural growth.

In England the dynastic problems of the monarchy can be traced back to the overabundance of sons of Edward III. After the death of Richard II, the succession went smoothly through Henry IV, V, and VI. Unlike his father, Henry V, the hero of Agincourt, Henry VI was not a well-liked or effective king. In 1450 a major rebellion took place, led by Jack Cade, an adventurer who claimed kinship with the Mortimers and used his compelling personality, intelligence, and military skills to exploit the political situation. It was not merely a peasant rising, but rather one that included mayors and other prominent citizens, and it indicates the level of discontent over the management of government. By 1453 Henry began to show signs of mental instability (perhaps inherited from his French grandfather, Charles VI) and was increasingly unable to rule. The two factions in the royal house, the Lancastrians and Yorkists, began to fight for supremacy. Warfare erupted in 1455. (Incidentally, the epithet Wars of the Roses was not used at that time, but was instead a poetic invention of the nineteenth century.)

The Lancastrians traced their royal lineage back to Edward III's son, John of Gaunt, Duke of Lancaster. Henry VI came from that line. The Yorkists, represented in Henry VI's day by Richard, Duke of York, traced their lineage from Edward III's third son, Lionel, Duke of Clarence, in the matrilineal line and from his sixth son, Edmund, Duke of York, in the patrilineal line. The Yorkists' argument was that their claim should have taken precedence because it was derived from the third son rather than the fourth. This position was largely unfounded. English law had never recognized succession through the female line when there was a possibility of male succession.

There were many causes for the Wars of the Roses, including general social unrest and political instability due to the inability of Henry VI to rule effectively. Underlying causes also included the widespread practice of *livery and mainte-nance* whereby lords employed followers or retainers who essentially formed small private armies. With the end of the Hundred Years War these men had returned from France and were quick to want to involve themselves in the rivalries that already existed in the royal family. Despite the military presence of these small armies, fighting during the Wars of the Roses was actually minimal. Of the thirty years during which the conflict lasted, only about thirteen weeks were spent in battle. The main impact of the conflict was the shifting succession that first brought the Yorkists and then the Lancastrians to power.

In 1461 Henry VI was defeated at the Battle of St. Albans and fled to Scotland with his wife and young son. Richard, Duke of York, had died the previous year, but his son took advantage of the situation and had himself crowned as Edward IV. He was nineteen when he became king. The first years of his reign were marred by his unpopular marriage to Elizabeth Woodville, daughter of one of the most ambitious and ruthless noble families in England, and by the defection of the Earl of Warwick (nicknamed the Kingmaker because of his role in putting Edward on the throne). As he matured, however, Edward proved himself to be a competent king, managing both the politics and finances of government much better than his predecessor.

When Edward IV died in 1483, his sons were still very young. His eldest, Edward (assumed to be the heir to the throne), was only twelve and his younger brother, Richard, was only nine. Edward V was named king but he and his brother were soon hustled off to the Tower of London "to ensure their safety" by their uncle, Richard, Duke of Gloucester. The two princes were never seen again, and in 1674 two small skeletons were found in the White Tower, presumed to be the young boys, probably murdered on the order of Richard, who took the throne as Richard III. The identity of the remains has never been confirmed, and Richard's role in whatever happened to the princes remains unestablished.

Without doubt, one of the most controversial kings in English history, Richard III continues to fascinate and repel. In August 2012 his body was located at the site of Greyfriars Church near Bosworth, where it was hastily interred in 1485. This discovery immediately reopened the old debates: was he really hunchbacked, deformed in both body and mind, as Shakespeare depicted him? In Shakespeare's play Richard conspired to have his older brother murdered (in the famous scene Clarence is charged with treason and is drowned in a "vat of Malmsey wine"), and Shakespeare leaves no doubt that it was Richard who murdered his two young nephews because they stood in his way of ascending the throne. Later historians have tried to find a more balanced assessment of Richard III. Shakespeare was certainly not unbiased, and much of his material was drawn from sources that sought to disparage Richard. Although it is true that Clarence was drowned, he probably was indeed guilty of treason against Edward IV, and we simply do not know what happened to the two princes. Interestingly, the body of Richard, found in what is now a parking lot, revealed ten battlefield wounds and evidence of scoliosis, which in his lifetime would have probably been revealed as one higher shoulder. His body was identified both through contemporary physical descriptions of his appearance and through modern DNA analysis. According to the archaeologist engaged in the project, the reconstruction of Richard's face through forensic archaeology (commissioned by the Richard III Society) revealed a face "warm, youthful, and earnest."

We will probably never know what the real Richard was like. In his lifetime he had both supporters and enemies, but the legality of his succession was certainly questioned when he took the crown as the last of the Yorkist kings. His main rival was Henry Tudor (Bolingbroke in Shakespeare's play), whose own claim was far from clear. The Tudors were not themselves royal, but Owen

Richard III, portrait by an unknown artist. Richard III is one of the most controversial of the English kings. He is accused of having murdered both his brother, the Duke of Clarence, and his two nephews in his quest for the English crown.

Forensic reconstruction of the features of Richard III. The reconstructed model of Richard's face accords well with his portrait (page 137) and at least physically does not show the monster portrayed by Shakespeare.

Tudor, Henry's grandfather, had served at court during the reign of Henry V, and he eventually married Henry's widow, the French Princess Katherine. Their son Edmund (half-brother to Henry VI) married Lady Margaret Beaufort, and it is through her that his son Henry claimed his right to the throne. She was descended from John of Gaunt, but through his mistress, Katherine Swynford. Thus, Henry's claim was both matrilineal and illegitimate; however, he was the closest living Lancastrian. He invaded England in 1485, having gathered a small mercenary army in France, where he had been living. They landed in Wales and then marched to the Midlands, where he met Richard's army at Bosworth Field on August 22, 1485. By evening Richard was dead and Henry Tudor had claimed the crown. His subsequent marriage to Elizabeth of York (daughter of Edward IV) united the houses of York and Lancaster. The Wars of the Roses had ended and a new dynasty was on the throne.

Although there were two brief attempts to reopen hostilities, Henry firmly maintained his hold on government. Both involved imposters, and both centered around the uncertainty of what had happened to the young Yorkist princes. In the first, a commoner named Lambert Simnel attempted to impersonate the Earl of Warwick, who was a cousin of the princes. He gained support from the Irish and French, but the king was not worried in the least. He knew that the real Earl of Warwick was being kept secretly as a prisoner in the Tower of London and that he was too feebleminded to ever press any claim to the throne. When Simnel was captured, the king took pity on him, and instead of ordering his execution, sentenced him to live out his days as a scullion in the king's kitchen.

The other challenge came from another imposter, Perkin Warbeck, who invaded England in 1496, claiming to be Richard, the younger son of Edward IV. He won the support of the Irish as well as the Scots. He had lived for many years in Scotland under the protection of the Scottish King James IV, but when he invaded England he was quickly captured and imprisoned in the Tower. Two years later he was executed, along with the real Earl of Warwick, ending any possibility of further challenges.

Once the political issues were resolved, Henry Tudor, now Henry VII, focused on establishing England more firmly in the changing political and cultural landscape of Europe. He and Elizabeth had four children and the dynastic marriages they arranged show clearly the changing milieu of the early sixteenth century. The eldest son, Arthur, was betrothed to Catherine, the second daughter of Isabella of Castile and Ferdinand of Aragon, monarchs of what was quickly becoming the richest territory in Europe following the discovery of the New World. The marriage took place in 1501 but Arthur died the following year, probably of tuberculosis. Catherine remained in England and eventually Henry realized that his dynastic aims could still be achieved through the marriage of the young widow to his second son, Henry. Henry VII's older daughter, Margaret, was married in 1503 to the Scottish King James IV, and the younger daughter, Mary, was married (after Henry's death) to the king of France, thus securing a number of key strategic alliances.

SCOTLAND AND THE EARLY STUARTS

The marriage between Margaret Tudor and James IV of Scotland is interesting on many counts. Although the desire to secure his northern flank is an obvious motivation, Henry VII's choice of the Scottish king as husband for his daughter reflects a greater importance placed on Anglo-Scottish politics than we have seen before, particularly as regards the increasing role of Scotland in the larger European context.

Politically, the fifteenth century had been difficult for the Scots. The direct male line of Robert the Bruce ended with the death of his son, David II, in 1371. The throne then passed to Robert II, son of Bruce's daughter Marjory and her husband, Walter, the high steward. Robert took the name Stewart and thus begins the Stuart dynasty (the name was changed to the French spelling in the mid sixteenth century during the time of Mary, Queen of Scots). In later years the belief was strong that the Stewart monarchs were cursed by bad luck, and the beginnings of the legend probably can be traced to this time. Robert's son, Robert III, was physically disabled, and the succession of Stewart kings that followed was characterized by murders, accidents, minority successions, and a variety of disasters, although there were successes as well.

Recognizing his inability to maintain control over the ambitious families around him, and fearing for the life of his young son (after his elder son had died in suspicious circumstances), Robert III put his son James on board a ship headed for France in 1406. The ship was captured by the English and the young boy was taken as a hostage to the English court, where he spent the next nineteen years under house arrest. He was treated kindly and allowed access to books and an education. He appears to have possessed another one of the Stewart traits, a love for learning and an aptitude for scholarship. He learned the rime royal style (seven 10-syllable lines, rhyming ABABBCC) then in vogue in the English court and composed his own poetry, written in an interesting mixture of Scots and Chaucerian English. Although there are surviving fragments of two or three other poems that he probably composed, he is best remembered for *The Kingis Quair* (*The King's Book*), which is a long allegorical romance apparently inspired by his falling in love with the young English Princess Joan Beaufort, whom he had seen walking in the courtyard during his captivity. When he was finally released from his long stay in England as hostage in 1424, he married her and brought her back to Scotland with him.

Although the image we have of King James in his youth is a pleasant one, in his later years he became more and more greedy and intolerant. He mounted a savage campaign against the Highlands, creating a strong resentment against the Scottish monarchy that had not been there previously. He also introduced legislative reforms, based mostly on English models, on an unprecedented scale: new administrative and financial reforms, laws concerning licensing, changes of representation in the Scottish Parliament, heresy laws, and other changes that offended the nobles and clerics who had flourished under the older systems. He recklessly spent the money that had been raised for his ransom and aroused animosity when he began exterminating members of his own family (the Albany branch, descendants of the fourteenth century Robert Stewart, Duke of Albany). A small faction of the aggrieved assassinated King James in February 1437. He left behind a six-year-old son.

Queen Joan, the "fair flower of England" in her youth, was wounded by the assassins in her efforts to save the king, and she immediately took her son to the safety of Edinburgh Castle, vowing revenge on the murderers. James II was crowned in Holyrood Abbey at the age of six. His face bore a flaming red birthmark that was widely rumored to mark him for an early death and a life filled with trouble. Superstition or not, the prophecies proved all too true.

During the minority of James II, another family was able to consolidate its fourteenth century gains and now came to prominence: the Douglases, who were divided into two branches, the Black Douglases and the Red Douglases. The Black earls (popularly, the good branch of the family) were descended from Sir James Douglas—the stalwart best friend of Robert Bruce—who was killed in battle while trying to fulfill his vow to take Bruce's embalmed heart to the Holy Land. The Red Douglases were descended from another James Douglas, the hero of the Battle of Otterburn, who fought against the English in 1388.

When he was nineteen, James II took personal control of the kingdom. He married Mary of Gueldres, a daughter of the powerful Duke of Burgundy (again illustrating the growing role of Scotland in continental politics) and began trying to subdue the factions that had held sway during his minority. Remarkably, he had great success, employing a mixture of bribery and threats to eventually end the power of the Douglases. By the age of twenty-five he had gained effective control of Scotland and began extending some of his father's more tolerable reforms. He created his own network of support by cultivating some of the nobility who had been ill treated by the Douglases and by marrying his sisters to strategic European dynastic partners. It began to appear that the prophecies had been in error. But along with his mother's courage and his father's tenacity, James had inherited the Stewart family's fascination with new ideas. His scholarly interests (coinciding with his political interests) focused on new military technology, in particular, the new hooped bombards (staved cannons). In 1460 James briefly involved himself in the Wars of the Roses on the Lancastrian side and used that as an excuse to try to recover Roxburgh, which had changed hands several times during the Scottish Wars of Independence. He brought his troops south, along with a magnificent new cannon, the Lion. As he stood by the great bombard, watching to see how it worked, it exploded. He left behind three sons. The oldest was nine years old.

Again, Scotland was faced with a minority ruler, another period of regency, and another return to virtual anarchy. The family that rose to the top this time was the Boyds. They rose from obscurity during this period and nearly as quickly disappeared from high politics. They were not as conniving and ruthless as the Douglases had been, although they were involved in a plot to kidnap the young king. After three months in the custody of Sir Alexander Boyd and a motley group of Border lords, including the Hepburns, Lindsays, Flemings, and Kerrs, the teenage James III appeared in public, saying that they had acted with his approval, and Sir Alexander became his master of arms, guardian, and chamberlain. Sir Alexander negotiated the 1469 marriage terms between James III and Princess Margaret of Denmark, following his father's precedent of choosing a European bride. Relations between Denmark and Scotland became less than amicable when the Danish king admitted that he only had two of the sixty thousand florins he had promised as a dowry for his daughter. Sir Alexander lost his head in the debacle, and the Danish king pawned the islands of Orkney and Shetland to James as payment for the dowry shortfall. Having now reached his majority, James concluded a treaty with Edward IV of England; went to war with the remnants of the MacDonald Lords of the Isles; and eventually forced their surrender of the earldom of Ross, which had been a point of contention for several generations. These territorial changes brought the kingdom of Scotland to its modern borders.

It appeared that James III was off to a better start than his predecessors, but he was more interested in scholarship and culture than in politics and war, and by the standards of his day, he did not have the traits necessary for a good king.

Perhaps he knew his family history too well: He did not trust the great noble families and instead surrounded himself with artists, musicians, astrologers, and alchemists. Looking back, we can see that in fact James III is an excellent example of Renaissance tastes and sensibilities, but to his contemporaries, his choices were incomprehensible and suspect. Public opinion favored the king's two brothers, Alexander, Duke of Albany, and John, Earl of Mar. Both were athletic, martial young men, much more to the taste of the nobility than the scholarly and introverted James. James probably realized that his brothers constituted a threat by their mere popularity, but an elaborate story began circulating that one of the king's favorites, Robert Cochrane (the architect of Stirling Castle) had persuaded the king that his brothers were using magical arts against him, seeking his death through the manipulation of waxen figures. The two were imprisoned in Edinburgh Castle. John, Earl of Mar, died from illness (or more likely from an excessive bleeding treatment), but Alexander, Duke of Albany, escaped. It was a swashbuckling exit. He killed his jailers and he and a page boy escaped down a rope of sheets tied from the window. The page boy slipped and fell, breaking his legs, but Albany safely descended and walked all the way to Leith, about fifteen miles away, carrying the boy. From Leith he fled to France, abandoning his land and title.

The dichotomy between the ideas of kingship held by the king and by his nobles widened as time went on. The king was not helped by a series of bad harvests and a return of the plague. Popular opinion was that he sat in his rooms with "masons and fiddlers," doing nothing while the people suffered. In truth, there was probably very little that James could have done to address the immediate problems of famine and disease, but his patronage of artists, musicians, scientists, and architects was seen as worthless and despicable. Cochrane in particular was the target of much hostility from the nobles. The story goes that, when James reluctantly went to war with the English in 1482, the disgruntled noblemen, unwilling to fight for a king who surrounded himself with such lowborn favorites, met at Lauder Kirk in Berwickshire. None of them wanted to risk confronting the king until Archibald Douglas, the young Earl of Angus, exclaimed "I'll bell the cat!" and went to the king demanding the removal of his favorites. James refused and six of his favorites were seized and hanged above the Lauder Water, including the colorful Robert Cochrane, who died demanding that he be "hangit with a silken cord and not ane tow of rope like ane thief."

The lords effectively captured the king and took him back to Edinburgh. Albany arrived on the scene, negotiating terms to his own benefit with Richard, Duke of Gloucester, who agreed to depart. Albany released and "restored" his brother to the throne, with all likely intent of taking the throne at some future time. The next year he got into an altercation with the Border lords and again fled to France, where he was killed in a tournament, leaving James on the throne, but no more in control than he had ever been. The death of Queen Margaret in 1486 left the grieving king more alone than ever. He still sought the company of his scholars, including Bishop Elphinstone (later founder of the University of Aberdeen), relishing learned conversation and savoring the books and poetry that he had loved all his life. The only real interest he took in government was in trying to bolster the royal revenues. He was determined to claim the dues of Coldingham Priory and ended up triggering a revolt by the Border lords, who still harbored grievances from earlier in his reign.

In 1488 James agreed to meet the rebels at Blackness to negotiate. He was accompanied by a small army and his fifteen-year old son, James. It is entirely unclear what role the young man played in the rebellion. He may have been part of it, he may have been an unwilling hostage, or he may have felt that his presence would help protect his father. Whichever was the case, there was no battle, the rebels dispersed, and the king dismissed his army to return to Edinburgh. However, the rebels re-mustered their troops and fell upon the king and his small bodyguard at Sauchieburn. The king was killed, although the specific circumstances are unknown and have been the subject of much conjecture.

JAMES IV AND THE SCOTTISH RENAISSANCE

James IV took the throne filled with a deep sense of guilt. Although his involvement with the rebels is not clear, he seemed to feel that he was at least partly to blame for his father's death, and he wore an iron chain of penance

James IV of Scotland by an unknown artist. James IV was Scotland's Renaissance king, beloved by his people and often thought by historians to be the best of the Stewart kings. He was killed at the Battle of Flodden in 1514 leaving behind an infant son.

around his waist for the rest of his life. Despite the dark start to his reign, he was a charismatic young man and easily the Stewart best liked by both historians and contemporaries. With him the Scottish renaissance came to full flower.

James's court was modeled on that of Burgundy, perhaps the epitome of northern culture during the fifteenth century. In his memoirs the Spanish ambassador Pedro de Ayala wrote a lengthy description of the king in which he noted that

> he is of noble stature, neither tall nor short, and as handsome in complexion and shape as a man can be. . . . His knowledge of languages is wonderful. He is well read in the Bible and other devout books. He is a good historian. . . . He is active and works hard. When he is not at war, he hunts in the mountains. . . . He is courageous, even more so than a king should be. I have seen him often undertake most dangerous things in the last wars. . . . He is not a good captain because he begins to fight before he has given his orders. He said to me that his subjects serve him with their persons and their goods, in just and unjust quarrels, exactly as he likes, and that, therefore, he does not think it right to begin any warlike undertaking without being himself the first in danger. His deeds are as good as his words. For this reason, and because he is a very humane prince, he is much loved.

The description reminds us that he was indeed a man and a prince of the Renaissance era. Unlike his father, he combined the traits of soldier and scholar, and he knew how to win people rather than alienate them. Accounts of James attest to his Renaissance zeal for learning everything: poetry, engineering, artillery, ship building, music, medicine, and alchemy. His court was filled with music and dance. He loved ritual and dressed in the latest, richest fashions, but he also insisted on personal knowledge of the commoners, talking to them and learning about their viewpoints with respect. He was the first of the Stewart kings to learn Gaelic and to go to the Highlands himself. He maintained an ongoing campaign to bring the Highland chiefs under the authority of the monarchy, but he did so with greater understanding of their culture than any of his predecessors (or arguably, his successors). Ayala's reference to his linguistic skills is well documented. James knew seven languages and regularly conversed with his ambassadors in their own languages; he could speak to the clerics in Latin as well. During his reign the University of Aberdeen, Scotland's third university, was founded and he passed the Education Act of 1496, requiring eldest sons of landowners to go to school to learn "perfyte Latin" and study law. (He was quite likely influenced in the latter cause by his father's friend William Elphinstone, bishop of Aberdeen.)

Inheriting the Stewart love for learning, James studied with physicians. There is documentation of his payments to subjects who volunteered to let him draw their blood and pull their teeth (for those requiring a doctor or dentist this was seen as a good opportunity!). Similarly, he probably performed alchemical experiments, working closely with the court alchemist, John Damian. Although we now think of alchemy as primarily focused on turning lead to gold, at that time it was essentially the only branch of experimental science or what is more correctly called natural philosophy. One vivid account of the work of John

Damian survives. In addition to his work on metallurgy, like da Vinci, he was trying to discover the secrets of flight. In 1507 he convinced the king that he could be in France before the king's ambassador, who had left a few days earlier. The court assembled on the battlements of Stirling Castle. One onlooker reported: "This Abbot [Damian] took in hand to fly with wingis. . . . He made a pair of wingis of fedders and flew off the walls of Stirling but shortly he fell to the ground and brak his knee bane." The intrepid Damian survived and explained to the king that the experiment had failed because "there was som hen fedders in the wingis." No further documentation survives regarding this particular research project.

Perhaps with greater practicality, James introduced the printing press to Scotland in 1507. (The first printing press in England was established by William Caxton in 1476.) It was intended primarily to serve the church, and indeed the beautiful *Aberdeen Breviary* was one of the first printed books in Scotland. It soon took on other functions, producing books of law and also collections of the new forms of poetry now being popularized in the king's court.

In Scotland the renaissance blossoming of culture was not as much pictorial as verbal. During James's reign both Gaelic and Scots poetry flourished. For a variety of reasons, Scotland is not nearly as rich in Gaelic manuscripts as Ireland, although it is very likely there was an equivalent amount of composition during the late Middle Ages. One rare survivor is the highly significant *Book of the Dean of Lismore*, written during James's reign. It contains primarily Gaelic material, although its inclusion of fragments in both Latin and Scots suggests a multilingual audience. The fact that the manuscript contains both Irish and Scottish Gaelic poetry provides evidence for the evolution of the language during this period, as well as documentation of the continued cultural exchange between the Gaelic-speaking regions of Ireland and Scotland.

In the Scots language, this period was a time of great innovation and maturity. Although Barbour and Blind Harry wrote their poems on the Wars of Independence earlier, the poets of the late fifteenth and early sixteenth century are regarded as the first to produce distinctively Scottish literature. It is called the Age of the *Makars*, a Scots word meaning those who make or build, reflecting highly developed craftsmanship. The three best known poets of this era are Robert Henryson, who began writing during the reign of James III; William Dunbar; and Gavin Douglas. They benefitted from the printing press, which helped disseminate their work. (In contrast, Gaelic writing used a different type of script than English, Latin, or Scots and therefore could not be printed on a standard printing press. It was not until the seventeenth century that this was resolved.)

James clearly saw himself and Scotland as part of the larger world of European politics. He called for a crusade against the Turks to be led by himself. (Nothing came of this except the annoyance of the Warrior Pope, Julius II, who regarded the Scottish king as something of an upstart.) He also negotiated with Henry VII to sign the Treaty of Perpetual Peace with England in 1502 and sealed it by his marriage to Margaret Tudor in 1503. The wedding was a sumptuous affair, strongly evoking images of Renaissance pageantry. Margaret's hair was loose under a new crown that had been made for her. Her dress was white damask embroidered with gold and lined with crimson velvet. The king wore a gold doublet and crimson hose with an over-jacket of crimson and black, along with a white damask cloak and a black velvet bonnet, which was adorned with a single great ruby. There was a great feast after the ceremony, with a boar's head, roast swan, and some sixty other dishes. The celebration went on for five days, with music, dancing, acrobats, and tournaments. The court poet, William Dunbar, even composed a poem, "The Thistle and the Rose," in honor of the event. Despite the courtly celebration, it was a state marriage: the new queen was only thirteen and the king was thirty.

It was James's involvement in European politics that led to disaster. Henry VII died in 1509 and he was succeeded by his second son, Henry VIII. In 1512 Henry joined the Holy League, which the pope and the Holy Roman emperor had formed against the French king. The French reminded Scotland of the Auld Alliance between France and Scotland and called on Scotland to go to war against England. Pope Julius II informed James that he would be excommunicated if he broke the truce with England. Caught in an impossible situation, James finally made the decision to go to war against the English.

On September 9, 1513, the Scottish army, composed of the "flower of Scottish chivalry"—more than twenty thousand lords, burgesses, borderers, and Highlanders—met the English army at Branxton Lea in the Flodden hills. The battle was a rout. The English were better equipped and better trained. Worst of all, the king's tactics proved true to Ayala's words. "Fighting like a common soldier," he charged into the midst of battle, leaving no clear orders for his troops. It is impossible to know exactly how many Scots died that day. The English claimed that it was twelve thousand, a number probably not far off the mark. Thirteen earls, along with the king's natural son Alexander, bishop of St. Andrews, died beside their king. Countless burgesses, farmers, and laborers—men from the Highlands, from the Borders, and from all of Scotland—fell that day. When the king's body was found it was full of arrows, one hand hung by a strip of flesh, and his neck was severed. Oddly, the iron chain that he had worn since he was fifteen was missing. Because of this, the rumor started immediately that the king was not really dead. Nonetheless, those who had known him in life said the body was his and it was conveyed to Newcastle and from there to London. Catherine of Aragon considered sending it to her husband, Henry VIII, who was in Flanders at the time, but decided against the idea, sending the king's bloodstained surcoat instead. The body was then sent to the monastery at Sheen in Surrey, where it remained unburied for many years. Elizabeth I's master glazier saw it, and intrigued by its incorrupt state, took the head home and kept it on display for a time. It was finally buried in an anonymous grave at St. Michael's in Wood Street.

In Scotland, the disaster of Flodden was beyond comprehension. There was no one left. The king was dead. The archbishop of St. Andrews was dead. Over forty lords were dead, along with countless burgesses and commoners. The king left behind an eighteen-month-old son.

IRELAND'S POLITICS AND THE GAELIC REVIVAL

For historians, Irish politics of this time period, similar to politics in England and Scotland, tended to obscure the great cultural revival that was going on during the latter fifteenth and early sixteenth centuries. There were two aspects of the revival: one internal and one external. With the decreasingly effective power of the English lordship, the Gaelic chieftaincies had revived and with them came a great resurgence in Gaelic literature and culture. Moreover, the Irish chieftains maintained close ties with continental Europe, through both religion and trade, and thus were aware of the broader cultural changes taking place during the fifteenth century.

Politically, by the fifteenth century the English controlled only the Pale, which encompassed Louth, Dublin, Meath, and Kildare, including the two important port towns of Dublin and Drogheda. In this area English was spoken and English laws and customs were observed. The gentry of the Pale included such families as the Plunketts, Cusacks, Barnewells, and Stanyhursts. Their income derived from their estates within the English lordship and they looked to the English Crown for military and political protection. However, they also maintained close relationships with their Gaelic neighbors, sometimes intermarrying with the powerful Gaelic clans. They considered themselves to be English and sent their sons to study at Oxford or Cambridge or to study law at the Courts in London. They also observed the English law of primogeniture, ensuring that their estates passed intact to the next generation. During the fifteenth century the Irish Parliament (first established in 1297 and composed of lords and commoners from the English lordship) met regularly and passed legally binding statutes, which, however, could be enforced only within the decreasing lands of the Pale.

The most famous of the fifteenth century Irish Parliaments was Poynings Parliament, held in 1494. Sir Edward Poynings was lord deputy of Ireland, sent by Henry VII in an attempt to restore peace after a rising of Gearóid Fitzgerald (Gerald the Great), eighth Earl of Kildare, whose lands and allegiances straddled both the English and Gaelic lordships. Poynings was a military man, and he arrived with six hundred soldiers. Kildare was arrested and sent to London. Poynings called a Parliament to meet in Drogheda that immediately passed an act of attainder against Kildare, along with forty-eight other pieces of legislation aimed at subduing the Gaelic Irish. He ordered an increase in the defenses around the Pale, outlawed the practice of *coyne and livery* by which lords maintained their own private armies, and reiterated the laws against wearing of Irish dress and the use of the Irish language and customs that had first been articulated in the Statutes of Kilkenny in 1366. The fact that the laws kept being reissued strongly implies that they were unable to be enforced effectively. One far-reaching statute that was passed by this Parliament (although its full impact was probably not realized at the time) was what came to be known as Poynings Law, which required that no Parliament could be held in Ireland unless the lord deputy and the council first asked permission from the king and told him the laws that they intended to pass.

In September 1496 Kildare was sent back to govern in Ireland, leaving his son Gearóid Og (Young Gerald) behind in the English court as a hostage. The English consensus by this time was that no other man could gain the submissions of the Irish chieftains and rule as effectively as Kildare. (His loyalty seemed secure because the Yorkist threat that had been involved in his rebellion was now removed.) One English agent wrote enthusiastically,

> His grace could have put no man in authority here who in so short a space and with so little cost could have set this land in such good order as it is now but this man only. I trust the King shall have a great treasure of him.

For the rest of his life, the Earl of Kildare ruled in the name of the English king, but he maintained his complex web of allegiances and fundamental outlook as a Gaelic lord. When the elder Kildare died in 1513, the new English king, Henry VIII, failing completely to understand Irish politics, appointed Kildare's son Gearóid ninth earl, lord deputy, with no hesitation. The young man had been raised in the English court, he had an English wife, and of course he would be loyal to the English Crown.

Although Henry VIII might momentarily have felt secure in his Irish possessions, the reality was quite different from his expectations. Theoretically the English kings might be the rulers of Ireland, but outside the rapidly shrinking Pale, Ireland lay in the hands of the powerful Gaelic lords who wanted no part of the English monarchy. In 1515 Henry received a report on Ireland stating that there were "more than sixty counties . . . inhabited by the King's Irish enemies [and] more than thirty great captains of English noble family that followeth the Irish order." The author also listed more than ninety lordships, ruled over by their own lords, or "as he is called in English, 'the captain of his nation.'" For the Irish, politics largely consisted of sometimes rapidly shifting clan feuds and alliances and sometimes deep animosities going back for centuries. These clan associations were incomprehensible to the English, based as they were on Gaelic law, communal identities, customary practices, and complicated marital connections. In general, the larger lordships sought to expand by annexing neighboring territory; thus, they were often at odds with their immediate neighbors and in alliance with whomever was on the other side. Many of the traditional clan feuds become obvious simply by looking at a map: the O'Neills and O'Donnells, Desmonds and Maccarthys, Kildares and Ormonds, Burkes of Mayo and Burkes of Clanrickard, and so forth. In some cases, there might also be a struggle for supremacy within a family, as was the case of the Geraldines of Kildare and of Desmond.

It would be overstating the situation to draw direct comparisons with the principalities of renaissance Italy, but there were indeed some functional similarities in terms of both politics and culture. Each lordship sought to command more power and wealth, and one of the ways to expedite this process was through the visible trappings of wealth and power. Gaelic Ireland had no grand palaces and piazzas to decorate, but part of the Gaelic resurgence was aimed at commanding patronage for those elements of culture most valued by the Gaelic elites. One visitor to a Gaelic lord's court recorded his experiences:

> Wonderfully did I spend my time: a day listening to harp music, a day hunting in the bordering mountains, a day solving riddles and putting them in the company of guests and young women, sporting in the breasts of the mountains, drinking, playing chess, out along the coasts in sailing boats.

Of particular importance were the high poets, whose status had revived along with that of the Gaelic chieftains. They were still men of the old hereditary aes dána families, the O'Dalys, MacMhurrichs, O'Higgins, and others. From the Gaelic perspective their power was immense. There were three major categories of poetry: poems that incited one to war (*goltraighe*), to love (*geantraighe*), and to sleep (*suantraighe*). In addition, there were the praise poems (or the opposite genre of satire) that could completely make or destroy a man's reputation, as well as the genealogies and place lore that secured the place of the clan in the landscape memory. The poet was no mere rhymer, but rather a highly educated, aristocratic custodian of identity and history. The English (probably rightly in

Woodcut of the MacSweeney chieftain and his court (Derrick's Image of Ireland, *1581). The woodcut suggests the barbarity that the English colonizers saw in the Gaelic Irish, but some of the details such as the roasting of meat in a skin and the recitation of a poet to the accompaniment of a harpist are reasonably accurate. The three figures who surround the chieftain are clerics, as can be seen from their tonsures and Irish furred cloaks.*

this case) particularly disliked the poets as being promoters of Gaelic culture and thus subversive to English rule. Certainly competition among the Gaelic chieftains as patrons of the poets and the other earned elites (including doctors, lawyers, and harpists) was intense and thus helped escalate the expectations and standards of court culture.

THE IRISH RENAISSANCE LORDS

The interconnection between the chieftains and the poet-elites can be seen vividly in the life and work of Manus O'Donnell, a sixteenth century Irish lord who has been specifically likened to a renaissance prince. We have a description of his appearance that sets the tone: "[he wore] a coat of crimson velvet with aglets of gold, twenty or thirty pair over a great cloak of right crimson satin girded with black velvet and a bonnet with a feather set full of aglets of gold." His eye-catching splendor marks him as a man aware of the latest fashions of his day, but there is much more upon which to base his place in the context of Renaissance Europe.

O'Donnell was involved in the complicated politics of the early sixteenth century, for a time allying himself with the powerful Geraldine League. He had been engaged in a struggle to overthrow his own father and allied with Conn Bacach O'Neill (the ancient hereditary enemy of the O'Donnells), first marrying Conn's daughter Siobhán and later marrying Lady Eleanor Fitzgerald, sister of Gearóid Og, after Siobhán's death. His relationship with these two women is poignantly shown in the poetry he composed for them using the complex Gaelic literary meters. His elegy on the death of Siobhán reveals personal grief and love, and his courtship poem a few years later to Eleanor again shows him as a man of intellect, passion, and clever expression. (Sadly Eleanor deserted Manus when he withdrew from the Geraldine League in an effort to safeguard both his son and his land.) There are at least six other extant poems that are ascribed to Manus, all showing a knowledge of the classical Gaelic literary genres and contemporary imagery.

We know that O'Donnell was well connected in the European courts, as shown by diplomatic correspondence with the Scottish court, the French court, the English court, and the papacy. An odd piece of evidence survives from a papal agent: "[O'Donnell] was the best lord of fish in Ireland, and he exchangeth fish always with foreign merchants for wine, by which he is called in other countries, the king of fish."

Manus O'Donnell was also engaged in the architectural and military innovations of his time, building the great castle of Port-na-dtrí-namhad, and a smaller one at Lifford. He propelled the O'Donnells to the forefront of firearms use, although he suffered the consequences when his son Calvagh rebelled against him and won a decisive battle using a borrowed Scottish bombard, the *gunna cam* (the crooked gun). Despite his defeat, Manus remained on good terms with his son and supervised the lordship when his son was captured by Shane O'Neill in 1561.

All of these stories would show possible glimpses of an Irish renaissance prince, but the most telling piece of evidence is in what he considered his most significant life work: a recension of the life of Colum Cille, patron of the O'Donnells as well as the O'Neills. Many lords had commissioned works of piety in late fifteenth century Ireland, just as their contemporaries had done across Europe. What sets O'Donnell's work apart is that it was not merely commissioned. He makes it clear in the first paragraphs of the book that it was he who undertook the work himself:

> And be it known to the readers of this Life that it was Manus (son of Aodh, son of Niall Garbh, son of Toirdelbach of the Wine) O'Donnell who had the part of this life that was in Latin put into Gaelic, and the parts that were in difficult Gaelic made easy, so that it might be comprehensible for all. He collected and assembled that part of it that was scattered in the ancient books of Ireland, and dictated it from his own lips. It was a major task as he had to spend a lot of time studying how to place each part in its correct position, just as it is written here below.

He stated his purpose clearly:

> As I am not worthy myself to obtain what I ask from God, I pray to you Colum Cille to speak to him as one of his own household, to get grace from him for me so that I can properly finish this work that I want to do for you, so that it might be to His honour and the raising up of your name, and to the good of the people who read and listen to it, and to the good of my own soul and body, and to the Devils' dishonor and great hurt.

Here we have good evidence of the piety and orthodox religious views of a Gaelic prince and a view of patronage that extended far beyond the secular world. Throughout the text there is evidence of critical thinking and an attempt to reconcile the sometime heterodox folk traditions with late medieval doctrinal positions. Interestingly, O'Donnell's text also shows numerous examples of the application of humanistic methods to reconcile divergent texts. The whole project fits well with Renaissance interests in history and textual analysis. From the fragments he was striving to make a cohesive whole, with points of disagreement or omission noted so that the reader (or listener) could draw his own conclusions. It is unclear whether O'Donnell knew Latin himself or if he had assistance with the Latin texts, but he certainly knew both classical Gaelic and the substantially different Gaelic vernacular and sought to find an accessible usage for anyone who might consult the work. In this way his text is a crucial transition piece in the evolution of written Gaelic, and in many ways it mirrors the way in which Italian renaissance scholars both preserved and shaped language.

O'Donnell died in 1563, and it is worth quoting his obituary from the *Annals of the Four Masters* as a testimony to a man who in many ways exemplifies the cultural changes from medieval to modern and shows evidence of an Irish renaissance:

> O'Donnell (Manus, son of Aodh, son of Niall Garbh . . .) a man who never allowed the chiefs in his neighborhood and vicinity to encroach upon any of his superabundant possessions, even to the time of his disease and infirmity; a fierce, obdurate, wrathful, and combative man towards his enemies and

opponents . . . and a mild, friendly, benign, amicable, bountiful, and hos-
pitable man towards the learned, the destitute, the poets, and the ollamhs,
towards the religious orders and the church, as is evident from the accounts
of old people and historians; a learned man, skilled in many arts; gifted with
a profound intellect, and the knowledge of every science, died on 9 February,
at his own mansion-seat at Lifford . . . and was interred in the burial place of
his predecessors and ancestors at Donegal, in the monastery of St. Francis,
with great honour and veneration, after having vanquished the Devil and
the world.

In discussing the Irish renaissance, one historian used a quote from
Aristotle, "one swallow does not a summer make," and then went ahead to identify several possible examples of Irish renaissance-like lords. O'Donnell is a striking and early contender, but there were indeed others. Silken Thomas, the tenth
Earl of Kildare, has been mentioned in this context (both for his complex and
double-dealing diplomacy as well as for his lavish fashion tastes that prompted
his nickname), but his upbringing, politics, and cultural outlook belong more
to the English and European courts than to those of the Gaelic Irish lordships.
Although he illustrates the broader political awareness of the Irish lords during
this period, he is not a good example of internal cultural changes.

A better case might be made for Silken Thomas's half-brother, the eleventh
Earl of Kildare. By the time of his succession in 1537, the English conquest was
gaining force, and what had been a strongly resurgent Gaelic culture was now
on the defense. Gearóid had spent time in the English court and was something of a cultural chameleon, partaking of both European and Irish outlooks,
but he came to be strongly associated with Gaelic politics and identity. His
place in this discussion is not so much because of his own actions, but rather
because of the ways in which he was perceived by the Irish. The English nicknamed him the Rebel Earl, but to the Irish he was the Wizard Earl, whose story
was conflated with one of his ancestors and was used as strong supernatural
political propaganda.

He was the namesake of another Gearóid, who was a powerful chieftain of
the fourteenth century. The earlier Gearóid was a noted leader and a composer
of Gaelic love poetry, and the Irish annalists noted that "Ireland was full of the
fame of his wisdom." His stronghold was at Lough Gur in County Limerick, the
center of the sovereignty of Munster. An elaborate story explained how Gearóid's
father had lain with Aine, the goddess of Munster, and from this union the fourteenth century Gearóid was conceived. The story was either invented or perhaps
revived by his sixteenth century descendant, who used it to strengthen his claim
to the leadership of the Fitzgeralds. (There are interesting parallels with the use
of magic and popular culture in the aura that surrounded Owain Glyn Dwr and
his rebellion.) With the invoking of this supernatural pedigree, the current
Gearóid was quickly transformed into the champion of the Gaelic Irish, destined
to lead the Irish to victory against their (English) foes.

Interestingly, the whole elaborate story of the fourteenth century Gearóid
was not original to the Irish or to the Fitzgeralds. It was borrowed wholesale
from the legend of Frederick Barbarossa, which was circulating in Italy at the

Lough Gur, Ireland. Legend says that the Wizard Earl can still be seen every seven years riding his steed out of the depths of Lough Gur to lead the Gaelic Irish to victory.

time among agents who were associated with the Fitzgeralds. It appears that this is an interesting case of deliberately appropriated political propaganda. Inspiring as the story might have been, reality intervened and the "wizard earl" was captured and held in London in semi-captivity until his death in 1585. However, the interconnection between traditional stories and folklore and the rise of what we may perceive as emergent nationalistic identities is striking and parallels a similar pattern in other parts of Europe. As several Irish historians have pointed out, the Gaelic cultural revival and the emergence of a distinctively Irish, Gaelic, and Catholic identity during the fifteenth century figures prominently in the cultural clash and the subsequent establishment of Ireland as the first example of English colonial rule. Significantly, Gearóid's legend did not end with his death. As late as the nineteenth century the beleaguered Irish still told the tale that Gearóid could be seen riding forth from the depths of Lough Gur every seven years, still seeking the victory of the Gaelic Irish.

THE ENGLISH RENAISSANCE: HENRY VIII

Before leaving aside the concept of a British renaissance (or more accurately, renaissances), it is important to note the existence of a strong cultural revival in England during the early years of the reign of Henry VIII. Although the full importance of the political and religious changes of his reign will be considered in the following chapter, it should be noted here that Henry himself could well be considered as a Renaissance prince on the model of his continental contemporaries. He was a skilled poet and musician, he could read and write

Field of the Cloth of Gold, *anonymous artist. This depiction of the magnificent tournament and spectacle that was held in 1520 for the meeting of Francis I of France and Henry VIII of England dramatically attests to England's claim for involvement in Renaissance pageantry in the same style as the rest of Europe.*

in several different languages, and he was able to apply his considerable intellect in understanding the subtle nuances of humanistic scholarship in both theology and politics. His image as a young Renaissance prince is perhaps best exemplified by the extensive pomp and ritual surrounding his meeting with Francis I at the magnificent Field of the Cloth of Gold pageant to celebrate the treaty of 1514 between the English and the French (forged in the wreckage of the Scottish defeat at Flodden).

The contemporary painting commemorating this event captures the visual lushness of conspicuous consumption on a scale certainly never before seen by the British. Henry, with his love of jousting and desire to be part of continental power, was in his element at the great tournament in Calais. Behind the tournament was arguably one of the strongest examples of Renaissance ideas and taste in England: Cardinal Thomas Wolsey, in many ways creator of Henry's sovereign persona. Before his fall from power in 1529 Wolsey was a great cultural connoisseur and a patron of artists and scholars. He was responsible for the design and building of Hampton Court, which was later annexed by the royal household. In addition to Wolsey, Henry's court contained poets and musicians, as well as arguably the greatest British humanist scholar, Sir Thomas More, friend of Erasmus and author of *Utopia* (1516). It is a fascinating proposition to consider what the blossoming world of the British renaissance could have been if the turmoil of the Reformation could have been avoided.

SUGGESTED READING

Blackie, Ruth, Gordon Donaldson, and Douglas McKenzie. *James IV: A Renaissance King*. Edinburgh: Birlinn, 1997.

Bradshaw, Brendan. *And So Began the Irish Nation*. Surrey, UK: Ashgate, 2015.

Canny, Nicholas, ed. *The Origins of Empire: British Overseas Enterprise to the Close of the Seventeenth Century*. Oxford: Oxford University Press, 1998.

Collins, M. E. *Ireland, 1478–1610*. Dublin: The Educational Company, 1980.

Cosgrove, Art, ed. *Medieval Ireland 1169–1534*. Vol. 2 of *A New History of Ireland*. Oxford: Oxford University Press, 1987.

Crawford, Robert. *Scotland's Books: A History of Scottish Literature*. Oxford: Oxford University Press, 2009.

Daiches, David, ed. *The New Companion to Scottish Culture*. Edinburgh: Subterranean, 1993.

Edwards, R. Dudley, Art Cosgrove, and Donal McCartney. *Studies in Irish History, Presented to R. Dudley Edwards*. Dublin: Dublin University Press, 1979.

Goodman, Anthony. *The Wars of the Roses: Military Activity and English Society, 1452–97*. London: Routledge, 1981.

Lander, J. R. *Conflict and Stability in Fifteenth-Century England*, 3rd ed. London: Hutchinson University Press, 1977.

Prebble, John. *The Lion in the North*. Harmondsworth, UK: Penguin Books, 1971.

Ross, Charles. *Edward IV*. London: Eyre Methuen, 1974.

———. *Richard III*. Berkeley, CA: University of California Press, 1981.

Chapter 10

The Age of Reformation

In Europe Christendom was shaken on October 31, 1517, with Martin Luther's posting of the "Ninety-five Theses," challenging the authority of the Roman Catholic church. In Britain the Reformation arrived piecemeal and in different forms, but with huge impact on all three kingdoms. Although the Church had been the focus of much disagreement since the Middle Ages, it had provided channels of shared outlook and, at least to some extent, was a unifying force in Europe. With its structures and beliefs called into question by the Reformation, great instability in politics and society ensued. Religion now shaped and was shaped by regional identities and the resulting conflict affected all of Europe as well as the British Isles.

HENRY VIII AND THE ORIGINS OF THE ENGLISH REFORMATION

Most historians now agree that in fact Luther did not start the Reformation. Rather, evidence of anticlericalism and changes in popular religious beliefs and practices dating to the late fifteenth century indicate that dissatisfaction with the institutional church and the idea of religious reform certainly predated Luther. In this respect, Britain was no different from the Continent. The moral laxity of the Renaissance popes together with increasing social strains that were largely unaddressed by the Church led many Christians to a sort of do-it-yourself religious life focused on pilgrimages, sacramentals, and a personal relationship with the saints as exemplified by de Voragine's immensely popular compilation of legends of the saints, *The Golden Legend*. Particularly in rural communities and in outlying areas, many people's religious life was dependent on the wandering Franciscan or Dominican friars who traveled through Britain and the Continent preaching, saying Mass, and listening to confessions. It would be incorrect to say that the religious beliefs and practices of the common people were necessarily heterodox, but they were often personal rather than institutional.

Against this overall backdrop, the Reformation arrived in England in the form of the king's "Great Matter." This was the euphemistic shorthand used in court circles to refer to Henry VIII's desire for a divorce from his wife, Catherine of Aragon. By 1527 it was becoming clear that she was not going to bear him the son he so desperately wanted as heir. She had given him a daughter, Mary, but a sad litany of miscarriages and stillbirths had yielded no son. By 1527 everyone knew that she was too old to have more children, and besides, Henry's

Henry VIII, copied from a portrait by Hans Holbein. This portrait depicts Henry in his middle years, with the elaborate and costly clothing that he favored.

eye had fallen on an enchanting young lady-in-waiting, Anne Boleyn. Anne's sister, Mary, had already become Henry's mistress, but Anne was too clever to follow in her footsteps. She wanted no less than marriage, and Catherine was in the way. Anne's lineage was not lofty, but she was of noble birth and by all accounts she was beautiful and vivacious, and Henry wanted her for his queen.

It is debatable how much was merely an excuse and how much was an actual moral dilemma for Henry, but it was at this time that he suddenly began questioning the validity of his marriage to Catherine. Because she was the widow of his brother Arthur, and hence was legally of too close a kinship, a dispensation had to be granted at the time of the marriage, and Henry now questioned whether it had been given in error. Henry was himself an able humanist scholar and had an extensive knowledge of theology. (Ironically, given what was to come, the pope had named him Defender of the Faith for his writings refuting Lutheranism.) He argued that the bonds of kinship were too close and that clearly God was showing his displeasure by not giving Henry a son. The pope, Clement VII, tried every means he could think of to avoid the issue.

To the great powers of Europe, England was viewed as ineffective and rather peripheral (specifically, Henry had failed to provide any resolution to the conflicts between the French and the Spanish or to address the threat from the Ottoman Empire). Catherine, on the other hand, was extremely well connected. She was the daughter of Ferdinand and Isabella of Spain (arguably the most powerful territory of the sixteenth century), and she was also the aunt of Charles V, who in 1527 ruled Spain, the New World, northern Italy, the Netherlands, and the Holy Roman empire. In addition, in his role as Holy Roman emperor, Charles was the primary defender of the Catholic church; it was he who convened the Council of Worms in 1522 that challenged Luther's heresy. Moreover, the troops of Charles V, as part of the ongoing dynastic Habsburg-Valois conflict, were currently occupying Italy. Given all of these factors, the pope was in no hurry for the nephew to come to the defense of his aunt. And so the king's Great Matter stalled in the papal courts as the pope fervently hoped that it would resolve itself with the death of Henry, or Catherine, or Anne; or that the infatuation would end; or whatever else the fates might offer.

With increasing anger and frustration, Henry demanded that his chief minister, Cardinal Thomas Wolsey, solve the problem. Wolsey had been a brilliant diplomat and skilled chief minister for Henry. His rise to power had been dramatic, and from 1513 on he had held increasingly influential positions as Henry gave him favor after favor for his service. He had been elevated to a cardinalate in 1515 and three years later became papal legate in England, thus outranking the archbishop of Canterbury and serving as direct liaison with the pope. In this position, he ought to have been able to obtain the annulment of marriage that Henry sought. In 1529 Wolsey managed successfully to petition the pope to convene a court in London to hear the case. Wolsey himself was one of the judges. The hearing focused on several issues: the validity of the original dispensation, whether or not the marriage between Arthur and Catherine had been consummated, and whether impediments still existed even after the granting of the dispensation. Before a formal decision on the case could be made, however, the pope recalled the case to Rome.

From Henry's perspective, Wolsey had failed. Henry stripped him of all his titles and properties, leaving him only the archbishopric of York, and instructed him not to meddle at all in political affairs. Wolsey, however, continued to correspond with the French (probably hoping they might intervene in the annulment case) and Henry summarily ordered him to London. It is quite possible that he would have been executed but he died before he arrived.

Wolsey was succeeded as chancellor by Sir Thomas More, author of *Utopia* and one of the greatest intellectuals of the sixteenth century. A devout Catholic, More opposed the divorce on moral grounds. At first Henry agreed that More need not be involved in the continuing annulment case and instead called Parliament to gain support for his position. This Parliament, called in 1529 and lasting until 1536, is nicknamed the Reformation Parliament. The legislative changes made by this Parliament did not bring about the Reformation all at once, but instead gradually eroded the power of the Church by enacting reforms concerning probate and wills and by challenging the rights of the Church to promulgate canon law in England without the approval of the king.

By 1532 More had had enough. He resigned his office over what he saw as an overstepping of the king's authority and a misuse of secular power in religious affairs. As a devout Catholic, More held firmly to his beliefs and adhered

Sir Thomas More. Friend of Desiderius Erasmus and the best known early Tudor humanist. This portrait, by Hans Holbein, depicts More wearing the "collar of S's" as English chancellor before his clash with Henry VIII over the issue of Henry's divorce.

to the authority of the Catholic church. He and his family hoped by his retiring to a private life that he might escape the king's wrath, but three years later, still firm in his beliefs, he was executed for treason. A near-contemporaneous biography written by his son-in-law William Roper describes the personal and intellectual life of the great humanist, showing his love for his wife, his interest in his talented daughter Margaret's education, and above all his enduring piety, even as he was caught between his duty to the king and his duty to the Church. Roper called More "a man of singular virtue, and of a clear, unspotted conscience." More was canonized in 1935.

CRANMER, CROMWELL, AND THE START OF THE ENGLISH REFORMATION

In 1532, a change in personnel helped lead to the legislation that established the Reformation in England. Sir Thomas Audley assumed More's position as chancellor. Audley did not play an active role in the subsequent events, but, unlike More, he complied with the king's wishes. That same year, the archbishop of Canterbury, William Warham, who had opposed the divorce, died and was replaced by Archbishop Cranmer, a Cambridge theologian with reformist leanings. Perhaps most importantly, Henry had a new chief secretary, Thomas Cromwell. Cromwell was neither scholar nor cleric, holding no university degree

Thomas Cromwell, by Hans Holbein. Cromwell was the principal secretary to Henry VIII and was responsible for drafting the legislation in 1533 that started the English Reformation.

and having spent some time as a mercenary soldier. He had for a time been in Wolsey's service and perhaps from him had learned that holding several positions was the key to success. An adroit diplomatic strategist, he recognized that the standard diplomatic channels would never give Henry his desired divorce.

Instead, working closely with Archbishop Cranmer, Cromwell drafted the Act in Restraint of Appeals, which effectively gave legal authority over religious affairs in England to the archbishop of Canterbury rather than the pope. Ostensibly, it only forbade English clerics from seeking appeals in Rome, but the statute went on to explain that the pope's authority in England had always been a usurpation and that the English church was independent of Rome. Passed by Parliament in 1533, the Act in Restraint of Appeals gave the king full authority over the church in England. It transferred the spiritual powers of the pope to the archbishop of Canterbury. The Church was now the Church of England, a national secular institution independent of Rome.

In 1536, the still-convened Reformation Parliament furthered England's break with Rome by passing the Act of Supremacy. This key piece of legislation formalized Henry's title as the supreme head of the Church in England, gave him the legal right to appoint bishops and archbishops, dissolved any monasteries with an income of less than £200, and imposed penalties on anyone who advocated papal jurisdiction within England. By 1539, terms had

The ruins of Glastonbury Abbey. One of medieval England's greatest monastic houses, Glastonbury was dissolved by Henry VIII in 1536. Its revenues were taken by the Crown and the buildings and furnishings were destroyed as part of the Reformation policy of iconoclasm.

been negotiated with the larger monasteries, and the official suppression was ratified by Parliament. All revenues of the now abandoned and destroyed monasteries reverted to the Crown. The English Reformation had begun.

At the same time, the king's Great Matter took a dramatic turn. In January 1533 Henry secretly married Anne Boleyn, who had either become pregnant or conceived shortly thereafter. In the spring of that year, Archbishop Cranmer gave Henry his divorce and proclaimed the marriage valid. Anne was crowned in June and in September gave birth to Henry's long-awaited heir . . . but, to his consternation, the child was a girl. She was named Elizabeth and Henry reconciled himself to trying again. Anne was young and surely next time she would bear a son. Three years later Anne conceived again, but this time she miscarried. Rumors circulated that she had given birth to a deformed stillborn son. Henry's ardor had cooled by this time and he did not object to charges that were brought against her for witchcraft and adultery. She was executed for treason in 1536, and Archbishop Cranmer produced theological documentation proving that the marriage had actually been invalid.

Catherine of Aragon died that same year and Henry promptly remarried, this time to Jane Seymour. She gave him a son, Edward, in 1537, but died of complications of childbirth. Henry married three more times (to Anne of Cleves, whom he divorced; Kathryn Howard, whom he had executed; and Katherine Parr, who survived him), but Edward was his last child.

The six wives of Henry VIII. In order of marriage, Catherine of Aragon was divorced by Henry, Anne Boleyn was accused of adultery and treason and was beheaded, Jane Seymour died of childbirth complications, Anne of Cleves was divorced, Kathryn Howard was accused of treason and beheaded, and Katherine Parr survived the king.

THE BROADER CONTEXT OF THE REFORMATION IN ENGLAND

The English reformation has been described variously as the "reformation from the top down" or "the reformation that never was," in reference to the legislative rather than the spiritual nature of reform in England. Most recent historians, however, challenge that view, seeing many similarities to the European reformations in the spiritual landscape in England, both before and after the official Reformation. For a variety of different reasons, Reformation history was long discussed only in its specific contexts—the Lutheran reformation or the Calvinist reformation—or it was lumped together (mostly by nineteenth century historians with their own political or religious agendas) as the Protestant reformation, seen as a monolithic reform movement that protested against all the abuses of the Catholic church. In contrast, contemporary historians argue that, although there were specific national contexts for reform movements, there was also a great deal of shared scholarship and intellectual viewpoints that extended across Europe. Although it would be an extreme oversimplification to say that the printing press was responsible for the Reformation, the role of shared scholarly interpretation and the debate of printed texts, both scriptural and interpretive, should not be discounted.

There is no doubt that all of Europe in the last years of the fifteenth century was suffering from spiritual challenges. The abuses connected with indulgences noted by Luther were very real, and a combination of what was seen as greed, inefficiency, and immorality led to an overall dissatisfaction with the institutional church among both scholars and the laity. Among the educated, better access to texts (the scriptures, writings by the church fathers, analysis by theologians, and so forth), along with the new methods of humanism taught in the universities, encouraged debate and personal interpretation. The community of learned elites was relatively small and friendships such as that shared by Thomas More and the leading Dutch humanist, Desiderius Erasmus, illustrate the common intellectual background of the men who became the leaders of the various reform movements. For some, nothing less than a break with Rome could address their theological concerns; for others, the desire to reform the established Church was the primary motivation. Over the course of the first four decades of the sixteenth century, nearly all regions of Europe produced religious reform movements. In one way or another, all were involved both with elite theology and with popular religious outlooks and practices. Eventually all came to be connected with the national identities of the emerging states of early modern Europe. Likewise, in the case of Britain, very different reformations took place within the three kingdoms of England, Ireland, and Scotland, as well as within the region of Wales, and all became aligned with the identities of the different polities.

THE IMPACT OF THE REFORMATION IN ENGLAND

Legislating changes in religious ideology and institutions did not necessarily mean that a population was willing to accept them. Historians have long speculated about why Parliament passed the Reformation statutes. Henry's motivation was clear; Parliament's was not. Perhaps fear of the king's wrath was sufficient incentive, perhaps the burghers in the House of Commons saw possible financial gains, perhaps they were all so disillusioned with the Church that they regarded any change as an improvement, or perhaps they just did not care. None of those reasons seems quite sufficient. It is true that our perception of the Reformation period is largely drawn from hindsight. We must remember that even many of the reformers did not view what we now call the Reformation as a permanent break with the existing institutions. (Luther, most notably, insisted that he never intended a break with the Roman church.) Perhaps those who passed the legislation in England merely thought of their actions as a temporary expediency to placate the king. However, much evidence suggests that religious life greatly occupied the thoughts and actions of ordinary people during this time. It seems highly unlikely that such would not have been the case with the members of Parliament, who represented a reasonably well-educated, civically committed, and culturally aware portion of the population.

Contrary to old textbook models of a diseased and moribund Catholic church on the eve of the Reformation, from the 1970s on scholarship has focused on the vibrant and dynamic spiritual life of late medieval Catholicism. Judging by a wide array of sources—from testaments and spiritual donations to commissions of prayer books, donations of altar goods, pilgrimages, attendance at sermons preached by itinerant friars, composition of religious poetry, circulation of religious texts, and many other types of documentation—it seems clear that spirituality figured prominently in the lives of everyone from rich to poor, young to old. Popular religion was based on Catholic theology and sacramental observance and therefore changes from above had a serious impact on the access to the channels of religious life deemed necessary to those whose lives and upbringing predated the Reformation.

Although Parliament passed the laws, there is evidence of much reaction against the changes. As early as 1536, the Pilgrimage of Grace in the north of England (starting in Lincoln and moving into Yorkshire) signaled dismay with the new reforms. The pilgrims at first focused their protest on the dissolution of the monasteries (long the center of religious life for ordinary people, particularly in rural areas) but the pilgrimage soon became a protest against reform in general. Those in rebellion believed in the authority of the old Catholic church and objected to the way in which Cranmer and Cromwell had seized power. Needless to say, the Pilgrimage of Grace was savagely repressed by the government. That did not, however, bring about conformity. Many powerful English noble families remained recusants (still practicing Catholicism and often adding secret chambers to their strongholds to hide the family chapel and conceal the household priest if necessary), and visits to traditional shrines and holy places continued, albeit clandestinely.

Although some parish priests were re-ordained under Anglican rules and continued parish life relatively unchanged, for many the loss of the monasteries meant major disruptions in basic social institutions as well as access to religious life. The monasteries had provided food for the hungry and nursing and medicines for the sick. The monks (while of varying degrees of scholarly attainment) were presumed to be literate and, especially in rural communities, could help write a letter or a will. It was often the monasteries that provided a basic education for young boys. They were inns for travelers, refuges for the old, centers of stability to withstand whatever life might bring. Nothing in the Reformation legislation provided any alternatives. In terms of religious life, not only did the monasteries provide Masses and confessors, they also provided a supernatural link with the saints who were believed to look after a community. Destroying their altars and buildings and desecrating cemeteries represented a profound break with a thousand years of religious life.

HENRY VIII'S LAST YEARS

The tensions produced by the Anglican reformation continued, and the last years of Henry's life were clouded by personal and political problems. Far from being the gallant courtier of his youth, Henry was now ill-tempered, old, obese, and suffering from incurable ulcers on his legs. Some historians have suggested that he suffered from syphilis, the scourge of the sixteenth century. In any case, his last wife, Catherine Parr, was more nursemaid than wife, trying to take care of the declining king and to provide some kind of affection for his three motherless children. Henry's will, drafted shortly before his death in 1547, provided for the succession by Edward and his heirs, to be followed by Mary and finally by Elizabeth. This would be the normal line of succession, but it overlooked the fact that both Mary and Elizabeth had been declared illegitimate by previous legislation.

Political tensions were closely connected with religious legislation. The conservatives had demanded and received some mitigation of the Reformation decrees in the Act of Six Articles, passed in 1539. These articles made it a heresy to deny transubstantiation (one of the main points of continental reform theology) and a felony to advocate the marriage of priests, as well as to receive communion in both kinds (bread and wine). By these terms, Archbishop Cranmer was himself a heretic. He was defended by Henry and remained in office as archbishop, but his wife was sent to Germany. What in many regions was the cornerstone of the Reformation—the printing of the Bible in the vernacular—had an odd, inconclusive twist in England. The Great Bible was printed in English in 1539 and reprinted in a cheap, easily available edition in 1540. However, a statute was passed in 1543 that forbade the reading of the scriptures, publicly or privately, by anyone except a man of the gentry or aristocracy. In the original statute women were excluded altogether, but an amendment later allowed noblewomen the privilege as well.

Most significantly, although the Reformation in England was not brought about by popular demand for reform, nonetheless, it established England as one of the new Protestant states, which by definition were in conflict with those of

Catholic Europe. In his youth, Henry had perceived England as an important part of the European diplomatic context, and even though much of his reign focused on internal affairs, not surprisingly, in his last years he turned back to this perspective. He was concerned (probably rightly) about the possibility of an invasion of England by the Catholic states and he strengthened his defenses, particularly along the southern coast of England. Having executed his old chief secretary, Thomas Cromwell, in 1540 for usurping powers that should have belonged to the king, Henry was now conducting his own international diplomacy. He turned to the old antagonism between England and Scotland and launched a campaign against the Scots, which culminated in a serious Scottish loss at the Battle of Solway Moss in 1542. The campaign profited Henry little, but in a sense it ushered in the Reformation era in Scotland. When the news of the defeat was brought to the Scottish king, James V, it was said that he died of a broken heart. He turned his face to the wall and uttered the prophetic last words "it came with a lass, and it will gang [go] with a lass," referring to the acquisition of the kingdom of Scotland by the Stewarts through Marjorie Bruce and his fear that the kingdom would end with the succession of his own newborn lass. His daughter, Mary, Queen of Scots, became queen when she was less than a week old, and arguably her reign, accompanied as it was by Reformation politics, ended the old kingdom of Scotland and ushered in a new era inextricably tied to religion.

THE SCOTTISH REFORMATION

Perhaps the most fascinating of the line of ill-fated and charming Stewart monarchs, Mary inherited a complex temperament and a complex kingdom. Her father, James V, had himself inherited the Scottish crown when a toddler. He was less than two years old when his father died on the bloody field of Flodden, and he spent his childhood in captivity, a pawn in the political affairs of his mother, Margaret Tudor; his stepfather, the Earl of Angus; and his uncle, the Earl of Arran. When he effectively became king at age sixteen in 1528 (following the banishment of the Earl of Angus), he was well liked and energetic. Although he had not known his father, he shared his father's love of learning and inventions, and he is remembered in Scots tradition as the *gaberlunzie* king who wandered the countryside disguised as a beggarman so that he could observe his subjects at their daily life. In spite of the disaster of Flodden, Scotland at this time was highly regarded in international politics and the young king was viewed as a good marriage prospect.

Strengthening the Auld Alliance with France was always an important part of Scottish diplomacy so it was no surprise that the king let it be known that he would favor a French marriage. He was first offered the daughter of the Prince of Vendôme. When he saw her portrait, he was not impressed and asked for an additional pension to accompany her £100,000 dowry. Nonetheless he went to France to conclude the marriage in 1536, but despite the additional monetary enticements, he could not bring himself to go through with the marriage. The French king then offered his own daughter, Madeleine, whom James had previously rejected. Apparently she looked more favorable by comparison, and the king accepted. They were married in 1537, but less than seven months later she died.

James was growing desperate and remembered being favorably impressed by a young widow whom he had met at the wedding, Mary of Guise. Her hand was being considered by Henry VIII (between wives at that point) and James hastily made an offer. They were married by proxy and she came to Scotland, bringing a dowry of a hundred thousand livres and family connections that would tie Scotland's destiny to the French Wars of Religion. Mary of Guise gave birth to her daughter, Mary, Queen of Scots, in 1542. Less than a week after her daughter's birth, she was widowed, and Scotland once again was plunged into a minority reign with a contested regency. Although Highland politics tended to favor the little queen's uncle, the Earl of Arran of the house of Stuart and next in line for the throne, the queen dowager, Mary of Guise, was well connected and determined to preserve her daughter's inheritance. Arran was open to reformist politics and even more open to an alliance with England (to counter the pro-French, pro-Catholic position of Mary of Guise and her allies). He was appointed governor in January 1543 and by spring an act was passed allowing the circulation of vernacular Bibles. By July a marriage alliance, the Treaty of Greenwich, was being drawn up to provide for the marriage of Mary, Queen of Scots, and Edward (to be the sixth) of England.

Wishy-washy to the extreme, Arran was now caught between English and Scottish politics. Fearing a backlash in Scotland, he refused to hand Mary over to Henry for safekeeping, but the damage had already been done. Mary of Guise, along with her staunchest supporter in Scotland, cardinal archbishop of St. Andrews, David Beaton, overturned the marriage treaty and reinstated James V's anti-heresy legislation, which had been abolished by Arran. In retaliation Henry launched a series of military campaigns against the Scottish Border, known as the Rough Wooing. Their main effect was to strengthen anti-English sentiment in Scotland and to help secure the pro-French, pro-Catholic position of Mary of Guise.

THE CONTINENTAL CONTEXT OF THE SCOTTISH REFORMATION

Although the official start of the Reformation dates to Luther's posting of the "Ninety-five Theses" on October 31, 1517, it took roughly two generations for the lines of religious conflict to be firmly drawn. At first it was not clear what the religious reforms really meant—spiritually, socially, or politically; it took one generation to determine the specifics of doctrinal positions and another to fully realize the points of conflict. In many ways the real catalyst of religious change in the sixteenth century was not Luther (who still upheld the traditional forms of political authority) but the next generation reformer John Calvin, whose unrelenting Scripture-based, legalistic doctrines demanded not only godliness in oneself and one's community, but also in one's rulers. Calvinism was not only a reform movement, but also a revolution in terms of society and politics.

John Calvin was born in France and published his *Institutes of the Christian Religion* in 1536. His theology was firmly based on scriptural texts and on humanistic scholarship, but his conclusions were very different from either those of the old Roman church or from the Lutheran perspective. The innovation in Calvin's theology was the doctrine of predestination. With meticulous scholarly analysis, Calvin argued that the scriptures show that man's salvation is predetermined. From the moment of birth (and probably before), God knows whether a soul is saved or damned and there is nothing that can change the outcome. Predestination assumes that a godly man will live a godly life, but no amount of good works will change the fate of one who is fated for damnation. That being the case, communities should aspire to contain only godly members of society, and anyone deemed ungodly should be removed by whatever means necessary. The definitions of godly and ungodly of course were in the eye of the beholder, or in this case, the believer.

A lawyer by both training and inclination, Calvin translated his theological conclusions into very specific rules of behavior that would be enforced by the elders of a congregation (the presbyters) through religious courts (the consistory). Having found only moderate support in France, Calvin moved his teachings (and his godly community) to the city of Geneva, which became a model for other Calvinist communities. One of Calvin's greatest admirers and strongest disciples was a young Scotsman, John Knox.

The international context of the growing religious tensions in Scotland was magnified by the events of the 1540s. In Scotland, reformer George Wishart preached to the east coast burghs and won many converts for his hard-line Calvinism before he was martyred by Cardinal Beaton in 1546. The accession of the nine-year-old Edward to the English throne in 1547 brought doctrinal changes to the Anglican church and a shift to a Calvinist interpretation in both laws and liturgy through the influence of Edward's tutor, the Earl of Somerset. He inflicted a savage defeat on the Scots at Pinkie, at least partly as a reprisal for the failed marriage negotiations, but he failed to capture the little queen. In July 1548 the Treaty of Haddington provided for her betrothal to the French dauphin Francis, and she was sent to France for safekeeping until she reached marriageable age. Although in many ways Mary's girlhood was idyllic, growing up as the cherished cousin in the luxuriant and cultured French court, she was not insulated from the growing religious conflict of France. Already the factional lines were being drawn between the upwardly mobile noble families, who espoused the Calvinist cause, and the entrenched Catholic party, represented by the houses of Guise and Valois. The French king, Henry II of the House of Valois, was popular and skilled in both war and diplomacy. His wife, Catherine de Medici, possessed both the reputation and ruthless ambition of her Medici ancestors. Together they—temporarily—kept the forces of religious division at bay.

Edward VI by Hans Holbein. Edward was sickly and reigned for only five years. His reign brought a Calvinist perspective to English Anglicanism.

In 1553 Edward died, and the oddities of the English Reformation and its interconnection with European politics again came into play. Because he died without heirs, Henry VIII's will was still in place, and the English throne was now claimed by Mary Tudor, daughter of the put-aside Catherine of Aragon, representative of their most Catholic majesties of Spain. There was the briefest of Protestant protest with the nine-day reign of Lady Jane Grey (descendant of Henry VIII's sister Mary), which was quickly suppressed by Mary Tudor and her supporters. To Mary's great rejoicing (along with that of all of Catholic Europe) England was now returned to the Holy Catholic Church. In 1554 while Mary Tudor celebrated her marriage to Philip II of Spain, Mary of Guise was officially appointed regent of Scotland.

It appeared to Catholic observers in Europe that the Reformation tide was turning in their favor. Although many did not agree with Mary's bloodthirsty persecution of English Protestants (as exemplified by the burning of 282 Protestant men and women in the Smithfield Fires), their opinion was counterbalanced by those who saw it as necessary and a just retribution for the Catholic martyrs of previous years. By these mid-century years, it was clear that the Reformation had changed from doctrinal differences to entrenched battle, with all sides determined to claim the ultimate victory of souls. It is a fascinating historical "what if" to ponder the outcome if Mary and Philip's marriage had pro-

Mary Tudor, by an unknown artist. Mary, the daughter of Catherine of Aragon, returned England to Catholicism during her short (five-year) reign. Her marriage to Philip II of Spain connected English politics to the Continent and was a source of great anxiety to English Protestants.

duced an English heir. As fate would have it, Mary died childless in 1558, only five years into her reign. With the accession of Elizabeth, England returned to Anglicanism.

Also in 1558, Mary Stuart (the Scottish ruling house had adopted the French spelling of the name by this time) and the French dauphin (heir apparent) married. Francis was given the crown matrimonial (the legal right to co-reign with his spouse, Mary) and a secret document was signed in which Mary bequeathed the kingdom of Scotland to the French monarchy if she died without heirs. To the fifteen-year-old queen of the Scots, the future must have looked bright and perhaps uneventful, but less than a year later, the French King Henry II was dead, killed in a freak accident while jousting at a tournament. The dauphin had become king and the queen of Scots was now queen of France. Within a very short time it was obvious that Francis had inherited none of the skills or vigor of either parent, and the court collapsed into chaos as the various family factions fought for control. These factions were defined not only by lineage but also by religious stance. In what would later culminate with the St. Bartholomew's Day Massacre, the French Wars of Religion were already taking shape.

The Burning of
Archbishop Cranmer.
*This woodcut illus-
tration is from*
John Foxe's Book of
Martyrs. *It provides
lurid testimony to
the reaction of
English Protestants
to the executions
ordered by Mary
in her efforts to
return England to
Catholicism.*

The first clear-cut challenge to the French monarchy, however, was a rebellion in Scotland triggered by the preaching of the Calvinist John Knox. Sometime during 1555, Knox returned to Scotland after a checkered career in which he had lived in Edward's England, served time as a galley slave, and been with Calvin in Geneva. His first well-known publication, a diatribe against female rulers titled "The First Blast of the Trumpet against the Monstrous Regimen [Rule] of Women," had not endeared him to Elizabeth, and he was probably genuinely motivated by the desire to return to Scotland to minister to the growing number of Calvinists in the Lowland burghs. Knox was already well known in Scotland, having assisted in the preaching of George Wishart and undoubtedly having been involved in the murder of Cardinal Beaton shortly after Wishart's execution. Knox claimed that Beaton's murder was a godly act and implied that Beaton and Mary of Guise had been lovers and conspired to murder James V.

The story goes that Knox always carried with him a great sword when preaching, and the image that emerges even from his own writings is that of a self-righteous troublemaker. Unlike his idol, John Calvin, who was noted for his unshakeable calm and coolness, Knox could always be found at the center of argument and strife. Scotland served him well. When he arrived in Edinburgh, religious discontent was already smoldering. He proceeded to the town of

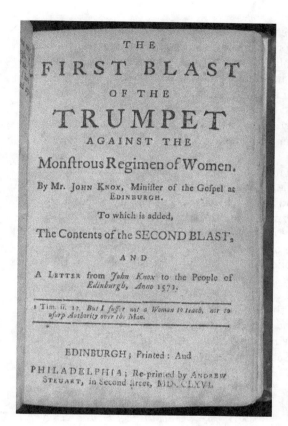

THE

.FIRST BLAST

OF THE

TRUMPET

AGAINST THE

Monſtrous Regimen of Women.

By Mr. JOHN KNOX, Miniſter of the Goſpel at
EDINBURGH.

To which is added,

The Contents of the SECOND BLAST;

AND

A LETTER from *John Knox* to the People of
Edinburgh, Anno 1571.

1 Tim. ii. 12. *But I ſuffer not a Woman to teach, nor to*
uſurp Authority over the Man.

EDINBURGH; Printed: And

PHILADELPHIA; Re-printed by ANDREW
STEUART, in Second ſtreet, MDCLXVI.

Title page of John Knox's "The First Blast of the Trumpet against the Monstrous Regimen of Women" (1571). Knox's virulent pamphlet was aimed at attacking the reign of female monarchs as contrary to the intentions of God. At this particular time in history there were many female sovereigns including Mary Stuart, Elizabeth Tudor, and Catherine de Medici.

Dundee, where a large number of Protestant sympathizers were gathered. Mary of Guise declared him an outlaw and summoned the Protestants to Stirling. Instead they went to Perth, a walled town that they viewed as defensible. There, John Knox's preaching sparked a riot that lasted for two days. Two monasteries and an abbey were stripped of their furnishings and destroyed, all the sacred images were desecrated, and the monks threatened with death. Mary of Guise brought in the troops and a civil war exploded. The Army of the Congregation, led by Knox, marched to St. Andrews and sacked the cathedral. The Reformation in Scotland had begun.

The young queen of Scots soon found herself engulfed in the religious upheaval. On June 11, 1560, Mary of Guise died. Knox rejoiced greatly and proclaimed that "God did execute his judgment upon her." In February 1561, the sickly Francis IX died, and in August of 1561 the grieving eighteen-year-old queen of the Scots returned home. Because she had refused to sign the Treaty of Edinburgh, giving England precedence over Scotland, she was not allowed passage through England. She disembarked on the fog-shrouded Firth of Forth, which according to Knox signified "the frown of God . . . with her [come] sorrow, dolour, darkness and all impiety."

Negotiations ensued between the queen and the provisional government in Scotland, represented by Mary's half-brother James Stewart, a prominent leader in the Protestant movement. Mary was allowed to practice her Catholic faith in private, and she agreed not to interfere with the Protestant Settlement of 1560. The Scots Council at this point was almost entirely made up of Calvinists. In return for Mary's agreement to these terms, James undertook to negotiate with Elizabeth to make official Mary's place in the English succession (as nearest relative through her grandmother, Margaret Tudor, in the event that Elizabeth did not have children).

Although much has been made of Mary's youth and frivolity, most current historians agree that she made a good attempt to exercise personal authority, with efforts to placate and find balance in an extremely difficult situation. She refused to accept any of the terms of the Acts of the Reformation Parliament (as inconsistent with her personal faith), but she did provide for a generous financial settlement for the holders of Protestant benefices. She also supported overthrowing the powerful Catholic Gordon family (Scottish politics at this time were still very greatly influenced by clan power and rivalries) and elevated her Protestant half-brother to the earldom of Moray. Mary tried valiantly to restore the visibility and grandeur of the Scots monarchy, making frequent progresses and establishing a vibrant and luxurious court. Of course, for Knox and the other hard-line Calvinists, the lavish court life was itself a sign of ungodliness, as was Mary's persistence in Catholic practice.

Mary, Queen of Scots, by an unknown artist. The young Scottish queen was seen by her contemporaries as beautiful and vivacious. As a Catholic, and next in line to the English throne, Elizabeth saw her as an extremely dangerous threat.

The uneasy compromises held only briefly. Although widowed, Mary was still very young, and the question of her marriage became a highly charged diplomatic and religious issue. For any queen regnant, there are no good choices, regardless of the religious dimension. To marry a foreign prince of equal status would potentially place the queen's realm in jeopardy of annexation. To marry a subject, even one of high noble status, was viewed as somewhat unnatural because that meant the man was subordinate to the woman (a view not favored by either Catholic or Protestant). Elizabeth's solution was to choose neither. With the intense instability of her reign, Mary probably could not have made that choice even if she had wished to. Eventually, she decided to marry Henry Stewart, Lord Darnley, her first cousin, next to her in line for the English succession. From Mary's point of view he was a good choice both because of his handsome appearance and because of his Catholicism. In July 1565 they married.

The marriage between Mary and Darnley set off a number of political repercussions. Elizabeth had shown no sign of acknowledging Mary as heir presumptive, and the added insult of joining together the two royal claims offended her greatly. Knox and his supporters railed against the thought of Catholic monarchy and possible alliances with Catholic Europe. Darnley himself was not happy. He coveted the actual title and authority of king, which Mary refused to grant him, giving him only the lesser title of king consort. By March 1566 Mary and Darnley had fallen out and he began secret negotiations with the Protestant party. His purpose was to try to deprive Mary of any support. The result was the murder of the queen's secretary and favorite musician, David Rizzio, in the queen's quarters, in her presence, when she was heavily pregnant with her son, James. (There were many speculations in the court, probably unfounded, that Rizzio was targeted because he was Mary's lover. More likely he was simply her trusted confidant.) Afraid that civil war was imminent, Mary made a great show of reconciliation with Darnley and held a grand ceremony of thanksgiving and baptism for the new baby in December 1566, attended by both Catholic and Protestant nobles. (No one missed the point that the baby, James, had a double claim to the English throne and was in fact the assumed heir even if Elizabeth, still unmarried and childless, refused to acknowledge his claim.)

Although the public celebrations implied the reconciliation of Mary and Darnley, the real situation was much different. Darnley, probably already ill with a disease that might have been tuberculosis or syphilis, did not attend the baptism of his son. It was increasingly clear that he had no political support from any quarter. Although there is still doubt as to Mary's personal complicity, there was already a plot afoot to murder Darnley. The deed took place on February 10, 1567. On that evening Mary went to visit her ailing husband where he was staying in the residence of Kirk o' Field, but left early. At midnight an explosion rocked the streets of Edinburgh. As one historian has noted, Darnley "was mourned by few, and the queen was not one of them."

Although Knox was quick to take the position that Mary and Rizzio had been lovers and that Mary had conspired to murder her husband, probably neither speculation would have been enough to bring about her downfall had she not made a fatal political error in promptly marrying James Hepburn, Earl of Bothwell, the man most Scots believed had been directly responsible for Darnley's death. Historians still debate her actions. Many have argued that infatuation combined with bad judgment lay behind them. Perhaps Mary already recognized that her enemies were multiplying; given Bothwell's reputation as a strong warrior, the epitome of the Border lord, perhaps she thought he represented safety. In any case, the events seem staged and theatrical. Bothwell "abducted" the queen, took her to his Border stronghold, and married her by Protestant rite on May 15, 1567. A month later, unwell and pregnant again, Mary met with a coalition of Scottish lords who sought to "liberate" her from a forced marriage. She negotiated safe passage for her husband to Denmark and then surrendered. She "voluntarily" abdicated on July 24, and her infant son James was crowned on July 29.

Although on the face of it, the turn of events looks personal and political, underlying the various positions were strong confessional motivations. The deposition of Mary and the assumption of the regency by the Protestant Moray ensured that no Catholic succession would take place. Moray made sure that James was raised Calvinist, and Scotland became yet another example of the process of *cuius regio, eius religio* (the religion of the ruler is the religion of the people) that was taking place across Europe. Although the term is associated with the Peace of Augsburg of 1555 that settled the religious wars in the German states, the concept had more far-reaching applicability. One way or another, governments and populations were coming into religious alignment. The religion of the ruler was the religion of the people—or in this case, the opposite process produced the same result, as the religion of the people forced the removal of a monarch of a different religion.

THE REFORMATION IN IRELAND

In many ways, Ireland can be seen as the exception that proves the rule in Reformation politics. In Ireland, alone among the regions of Europe, the religion of the government (Anglican England) and the religion of the majority of the population (Catholic) did not reach alignment. Instead, the struggle in Ireland represents one of the most virulent and long-lasting confessional disputes in Europe, dating from the Reformation era to the present day.

Catholicism, in both its institutional and popular form, was deeply entrenched in Ireland prior to the sixteenth century. Arguably from the early medieval period, and certainly from the twelfth century onward, religious offices and practices were closely linked to the Gaelic ruling elites, and their support of the Church is well documented in the Irish annals and extant examples of late medieval religious poetry and books of devotion. By the sixteenth century the old Anglo-Norman families of Ireland had become completely gaelicized and there was no discernible political or religious difference between them and the old original Gaelic families. The new political, social, and cultural group that emerged during the Tudor period consisted of those of English birth who now took up governing roles in Ireland. With the advent of the Anglican reformation the lines of demarcation became very complex indeed. Historians use the designation *Old Irish* to mean the old Gaelic and gaelicized families who retained their Catholicism during the Tudor period, *Old English* to mean those of English birth or descent who remained Catholic, and *New English* to mean the new English ruling elites, who brought with them Protestantism along with new political views.

Technically the Reformation arrived in Ireland in 1536 when the Irish Parliament passed legislation accepting the supremacy of Henry VIII as head of the Church in Ireland, although he was not named king of Ireland until 1541. In the Pale and in the old Anglo-Norman port towns there was a sense of tension, but little actual challenge to the new edicts. In Gaelic Ireland, the legislation was at first largely ignored, but two years later the *Annals of Ulster* note the event in curiously localized terms, illustrating the strong role of traditional religiosity in Ireland: "a hosting by [Lord Grey] the Saxon Justiciary . . . and the monastery of Down was burned by them and the relics of Patrick and Colum-cille and Brigit and the image of Catherine were carried off by them." A year later the *Annals of Connaught* recorded,

> The miraculous image of Mary at Trim, which had been venerated for ages by all the Irish, which used to heal the blind and the deaf and the lame. And all other sufferers; and the Staff of Jesus, which was in Dublin, where it worked miracles and wonders renowned in Ireland from the time of Patrick to this time . . . these were burnt by the English. More than this, there was no holy Cross or effigy of Mary or famous image in Ireland which they did not burn if it fell in their power; nor was there one of the Seven Orders which their power could reach in Ireland that they did not destroy; and on that account the Pope and the Church both here and in the east were excommunicating the English.

The Irish resistance to English iconoclasm and the destruction of the monasteries is consistent with the importance of the shrines and monasteries in pre-Reformation Irish religious life. There was no organized rebellion as with the Pilgrimage of Grace, but in the case of Ireland, the Gaelic hinterlands proved much more impossible to subdue. The English Crown, acting through a series of different English governors, used a variety of different measures from conciliatory to draconian, but all were ineffectual. Outside the Pale Catholicism endured, much to the chagrin of the English ruling elites.

Technically during Henry's time taking the Oath of Supremacy was not required for the Tudor scheme of *surrender and regrant* (a process through which the Gaelic chieftains would surrender themselves to the Crown, and in exchange for a promise of obedience and recognition of the king as overlord, they would have their land regranted to them, along with government assurances of authority over their followers). However, the hidden confessional agenda was apparent and became a matter of grave concern to the Catholic church. It was in fact, most likely that particular policy that led to the foundation of the first Jesuit mission to Ireland in 1542. Although many chieftains availed themselves of surrender and regrant, few seem to have considered themselves bound by its terms. As soon as they received their titles, they disappeared back into their Gaelic strongholds, impenetrable by the English—culturally, linguistically, and often geographically.

Meanwhile, the English government was trying to enforce the dissolution of the monasteries in Ireland as a means of rooting out Catholicism. Although the burnings and iconoclasm had been noted by the Irish as the first sign of the Reformation, overall this tactic too was more notable in its failure than in its success. The English government reformers might burn the buildings and destroy the sacred furnishings, but the monks and friars would usually be given shelter by the Gaelic lords, who would help to rebuild the damaged structures whenever possible. Some were claimed and used by the reformed church, but most in Ireland were later reoccupied by Catholic clerics. Even in the absence of buildings, many of the orders remained intact and many of the supposedly suppressed houses continued to be used into the seventeenth and eighteenth centuries. In addition to their protection from the Gaelic lords, the religious houses in Ireland continued to be supplied by Continental clergy and by the seventeenth century, continental seminaries were providing training for Irishmen who returned to Ireland to maintain the faith.

In the port towns and the Pale, it was much more difficult to avoid the encroachment of Reformation politics. Typically the residents were of English descent. They had long had an attitude of distinctiveness and superiority over the "mere Irish" (or wild Irish) of the Gaelic lordships, and it appears that the English reformers assumed that they would be compliant with the new Reformation views. That this was not the case was an endless source of bewilderment and consternation for the Tudor monarchs and governors, and it has remained a point of endless debate for the historians as well. The shift of the Old English of the port towns and the Pale from strong colonial supporters to strident recusants provides clues for the anomalous failure of the Reformation in Ireland.

Perhaps nowhere is the intertwining of religion and politics during this era clearer than with this group. They had been the local voice of the English colonizers, but with the Reformation and the overall mood of suspiciousness, the New English began to feel that the Old English were untrustworthy because of their Irish birth, and they were increasingly passed over for positions of governmental authority. Although most attended reformed church services as required, there was a suspicion among the newer arrivals that their observances were tainted by long exposure to the Gaelic Irish. Certainly because of a lack of Gaelic-speaking ministers, many pre-Reformation clerics retained their positions and their congregations often continued their traditional forms of piety. For the Old English, the use of Gaelic was not problematic, but for the New English, the language itself was viewed as fostering sedition. When the militantly Protestant Bishop John Bale arrived in his Irish See of Ossory in 1549, he was scandalized to note that "the communion . . . was there altogether used like a Popish Mass, with the old apish toys of anti-Christ, in bowings and beckings, kneelings and knockings." The Reformation had widened the gulf between the English and their colonial descendants, and as the Old English in the port towns and the Pale felt more and more estranged, they increasingly found their identity to be located in their Catholicism rather than in their ancestry.

Given the very slight inroads in Protestant reform in Ireland, not much changed during the reigns of Edward and Mary. When Lord Lieutenant Anthony St. Leger arrived in Ireland in 1550 (essentially acting as viceroy), one of his instructions was to enforce the first Act of Uniformity, enacted by Edward VI in 1549 to introduce the second *Book of Common Prayer*. From the evidence, only Bishop Bale seems to have followed this edict. Bale was a radical reformer, influenced by the teachings of the Swiss reformer Zwingli, and he attracted a few followers in his own diocese, but he undoubtedly contributed more to the formation of popular resistance to the new reformed policies. Those who had tolerated the Henrician policies now rebelled. Edward Staples, bishop of Meath, noted that

> divers answered that they would not come [to the sermon he was preaching] lest they should learn to be heretics. One of our lawyers declared to a multitude that it was a great pity I was not burned; for I preached heresy.

Mary's short reign affected little in Ireland. There were no martyrdoms and no real change in clergy. One monastery was restored (the Knights Hospitallers at Kilmainham), and for most of the population religious practices continued, little changed from their pre-Reformation foundations. Politically, there was a brief respite for the Catholic population of Ireland, but the discernible tensions from the Edwardian reforms had not been resolved. As we will see in chapter 11, for the Irish, the real Reformation era and its impact on religious and cultural life began with the accession of Elizabeth in 1558.

THE REFORMATION IN WALES

The advent of the Reformation in Wales followed much the same course as in the other regions of the British Isles. Late medieval Welsh religious practice focused on traditional religion, with strong connections to religious shrines, holy wells, and the religious houses established during the Middle Ages. Cistercian houses had once been dominant in Wales, but by the sixteenth century were waning. By the time of the Dissolution of the Monasteries under Henry VIII, there were only eighty-five Cistercians remaining in their monasteries, although the number of religious houses dissolved in Wales numbered forty-seven. As in the other regions, the loss of communal connections with the Welsh religious houses had a great impact on the lay population, and the destruction of traditional Welsh shrines and statuary heightened anti-English sentiment. During the Edwardian period, the destruction was even greater.

Although there was deep resentment among the Welsh, it did not translate into political action. It has been argued that, had Mary's reign lasted longer, Wales might have become a bastion of Catholicism similar to Ireland, as deeply entrenched as the old religion was among the Welsh. For a variety of reasons, the Reformation process took different shape in Wales. For one thing, there was no focused anti-Protestant movement. Even more importantly in Wales the English were successful in using the Welsh language as a vehicle of Protestantism, unlike the Gaelic language in Ireland. Three Welsh Protestant bishops, Richard Davies, Humphrey Llwyd, and William Salesbury, persuaded the English government that the Welsh could be converted most successfully through the use of the Welsh language. The Act of 1563 ordered the translation of the scriptures into Welsh, both promoting Protestantism and probably ensuring the survival of the Welsh language. In 1588 a Welsh Bible—still regarded as a literary masterpiece—was completed. The identification of Protestantism with the Welsh language is in many ways the key to understanding the difference in the acceptance of Protestantism in that region as opposed to Gaelic Ireland or, as we will see, the Highlands of Scotland. In those regions Protestantism was promoted through the English language and was thus viewed with hostility. In Ireland the first Irish Bible was not completed until 1685. The Scottish Highlanders had to wait until 1691 for access to Gaelic Bibles in Roman script; the first one specifically translated into Scots Gaelic was not published until 1801.

SUGGESTED READING

Bradshaw, Brendan. *The Dissolution of the Religious Orders in Ireland under Henry VIII*. Cambridge: Cambridge University Press, 1974.

Brigden, Susan. *London and the Reformation*. Oxford: Clarendon Press, 1989.

Corish, Patrick. *The Irish Catholic Experience: A Historical Survey*. Dublin: Glazier, 1985.

Cowan, Ian B. *The Scottish Reformation: Church and Society in Sixteenth-Century Scotland*. London: Weidenfeld and Nicolson, 1982.

Dickens, A. G. *The English Reformation*, 2nd ed. University Park: Pennsylvania State University Press, 1989.

Duffy, Eamon. *The Stripping of the Altars*. New Haven, CT: Yale University Press, 1992.

Elton, G. R. *Reform and Reformation: England, 1509–1558*. Cambridge, MA: Harvard University Press, 1977.

Guy, John. *Thomas More*. Oxford: Arnold, 2000.

Gwyn, Peter. *The King's Cardinal: The Rise and Fall of Thomas Wolsey*. London: Barrie & Jenkins, 1990.

Haig, Christopher. *English Reformations: Religion, Politics, and Society under the Tudors*. Oxford: Oxford University Press, 1993.

Ives, E.W. *Anne Boleyn*. Oxford: Blackwell, 1986.

Lynch, Michael. *Mary Stewart: Queen in Three Kingdoms*. Oxford: Blackwell, 1988.

MacCulloch, Diarmid. *Thomas Cranmer*. New Haven, CT: Yale University Press, 1996.

Meigs, Samantha A. *The Reformations in Ireland: Tradition and Confessionalism, 1400–1690*. London: Macmillan, 1997.

Pettegree, Andrew, ed. *The Early Reformation in Europe*. Cambridge: Cambridge University Press, 1992.

Scarisbrick, J. J. *The Reformation and the English People*. Oxford: Blackwell, 1984.

Scribner, Bob, Roy Porter, and Mikulas Teich, eds. *The Reformation in National Context*. Cambridge: Cambridge University Press, 1994.

Smith, Lacey Baldwin. *Henry VIII: The Mask of Royalty*. London: Cape, 1971.

Williams, Penry. *The Tudor Regime*. Oxford: Oxford University Press, 1979.

Chapter 11

Elizabethan Politics and Jacobean Tensions

The accession of Elizabeth in 1558 truly changed the face of the British Isles in terms of both its internal and international reputation and its relationships. In one way, it was not a new era, for Reformation politics continued to have a major impact, but in another, the Elizabethan era marked the transformation of Britain from a fairly minor power on the periphery to a major player in international affairs. The interconnection between Britain and the Continent intensified during what has been called the seventeenth century Age of Crisis. Under James VI (of Scotland)/I (of England), issues of divine right monarchy, inflation, intellectual transformation, and internal conflicts in the three realms he governed (England, Scotland, and Ireland) all affected Britain internally at the same time that Britain was establishing its role in an increasingly global society.

THE ELIZABETHAN RELIGIOUS SETTLEMENT

Although Elizabeth's accession to the Tudor throne was without incident, there was widespread uncertainty as to her personal religious beliefs and her official stance on religious matters. Having been declared illegitimate by the Catholic church, the daughter of Anne Boleyn must be Protestant, but there was a great difference between the Protestantism of Henry VIII and that of Edward VI. Elizabeth herself was something of a cipher. Astutely, she had avoided any public reaction to the policies of Edward or Mary. She had largely lived in seclusion, particularly during the troubled years of Mary's reign when there were various plots to depose the Catholic Mary and install the Protestant Elizabeth on the throne. When she became queen, she was twenty-six years old, highly intelligent, fluent in Latin and other languages, and well educated as a humanistic scholar. She understood theology, and for the most part, she had a good grasp of the viewpoints of her subjects.

Historians often regard the religious settlement enacted by Elizabeth's first Parliament in 1559 as a model of moderation, although by virtue of its middle-of-the-road quality it offended those at both ends of the spectrum: the Catholics and the Puritans. The settlement upheld the edict against papal supremacy and jurisdiction in England, and the queen took the title of supreme governor of the

Elizabeth I when a Princess, attributed to William Scrots. This portrait shows the sumptuous dress of the late Tudor period and already hints at Elizabeth's taste for decoration as well as a love of scholarship represented by the book in her hands.

church (in contradistinction to supreme head of the church, the title used by Henry VIII and Edward VI). This change could reflect a slight theological backpedaling or perhaps it merely reflected the premise of the Biblical Pauline epistles that a woman could not be head of anything.

The religious settlement of 1559 required the introduction of a new *Book of Common Prayer* (less radical and Calvinist than the 1552 version). It also implemented a return to liturgical practices dating from the beginning of Edward's reign, such as the wearing of the cope and a more traditional arrangement of the altar. Priests were again allowed to marry (although Elizabeth would have preferred a celibate clergy), and all clergy were required to swear the Oath of Supremacy. Interestingly, nearly all the parish priests did so, but nearly all the bishops refused (indicating a continuing loyalty to Rome). They were dismissed, leaving many vacancies to be filled, including the archbishopric of Canterbury. Elizabeth had difficulty filling this position, but finally settled on Matthew Parker, a Cambridge historian and humanist whose views accorded well with hers. Because of the dearth of candidates, some of the other bishoprics ended up being settled on Marian exiles, who had fled the Protestant persecutions of Mary Tudor's reign and were by definition more radical in point of view. The settlement was completed by the adoption of the "Thirty-nine Articles," a revised and slightly more moderate version of Archbishop Cranmer's "Forty-two Articles," outlining in detail the tenets and practices of the Anglican church. The "Thirty-nine Articles" were hereafter printed in the *Book of Common Prayer* so that all English subjects would know the terms of settlement.

From the Catholic perspective, the Elizabethan settlement allowed no real freedom of interpretation or practice. It was illegal for Catholic priests to perform the sacraments in England, and some, like Edmund Campion and John Fischer, were martyred. Many of the old English aristocratic families, particularly in the north, remained Catholic, maintaining their own secret household priests and altars. Some of these priests were men who were ordained during Mary's reign, and some were sent from Rome. The Jesuits were particularly active in the English mission, as well as the Irish. In 1569 a seminary was established at the University of Douai in the Spanish Netherlands for the training of English priests. (The university was established in 1560 by Philip II of Spain as a sister college to the fifteenth century University of Louvain.) The founder of the seminary (also called the English College), an Englishman named Walter Allen, commissioned the Douai Bible, a translation of the Latin Vulgate into English that was used by English-speaking Catholics up to the modern era. The Catholic threat, which was evidenced by both internal recusancy and fear of foreign invasion, continued to plague Elizabeth for much of her reign.

From the other end of the spectrum, the Puritans (Anglicans with a Calvinist perspective) also opposed the Elizabethan religious settlement. For them, it was too lenient. As their name implies, they sought to purify the Anglican church of anything that suggested Catholicism (or popery and superstition as they saw it). Although there was a range of Puritan extremism, most disliked the liturgy and the formal celebration of the sacraments and favored a stark Calvinist church with no vestments, decoration, or music. When the Puritans tried to force Elizabeth to back down on the clause that required ministers to wear vestments (a surplice at the least), she refused. These clerics were dismissed from their offices and founded their own nonconformist congregations in 1571.

ELIZABETHAN DOMESTIC POLITICS

During Elizabeth's long reign many social and cultural changes took place in England that would have long-lasting repercussions. A serious spiral of inflation had already set in by the end of Henry VIII's reign (with prices twice what they were at the beginning of his reign). Elizabeth tried to control inflation by ordering a return to coinage that had a high monetary standard, which had been debased during the reigns of Edward and Mary. (The practice of using metals cheaper than gold or silver to debase the currency was in common practice and then, as now, contributed toward less actual purchasing power.) This return to "good money" was partly prompted by one of Elizabeth's financial advisors, Sir Thomas Gresham, whose comment on debased currency—"bad money drives out good"—came to be called Gresham's Law. It held true until the standardized paper currency and governmental controls of the twentieth century altered fiscal practice. Despite the recoinage of 1560, inflation continued and by the 1590s prices had doubled again. This, combined with several disastrous harvests, resulted in a population that was sharply divided between the lavish court and the landless vagabonds who characterized both Elizabethan literature and reality.

Elizabeth loved music and pageantry and rich displays of wit and wealth. Her reign is remembered for her many progresses in which she traveled around England with her court, paying visits to the aristocrats and gentry of England. This was part of her appeal. Perhaps more than any previous English monarch, Elizabeth understood what we would now call public relations. She made sure that she was seen and always acknowledged her debt to the English people and her love for them. She was often a generous patron, but she had a sharp temper and could as quickly turn against one of her former favorites. When Walter Raleigh, whom she had knighted, married one of her ladies-in-

Elizabeth I by Marc Gheeraerts. This later portrait of Elizabeth (1592) is associated with her image as Gloriana, the heroine of Spenser's The Faerie Queen. *She is depicted standing on a map of England.*

waiting without her permission, she had both Raleigh and his bride imprisoned in the Tower of London. When Robert Dudley, Earl of Leicester (probably the man she came closest to marrying), became involved in a court scandal following the suspicious death of his wife, she had him banished from court. When Robert Devereaux, Earl of Essex and greatest favorite of her later years, failed her in accomplishing her Irish policies and rebelled against her, tearfully she had him executed. Nonetheless, she also attracted many noteworthy scholars and patrons to her court, including the flamboyant alchemist and mathematician John Dee and the poets Sir Philip Sidney and Edmund Spenser. Spenser's "Faerie Queen" was written as a panegyric to Elizabeth, and for many contemporaries as well as historians, her image as Gloriana has endured.

The seamy underside of the glittering court of Elizabeth was the world of the beggars and vagrants who had been displaced from their agricultural life by the beginnings of the enclosure movement (in which landlords dispossessed their tenants and fenced them out of the common lands held by their ancestors in order to convert the land to pasturage). As the displaced tenants fled to urban centers (especially the city of London) in search of food and employment, they encountered instead poverty, disease, and an environment in which anyone would do anything to try to survive. Elizabethan London was teeming with brothels, bear baiting, cockfighting, itinerant astrologers, legions of beggars ("impotent" if they were old or maimed, and "sturdy" if they were capable of working), and tricksters or *cony catchers* who made their living by swindling gullible clients in the shell game and other similar ploys.

Cony catcher's pamphlet, by Robert Greene (1592). Cony catching was a slang term used in the Elizabethan period to denote theft through trickery. The "cony" was the target and the catcher was the con man.

Legislation was enacted to try to regulate the expanding ranks of the poor and landless. It restricted the movement of the poor from their parish of birth, but enforcement was often ineffective despite the frequently draconian terms. The 1536 Poor Laws of Henry's Reformation Parliament (in place for most of the sixteenth century) had essentially delegated administration of the affairs of the poor to the parishes, with mixed degrees of success. The Elizabethan Poor Law (passed in 1601) codified licenses (such as sturdy beggars must be licensed to beg), punishments (vagrants could be run out of town, flogged, or pilloried), and relief structures (through which the poor could get some assistance, although still through the administrative structure of the parishes). In 1562 an act against gypsies was passed that upheld an earlier statute threatening deportation and confiscation of goods, but added that any person taken in disguise in the company of gypsies would be regarded as a felon and suffer death as well as confiscation of property. A year later, in 1563, Elizabeth passed her first law against witchcraft (making punishable by death any act of witchcraft that resulted in the death of another person).

Elizabeth's ability to carry out her policies was aided by the talented statesmen who served her throughout her reign. In many ways, the Elizabethan era marks the transition from a more personalized style of monarchy to a more institutional one under the Stuarts. Under Elizabeth the Privy Council retained precedence over Parliament, although Parliament would soon come to dominate English politics. For most of her reign, Elizabeth was aided by Sir William Cecil, later given the title of Lord Burghley. He was educated at Cambridge and had first served as principal secretary under Lord Somerset before holding the same title under Elizabeth. His role was as principal adviser on all matters, both domestic and international, and he was a highly astute diplomat. Other members of the Privy Council included Sir Francis Walsingham, chief "intelligencer," who oversaw a wide network of agents and spies in the European courts, and Sir Walter Mildmay, chancellor of the Exchequer, who, along with Gresham, was one of the best financial advisers of his day.

Elizabeth was cautious enough to listen to her advisors, although she usually made the final decisions based on her own authority. One of the most delicate domestic issues was, of course, the question of her marriage. In an age in which virtually all women were married or widowed and in which the need for a royal heir was paramount, the idea of a perpetually virgin queen was not entertained as even a possibility. Elizabeth was highly offended when Parliament petitioned her to take a husband, but for many years she successfully dangled the lure of possible marriage before a succession of foreign suitors (including her former brother-in-law, Philip II, and the French Prince of Anjou and Duke of Alençon). Probably the closest contender (and quite possibly the man she loved throughout her life) was Robert Dudley, Earl of Leicester. He, along with Cecil, knew her better than anyone in her court, and likely both men realized that she was too astute to let herself be caught in the trap of a queen—to share power with a subject or with a foreign prince. Although she played at marriage diplomacy, she probably made the decision while still a young woman that she would never wed and would instead join herself to England.

THE INTERNAL CATHOLIC THREAT

Politically, one of the greatest threats to Elizabeth's reign and to her religious settlement was the insidious problem of internal Catholicism. Recusancy within England appears to have been on the rise, and as had always been the case, England was wary of attacks that could come on her flanks, through either Scotland or Ireland. Scotland seemed reasonably secure. Mary Stuart's son, James, had been taken from his mother while an infant and had been raised by his tutors to espouse solid Calvinism. Although Scottish Calvinism differed in outlook from Elizabeth's moderate Anglicanism, there seemed little chance of Scotland reverting to Catholicism. (Elizabeth was probably unaware of the continuing adherence of the Highland regions to Catholicism. These regions had been little affected by the Reformation movement in the Lowlands and remained traditional in outlook, Gaelic-speaking, and governed more by local clan chieftains than by the Scottish monarchs.) Elizabeth staunchly refused to name an heir, but it was apparent to everyone as the years went by that she would have no children and therefore her cousin the Scottish king, James Stuart, was the de facto heir to the English throne.

The most pressing problem for Elizabeth was not James, but rather his mother, Mary, Queen of Scots. After her forced abdication in 1567, Mary escaped from Lochlevan Castle and raised a small force against her half-brother Moray. Defeated at the Battle of Langside, she fled to England, where she was imprisoned on orders of Elizabeth. Although popular culture has created many conversations between the two monarchs, there is no documentation showing that they ever met. Mary sent impassioned letters to Elizabeth, and Elizabeth acknowledged Mary as her cousin and an anointed ruler, overthrown by an unruly population. Nonetheless, Mary's existence represented a great threat to Elizabeth and her carefully crafted peace. Any plots, internal or foreign, that sought to restore England to Catholicism rallied around Mary. Even though deposed, by lineage she was next in line to Elizabeth and her piety was unquestioned. Time and again the plots swirled around her: the Northern Rebellion in 1569, the Ridolfi Plot in 1571, and other plots in 1583 and 1586. Time and again, Elizabeth turned a blind eye, opposing her advisors who called for the execution of the Scottish queen. Finally in 1587, probably in response to the worsening religious conflicts on the Continent, Elizabeth signed the warrant. Afterward, she insisted that she had not meant it to be carried out, but in Fotheringay Hall, attended only by her crying ladies-in-waiting and shivering pet dog, the dramatic and dangerous queen of Scots went to her death, at least temporarily removing the most immediate Catholic threat from within England.

Illustration of the execution of Mary, Queen of Scots. A later depiction of Mary's execution, it accurately shows the presence of her ladies-in-waiting and conveys almost biblical images of justice.

INTERNATIONAL POLITICS

One cannot separate the events of Elizabeth's reign from the larger context of European religious politics. The *cuius regio, eius religio* principle (religious alignment of ruler and population) continued to dominate continental political ideology throughout the second half of the sixteenth century, and as a defined Protestant state England could not help but be caught up in the surrounding conflicts of Europe. Throughout Europe, the great powers formed alliances or became embroiled in conflict resulting from their confessional identity.

In France, the religious tensions that had been brewing since the untimely death of Henry II had given way to a religious civil war, usually known as the French Wars of Religion. Henry had left behind a formidable widow, Catherine de Medici, and three exceedingly ineffective sons. The first, Francis IX (husband of Mary, Queen of Scots), died in 1562, and the years after his death were characterized by intense factionalism among several different aristocratic families who identified themselves partly on the basis of religion. Catherine, using all her Italian connections, strove to keep the French inheritance for her sons. The Catholic families of Guise and Valois vied for power, and the strident House of Coligny presented itself as champion of the French Protestants (those who were politically oppressed during this period were known as Huguenots and were sometimes clandestinely aided by the English).

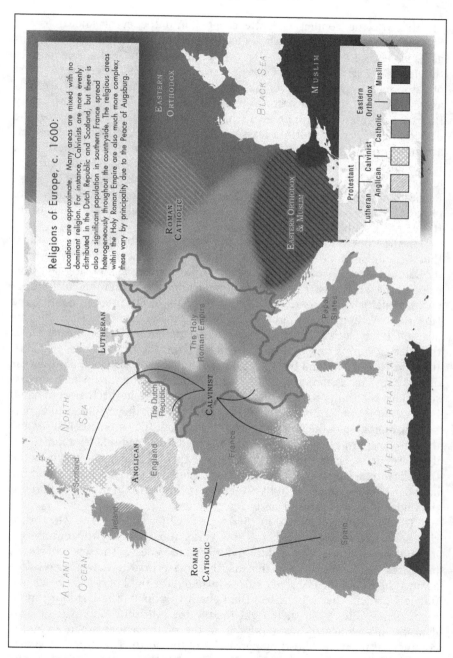

Religions of Europe, c. 1600:

Locations are approximate. Many areas are mixed with no dominant religion. For instance, Calvinists are more evenly distributed in the Dutch Republic and Scotland, but there is also a significant population in southern France spread heterogeneously throughout the countryside. The religious areas within the Holy Roman Empire are also much more complex; these vary by principality due to the Peace of Augsburg.

Religions of Europe, circa 1600. This map shows the distribution of religious confessions across Europe after nearly a century of Reformation conflict. By this time, in nearly all cases, the religion of the monarch and the population had come into alignment.

In 1572 the conflict violently erupted into the event known as the St. Bartholomew's Day Massacre. Arguably the worst case of early modern religious violence, the massacre was an orgy of killing in the name of religion in the streets of Paris. The conflict was not resolved until 1590 when the youngest of Catherine's sons (the Duke of Alencon with whom Elizabeth had flirted) was assassinated and the French crown passed to the king's brother-in-law, Henry Bourbon, a Protestant with no firm religious convictions. As the story goes, he declared that "Paris is worth a Mass" and converted to Catholicism. This act, accompanied by the reasonably generous toleration extended to the French Protestants in the 1598 Edict of Nantes, ended much of the religious turmoil and aligned France with a Catholic identity. These terms held until the 1685 Revocation of the Edict of Nantes by Louis XIV, which prompted the departure of most of the French Huguenots to what they viewed as friendlier territories (the Dutch Republic and the New World).

In the Holy Roman empire, the 1555 Peace of Augsburg literally required that the religion of the prince determine the religion of the principality (primarily Catholic or Lutheran in that region). In a territory comprising sixty-five principalities, this meant a shuffling of populations to match religious preferences. Nonetheless, in its role as a great power player in European politics, the Holy Roman empire was regarded as a Catholic territory, following the religious position of the elected emperor. Charles V, the monarch who had presided over the Diet of Worms and who had inherited Spain, the Netherlands, Northern Italy, the New World, and the Holy Roman empire, abdicated in 1558 (the year of Elizabeth's accession) and divided his territories, giving the Spanish succession to his son Philip (II) and his German territories to his brother Ferdinand. Both were fervent Catholics, and as Habsburg cousins they maintained a militant championing of the Catholic cause against both the Ottoman Muslims and the European Protestants. In 1571 the combined Holy League at least temporarily defeated the Ottomans at the Battle of Lepanto, bringing renown to the Catholic forces. However, the Protestants remained undefeated, even within the boundaries of Habsburg territory. The Dutch inheritance in many ways proved the undoing of the Spanish Habsburgs.

The Dutch Revolt started in 1566 and lasted for eighty years. (One historian has referred to this conflict as "the Vietnam of the sixteenth century" for its huge expenditures, loss of life, and inconclusiveness.) The seven northern provinces, with a population that had become primarily Calvinist, revolted against their Catholic Habsburg rulers, invoking the right of resistance against ungodly princes that was part of the Calvinist outlook. The Habsburg monarchs firmly believed in their right to rule these territories as part of their dynastic inheritance and were mindful of the rich revenues produced by the commercial towns and bustling port cities of the north. The Dutch Calvinists saw the English Protestants across the channel as their natural allies, and the Habsburgs (already on the offensive against heretics) saw the English as their natural enemies.

Moreover, by the 1570s, the Spanish were being harassed by English privateers in the Caribbean who were attacking Spanish ships carrying treasure and goods from the Spanish colonies of the New World. Sir Francis Drake is probably the most renowned (or infamous) of these sea dogs. Although technically he and others carried authorization by the Crown to attack ships of nations with which England was at war, the actions of these privateers were often indistinguishable from what would be termed piracy and contributed to the escalation of hostilities between Spain and England.

The ability of the English to endure and even to expand their economic and diplomatic influence in the face of the complexity of European affairs is nothing short of remarkable. Elizabeth adroitly avoided any permanent entanglements with the Spanish or French, and she maintained her role as a champion of the Protestants while doing little to invoke actual attack. The exception came in 1588 with the invasion of the Spanish Armada. Angered by Elizabeth's assistance to the Dutch and the execution of the imprisoned Mary, Queen of Scots, in 1587, the Spanish king, Philip II, was determined to subdue England and its Protestant heresy. He ordered the invasion of England by a flotilla of Spanish ships under the leadership of the formidable Spanish commander the Duke of Medina-Sidonia. Elizabeth mustered her navy and posted watches along the Channel. As the "Invincible Armada" approached, the wind changed, forcing the Spanish ships to drop anchor. The English took advantage of the situation; taking a number of old hulks, they loaded their cannons, set fire to them, and let them drift into the anchored Spanish fleet. The approach of these *hellburners* so frightened the Spanish that they cut the cables and fled in disarray, some being blown back across the Channel by the wind, and some trying to make it to the coasts of Scotland and Ireland where they were wrecked. Only a tiny number of the invincible fleet made it back to Spain. The English rejoiced in the "Protestant wind" that had helped bring them victory.

THE IRISH PROBLEM

The failed reformation in Ireland proved to be one of the most vexing problems of Elizabeth's reign. In some senses it was an internal problem, but the persistent Catholicism of the Irish made it an international problem as well. Elizabeth intended her religious settlement to incorporate all of her people, but clearly there could be no compromise with the increasingly entrenched and militant Irish Catholics. A variety of different policies were tried. Elizabeth named English bishops to Irish dioceses and established a new university in Dublin, Trinity College, to make available education for Protestant Irishmen. But the Anglican church of Ireland had little support outside the Pale. The Gaelic chieftaincies had not wavered in their Catholicism, and as more of the Old English of the port towns became avowed recusants, it was increasingly clear that the English government was having little effect on the religious outlook of the Irish population.

Some historians have argued that Ireland was the first example of English colonialism, and as such religion and politics were tightly interconnected in matters of identity and conflict. Although the idea of introducing loyal "plantations" (land confiscated from the Irish landowners and parceled out to English colonists) started under Mary and Philip (with the creation of Queen's County and King's County), the Elizabethan plantations have many hallmarks of later imperialism. During the 1580s the English government tried to force Protestantism on the natives of Munster. The Fitzgerald chieftain of this region rebelled against the English, casting himself as defender of the persecuted Catholics. When he was defeated, the English confiscated and laid waste to his land. They then brought in twenty-two thousand Protestant English men, women, and children as settlers in the new plantation. With their arrival, the old Catholic landowners of the area fell further into poverty and lawlessness, and a new social category was introduced in Ireland: the New English, who were English born, Protestant, and loyal to the Crown and were given their land at the cost of the Old Irish Catholics.

Through the actions of a series of Elizabethan governors, including Sir Henry Sidney (father of the poet) and Sir William Fitzwilliam, the English tried to force their religion and their government on an unwilling population. Whereas Elizabeth had succeeded so well in so many aspects of her government, she failed abysmally in understanding the Irish people or in enacting policies that would lead to a peaceful relationship. The sixteenth century culmination of hostilities was the 1594 revolt of the great Ulster chief, Red Hugh O'Neill, Earl of Tyrone. He had extensive support from the neighboring lords and probable aid from the Church. Elizabeth sent her current young favorite, the Earl of Essex, to negotiate with Red Hugh. (Essex had been given a charter for his own plantation in Ulster and so had his own agenda as well.) The negotiations failed completely; Essex fled back to England without doing battle and eventually was executed. It was not until 1603 that Red Hugh, along with a large contingent of Spaniards who had joined him, was finally defeated by the English at the Battle of Kinsale, under Lord Mountjoy, Essex's successor. Ulster was now taken over by the English, and in 1607 the remaining Gaelic Catholic lords who had been in alliance with O'Neill fled to the Continent in what is remembered as the Flight of the Earls.

Their departure left Ireland without its old leadership, but their efforts to foster support for the beleaguered Irish Catholics had a profound effect. By the beginning of the seventeenth century Irish seminaries were being founded on the Continent and the Irish Counter-Reformation was well underway. In the meantime Elizabeth had spent millions of pounds in trying to subdue the Irish and had instead created lasting enmity. Ireland remained the anomaly where *cuius regio, eius religio* did not hold. The religion of the ruler was not the religion of the people, and so it would continue into the seventeenth century.

JAMES VI OF SCOTLAND/I OF ENGLAND

Elizabeth died on March 24, 1603. She was the last of the Tudors, and as everyone knew, the English crown would pass to a new dynasty. Her successor was James Stuart, sixth of that name in Scotland and first in England. Knowing that the inevitable day would come, Cecil had been corresponding with James for years. They wrote in amicable terms and James made clear to everyone that he was king of Scotland and not just the (undeclared) heir to England. He had been king of the Scots since he was thirteen months old, following the forced abdication of his mother. There had been a series of regencies, and James was most influenced by his tutor, George Buchanan, the great Scots scholar and historian. He was a stern taskmaster, and under his tutelage James learned to apply his already formidable intellect, working for hours in the library that had been assembled in Stirling Castle: six hundred books in six languages. By the time he was ten James was able to translate the Latin scriptures into French and from French into English. He always spoke with a heavy Scots accent, but unlike his

James I, by Daniel Mytens. This portrait from 1621 shows James in the later years of his reign. (He died in 1625.)

grandfather and great-grandfather (James IV and V), he did not learn Gaelic and always had a strong bias against the people and culture of the Highland regions. Buchanan hated Mary and her religion with a passion and, if he did not pass along his virulence, his pupil certainly learned to be sympathetic to his martyred father and indifferent to the fate of his mother. His religious upbringing was strict Calvinism.

By the time he was eighteen, James had already learned to trust nobody and to rely on his own judgment and his own authority. John, Earl of Mar, derisively called him Jock o' the Slates for his love of scholarship, and a French visitor called him an old young man. Later in his life he was tagged the wisest fool in Christendom, and historians have often repeated the nickname. This unflattering view is not justified. James was in fact highly intelligent and his ideas on kingship were by no means outside the norm for his time.

When he took control of Scotland in his own right, James was forced to reach an understanding with the Scots Kirk that satisfied its wishes for autonomy as well as fit his own increasingly strong conviction about the absolute authority of a monarch. In this he proved ineffective. James negotiated hard and a compromise was reached whereby he could name bishops, but each would be subject to a presbytery of ministers and all ultimately under the authority of the General Assembly. (The structure of the Scottish church was complex. The smallest local unit of administration was the Kirk session, presided over by a committee of elders. This was under the authority of a regional synod, and the synods were under the authority of the national General Assembly. Throughout the early modern period there were strong differences in opinion between those who supported a presbyterian style of authority under counsels of elders and those who supported an episcopalian structure that included bishops. Not surprisingly, the episcopal alignment was usually favored by the monarchs.) Even this unbalanced agreement was further undermined by James's decision the following year to annex the episcopal revenues to the royal treasury, thus rendering the benefices worthless either as income for a loyal incumbent or as a bargaining point.

Besides the tension with the Kirk, James was faced with the difficulties of dealing with a touchy and always potentially treasonous aristocracy. The long succession of Scottish minorities and regencies had exacerbated the family-centered ambitions of the Scottish lords, and loyalty never could be assumed. In the Highlands, a century of lawlessness followed the dissolution of the old Lordship of the Isles in 1493, which had provided a stabilizing local influence, even while challenging the power of the Stewart monarchs. With its loss, the old clan warfare revived, particularly centering around the increasing power struggle between the Campbells and the MacDonalds. For the Gaels, this time period is known as the *Linn nan creach* (the Age of Forays), in which the king in Edinburgh was largely irrelevant.

Perhaps because of the long history of minority rules and contested regencies, James was very aware of his obligation to produce an heir. Although historians have raised questions concerning James's sexual orientation based on the continuing influence of young male favorites throughout his life, marriage was necessary, and contemporaries remarked on his apparent infatuation with Anne (or Anna) of Denmark, the young woman who was to be his bride. She was tall and blonde and amiable. She was also a Lutheran, which displeased Elizabeth, who would have preferred for James to marry his cousin Arabella Stuart. When Anne set sail from Denmark, terrible storms drove back the ships. In October 1589, in what one historian has described as "the one romantic episode of his life," James decided to go and bring her home himself. The wedding was celebrated in Oslo and James remained there for several months, enjoying his new father-in-law's hospitality, conversing with Danish scholars, and probably glad to be away from the troublesome Scottish Kirk and lords for a time. Eventually James and Anne had seven living children.

An odd consequence of James's marriage to Anne and the difficulties encountered with her voyage to Scotland was a new focus on the crime of witchcraft in Scotland. Similar to many statutes across Europe, an act of Parliament in 1563 criminalized witchcraft in Scotland, and there was a handful of trials, with a mixture of accusations of poisonings, injury by magic, bewitchments, and so forth. But in 1590 a cluster of accusations started that focused on a magical conspiracy against the king and queen. As evidence from the trials unfolded, the picture that emerged was a tangle of politics, diabolism, and magical treason. The witches (allegedly) had been commissioned by the Earl of Bothwell (nephew of Mary's third husband) to harm the king and prevent the ships from reaching Scotland. John Fian was the ringleader, and a contemporary pamphlet documenting his trial and execution spelled out his offenses. It was a sordid affair. Both Scottish and Danish witches had performed magic to raise the winds and sink the ships, and wax images and toad poison were to be used to kill the king. About seventy people were brought to trial for their supposed connection with this conspiracy.

The king's direct involvement helped to codify Scottish legal procedures connected with the crime of witchcraft as well as ultimately helping codify witchcraft theory through the publication of his book *Daemonologie* in 1597. Perhaps partly through his knowledge of Danish witch trials, and partly through his own assessment of the evidence contained in the testimonies of the North Berwick witches, James took the position that witchcraft was inextricably linked to diabolism (pacts with Satan) and that it was a mixed crime involving treason to both Church and state. This position linked Scotland more firmly to continental views of witchcraft than it did to the English model, which tended to deemphasize the role of Satan. The result was that punishments for witchcraft in Scotland tended to be more severe and were carried out more frequently. One historian has remarked that Scotland was "the most witch-ridden zone per capita" of any region in Europe during the early modern period, and witchcraft remained a capital crime in Scotland until 1721, considerably later than in England or on the Continent.

(19)

CHAP. X.

How fome Witches revelling in a Gentle-man's Houfe, ferved the Servants who furprifed them.

IT happened one time that a great number of Lancafhire Witches were rev-
ling in a gentleman's houfe, in his ab-
fence, and making merry with what they
found, the dogs not daring to ftir, they
having it feems, power to ftrike them
mute.—However, dnring their frolick-

Woodcut illustration of the Lancashire witches. This somewhat primitive woodcut was reproduced in a number of texts and helped promote images associated with witchcraft, such as a horned devil and witches on broomsticks.

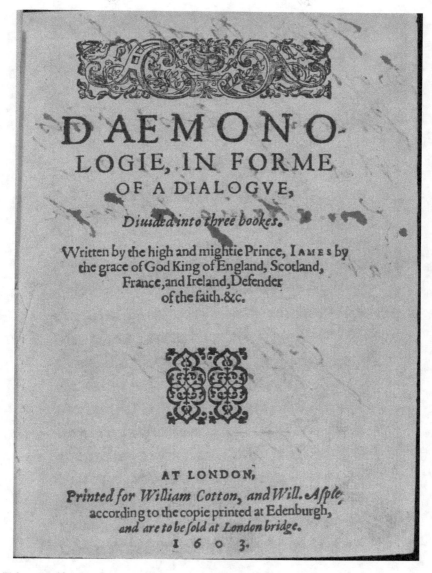

D AE M O N O-
LOGIE, IN FORME
OF A DIALOGVE,

Diuided into three bookes.

Written by the high and mightie Prince, I A M E s by
the grace of God King of England, Scotland,
France, and Ireland, Defender
of the faith.&c.

AT LONDON,
Printed for William Cotton, and Will. Aspley
according to the copie printed at Edenburgh,
and are to be fold at London bridge.
1 6 0 3.

Title page of James I's Daemonologie. *Published in 1603, James's attempt at codification of witchcraft theory strongly influenced evolving witchcraft laws in both England and Scotland.*

In addition to his treatise on witchcraft, the scholarly Scottish king also wrote two books detailing his political theories: *The Trew Law of Free Monarchies*, written in 1598, and *Basilikon Doron* (1599), an instruction guide to his young son Henry concerning the nature of a king's authority and a guidebook for governing. Much has been made of James's overbearing absolutism,

Title page of James I's Basilikon Doron. *James's treatise on government was written in 1599 before he ascended to the English throne. It illustrates clearly his theological and political justifications for divine right monarchy.*

although in fact his actual governing was not much different in style from Elizabeth's or that of many of his other contemporaries. He merely wrote down his political philosophy so that it could be examined in careful hindsight. His political writings certainly make it clear that he believed in divine right monarchy and the right of a king to rule without interference. On the other hand, in practice, both in Scotland and in his later years as English king, James was careful to acknowledge other institutions of authority, even when they were irksome or did not uphold his choices. Divine right, as a theory, derived from the medieval Doctrine of the Two Swords, in which God's will on earth was rendered through the two institutions of Church and monarchy, and as such, was a view held by most early modern monarchs.

ACCESSION TO THE ENGLISH THRONE

On March 27, 1603, Sir Robert Carey rode into Edinburgh bringing the news that Elizabeth was dead. Four days later James was proclaimed king in London. In April he started the long journey south, departing from his Scottish subjects with the assurance that he would return every three years (a promise he did not keep). James claimed that the Scots reacted to his departure with tears and the English with rejoicing. That may well be regarded as an overstatement on both counts. Although the Scots may have felt forsaken by their king, in many ways an absentee monarchy worked to their advantage, allowing the governing institutions in Scotland to work more smoothly. As for the English, many were dismayed by the prospect of a king from the barbarous north. In person James was blunt spoken and often coarse, and his manners were uncouth. He was sloppy in dress and gave the appearance of an unpleasant corpulence due to the padded armor he always wore under his clothing (a sensible precaution given the tenor of Scottish politics). The English found his accent hard to understand and his bluntness abrasive. In all ways, James and his court could not have been more different from the formal and feminine atmosphere of Elizabeth's reign.

James's great desire was to see a true union between the two halves of his kingdom. He argued (logically enough from his perspective) that God had created it as one island and therefore it should be joined. (Needless to say, Ireland was more problematic.) And following the logic of divine right, James believed that God had given him the position of deputy over both halves and so the idea of a Great Britain would seem to be what was intended. Neither the Scots nor the English wished to see any loss of independence, and in many ways each regarded the other in negative terms and both had no desire to merge their administrative structures. Moreover, the religious differences were substantial, and although James was of the opinion that the religious problems could be addressed, his constituents on both sides of the border were not convinced. When he made clear that he wanted his title to be king of Great Britain and Ireland, Parliament refused the necessary ratification. He still used the title, but it was by proclamation, not statute.

In England the threat from nonconformists of both extremes (Puritan and Catholic) was still unresolved from Elizabeth's reign. Theoretically everyone was to abide by the Elizabethan settlement, but there was not an actual consensus. As early as his journey south, James was met by a group of Puritans bringing to him the Millenary Petition (which was said to have a thousand signatures, although in reality they were probably much fewer). The petition asked for shorter church services, simpler (or no) music or vestments, and no signs of popery such as the cross or wedding rings.

James agreed to discuss these matters and in 1604 called the Hampton Court Conference. The conference made the king's position clear, though not to the liking of the Puritans. They had assumed that, with his Calvinist upbringing and having been used to a presbyterian system in Scotland (one under the authority of a council of elders), he would support presbyterianism in England. Not so. The king gave the assembled conference a long erudite lecture on church history and then thundered, "No bishop, no king!" James was in fact a staunch supporter of episcopalianism (rule through bishops) and hated the presbyterian system. A presbyterian church, he pointed out, agreed as well with monarchy as God agreed with the Devil, and he wanted to hear no more of the Puritans' demands. Before the conference adjourned, some committees were established to examine points of reform, although nothing much came of their deliberations. The one exception was agreement on a new translation of the Bible. This would be the King James Version, which was the work of forty-seven scholars, all members of the Church of England, though representing both ends of the religious spectrum. James himself offered his perspective on certain points of translation, ensuring that the new text met with his views (and those of the Elizabethan settlement) concerning the Anglican state.

On the Catholic side it could be difficult to even identify the opposition. There were many who officially conformed by attending required Anglican church services, but who still secretly practiced Catholicism. Some merely wanted the right to legally practice their faith; some wanted nothing less than a return to Catholic monarchy. The most dramatic example of Catholic extremism came in 1605 with the Gunpowder Plot. A small group of conspirators, including some holding minor positions in the government, conceived the idea of blowing up the Parliament building during the ceremonial opening of the 1605 Parliament session. With most of the officials dead, they reasoned, it would be an easy matter to reinstate a Catholic government. Led by the arch-conspirator Guy Fawkes, they contrived to fill the basement of the Lord's Chamber with gunpowder. Just as Fawkes was about to light the fuse, the plot was discovered and he was apprehended. He was found guilty of treason and executed. The anniversary of his arrest, November 5, is remembered as Guy Fawkes Day, still celebrated in Britain. For many years the anniversary was a time of anti-Catholic harassment, but in modern times the celebration has evolved into something more like Halloween with pranks, costumes, bonfires, and children demanding a "penny for the Guy" (small effigies representing the conspirator) and culminating in the burning of the effigies in bonfires.

In addition to the religious tensions that still persisted, Elizabeth had left James with other mounting problems, including major fiscal issues. The Tudors had always been openhanded in their patronage and lavish in their court life. During the last years of Elizabeth's reign, enormous amounts of revenue had been spent in trying to militarily subdue the Irish. The result was a nearly empty royal treasury. England still operated on the medieval principle that monarchs should be able to live on their own revenues except in times of crisis when taxes could be levied. Because England was at war for most of the later part of Elizabeth's reign (both with the Spanish and with the Irish), Parliament had granted a certain amount of taxation, but these sources of income were not permanent, and there was no theoretical agreement on what taxation a monarch could request in times of peace. In the early modern era this practice was hopelessly out of date, and it was compounded by the soaring inflation of the sixteenth century. Historians have been quick to blame the Stuarts for their unsound fiscal policies; however, there is evidence that James clearly understood the problem and tried to resolve it, but he had few resources on which to draw.

IRELAND

In Ireland the accession of James was met with great rejoicing and Te Deums were sung in the city of Waterford. Churches were rededicated in Kilkenny, Clonmel, Cashel, Cork, and Wexford, and bells of celebration were rung across the land. For the Irish the accession of James, a Scot, not an Englishman, and the son of Mary Stuart, martyred for her faith, must mean that their time of persecution was over. The celebration was brief. In July 1605 James issued a proclamation stating that

> we hereby make known to our subjects in Ireland that no toleration shall ever be granted by us. This we do for the purpose of cutting off all hope that any other religion shall be allowed save that which is consonant to the laws and statutes of this realm.

James went on to reinvoke the Elizabethan laws against recusancy and to require that all loyal subjects attend Protestant church services. He also called for the expulsion of all priests and Jesuits from Ireland by December 10, 1605. (The need for this stipulation shows us that the Catholic reformation was in fact gaining ground during Elizabeth's reign.) James's edicts were enforced quickly and harshly, and the Irish Catholics were once again reminded that they were under persecution.

Ulster remained a particular problem for James as it had been for Elizabeth. The Rising of 1591 was still fresh in everyone's memories, and despite Elizabeth's eventual military victory, many insurgents remained. Ulster had in many ways been the focal point of anticolonial, anti-English, and anti-Protestant sentiment. This ancient kingdom had once been the dominant power in Gaelic Ireland, and especially with the defeat of the Fitzgeralds of Munster, the O'Neills and O'Donnells of Ulster provided the main Gaelic (and Catholic) leadership

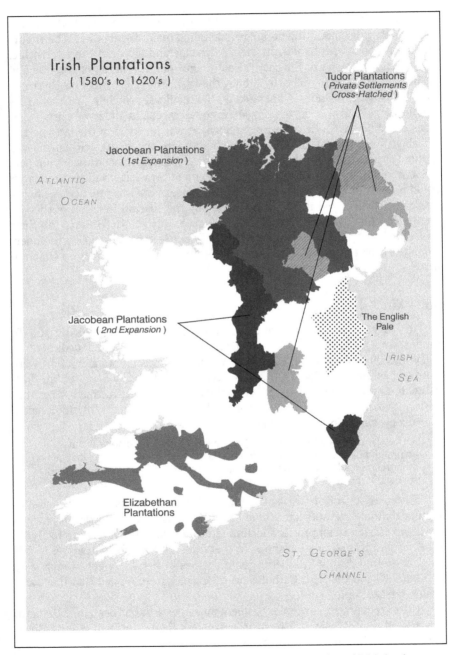

Irish plantations (1580s to 1620s). This map shows the expansion of Irish land brought under English control through the formation of plantations. From only two plantations (Queen's County and King's County) during the time of Mary Tudor, the amount of territory rapidly increased under Elizabeth I and James I.

of Ireland. With their defeat in the Nine Years War, Ulster had been divided into counties that were subject to the authority of the English monarchs. When the Catholic lords initially fled in 1607, they intended to go to Spain, but they ended up being sheltered by the papal court in Rome, where they and their descendants continued to play a major role in Irish politics throughout the seventeenth century. Their departure made the Ulster question even more urgent.

The solution of James and his advisers was a new plantation scheme. Under the new scheme Ulster was divided into six new counties (Armagh, Cavan, Fermanagh, Tyrone, Derry, and Donegal) that were designated as Crown property. Aside from some remaining church properties, the land was available for colonial settlement by servitors (those who had served the king in Ireland) and undertakers (who agreed to bring over both English and Scottish settlers and establish new communities). Only a few of the original owners retained their status and holdings, with the stipulation that they must be able to produce official English-style leases (which had never been part of Gaelic landholding) and that they agree to adopt English housing and farming methods. There was indeed a large influx of immigrants, but instead of creating lots of little Pales in which the new colonizers were to be insulated and protected from the wild Irish, the new immigrants dispersed and the undertakers, if unable to recruit enough suitable planters, often accepted native tenants, thus practically guaranteeing conflict between the new (Protestant) landholders and the disenfranchised and impoverished original owners. Additionally, the religious mix was a volatile one, with the Old Irish Catholics now living side by side with Anglicans and Scottish Calvinists. Many of the roots of the modern Irish problem can be traced directly to the Ulster plantation.

SCOTLAND

After moving his court to England, James returned to Scotland only once in 1617. After having been in England for several years, he boasted, "Here I sit and govern by my pen. I write it down and it is done, and by a Clerk of the Council I govern Scotland now, which others could not do by the sword." He could not have been more mistaken. In his absence the Kirk was gaining ground and taking more and more authority to itself, and the Highlands, which had never been successfully ruled from Edinburgh, let alone London, were in an escalating power struggle between rival chieftains (primarily the Campbells and MacDonalds) for control of the region that had been the Lordship of the Isles. These were not just archaic clan feuds, but rather an alignment with the political issues of the day. Clan Campbell stood for Protestantism; Anglo-Scottish culture; industry and commerce; and when it suited, the king's politics. As early as 1578, James had given the Campbells special lieutenancies to keep the Highlands in control, and after 1603 they were given "orders of fire and sword" by the king (the legal right to make war) to subdue any rebellious clans. Clan Donald (representatives of the old Lordship of the Isles) stood for Catholicism and the traditional Gaelic language, culture, and way of life. James was warned by the wise Andrew Knox, bishop of the Isles, that destroying one clan only to elevate another would never achieve success. As it was, the hostilities between Clan Campbell and Clan Donald would continue to color Highland politics well into the eighteenth century.

James had never made a secret of his disdain for the inhabitants of the Highlands and islands. In his instructions to his son he advised him "to reform and civilize the best inclined among them, rooting out or transporting the barbarous and stubborn sort and planting civility in their rooms." James tried the same policy he had used in Ulster, demanding that landholders produce official leases, and he tried to organize plantations of Lowland colonists in Kintyre, Lochaber, and the Hebrides. The scheme failed miserably. Any potential colonizers were easily driven out by the still-powerful MacLeods and MacLeans, and besides, the land was not desirable enough for the colonizers to want it.

In desperation, James tried for sweeping cultural reform. He appointed a commission to extend the authority of the king into the Highlands, and in 1609 the commission produced the Bond and Statutes of Iona. The statutes called for the chieftains to agree to obey the king and his laws and extended the authority of the reformed church in the Highlands. They also provided for the control of the production of alcoholic beverages; the suppression of idle vagrants, beggars, and bards (who helped to perpetuate traditional Gaelic culture); the limitation of the retinues of the chieftains; the prohibition of firearms; and the insistence that heirs be sent to the Lowlands to be educated. The statutes were renewed in 1616 with the added provision that no one in the islands could inherit property unless he could read, write, and speak English. Some chiefs signed the document and there are some examples of chieftains' sons being sent south for their education, but many chieftains simply ignored the terms for as long as it was possible. In hindsight, the Statutes of Iona can be seen as representing increasingly hard-line attitudes toward Highland culture. In many different ways they had an enormous impact on Highland society, contributing to the debasement and eventual outlawing of the Gaelic language and other aspects of Highland culture during the eighteenth century.

JAMES'S LATER PARLIAMENTS

Although James had never been particularly successful in his dealings with Parliament, relations worsened as time went by and no resolutions were reached on the issues that had plagued the kingdom since his accession. One Parliament, called in 1614 and nicknamed the Addled Parliament, sat for only two months and produced no legislation. When James dissolved it he threatened to call no more Parliaments, commenting to the Spanish ambassador that he could not understand why his predecessors had created the institution. He managed to go for seven years without calling Parliament, but in 1621 an international crisis required deliberation and action. In 1618 war had broken out in the Holy Roman empire. It was a complicated situation: partly a religious war, partly a territorial dispute, and partly a challenge to the authority of the emperor. The conflict, which was to become the Thirty Years War, could not be ignored by any European ruler, but James was even more closely involved. His son-in-law was one of the main combatants.

The Holy Roman empire was an immensely complex territory. Dating back to the Middle Ages, it was governed by an elected emperor. Normally the title passed in dynastic succession from father to son and was merely ratified by the seven elector princes. However, in 1618, a novel and catastrophic situation occurred. Of the seven electors, three were Catholic (the archbishops of Mainz, Cologne, and Trier) and three were Protestant (the electors of Saxony, Brandenburg, and the Palatinate). The tiebreaker vote would be the seventh elector, the king of Bohemia. However, the kingship of Bohemia was in dispute. The two claimants were Ferdinand II, who was Catholic and the heir to the emperor, and Frederick of the Palatinate, who was Protestant and James Stuart's son-in-law (married to James's daughter Elizabeth). When the old emperor Matthias died in 1618, the Bohemian conflict became a crisis. Whichever man won Bohemia would also win the empire.

It was a total quandary for James. Ferdinand was the heir and by divine right theory had every right to his authority. However, England should be supporting the Protestant cause, which appeared to be somewhat on the wane during the early years of the seventeenth century. There was also the matter of Spanish diplomacy: James was trying to broker a marriage for his son and heir, Charles, with the Spanish Infanta, but he should also show support for his daughter Elizabeth. Above all, James hated war and knew England did not have the resources for involvement in what was already looking like a long and difficult conflict. Finally he made the decision in 1621 to call Parliament. Parliament took the stance that England should intervene in the defense of Protestantism. Reluctantly James agreed if Parliament would give him the money for a war. It refused as long as he maintained the Spanish alliance. Angry, James insisted that foreign policy was the prerogative of the king, not Parliament. In the end Parliament did not vote enough money for any effective intervention and England stayed out of the Thirty Years War.

James was not well in his last years. In 1624 he suffered a stroke and the last Parliament, which resolved to revive the war with Spain, was presided over by his son Charles and James's great favorite, George Villiers, Duke of Buckingham. In March 1625 James died and his son Charles inherited the crowns of three kingdoms, along with the insolvency and all the unresolved problems of his father's reign.

SUGGESTED READING

Bossy, John. *The English Catholic Community, 1570–1850*. Oxford: Oxford University Press, 1976.

Brady, Ciaran. *The Chief Governors: The Rise and Fall of Reform Government in Tudor Ireland*. Cambridge: Cambridge University Press, 1994.

Canny, Nicholas. *The Elizabethan Conquest of Ireland*. Hassocks, UK: Harvester Press, 1976.

Collinson, Patrick. *The Elizabethan Puritan Movement*. Oxford: Oxford University Press, 1967.

Ellis, Steven. *Tudor Frontiers and Noble Power: The Making of the British State*. Oxford: Clarendon Press, 1995.

Falls, Cyril. *Elizabeth's Irish Wars*. Syracuse, NY: Syracuse University Press, 1997.

Houston, S. J. *James I*. London: Taylor & Francis, 1973.

Johnson, Paul. *Elizabeth: A Study in Power and Intellect*. London: Weidenfeld & Nicolson, 1974.

Jones, Norman. *The Birth of the Elizabethan Age: England in the 1560s*. Oxford: Blackwell, 1993.

Levack, Brian. *The Formation of the British State: England, Scotland, and the Union, 1603–1707*. Oxford: Clarendon Press, 1987.

MacCaffrey, Wallace T. *Elizabeth I*. London: Edward Arnold, 1993.

Mattingly, Garrett. *The Armada*. Boston: Houghton Mifflin, 1959.

Moody, T.W., F. X. Martin, and F. J. Byrne, eds. *A New History of Ireland*, vol. 3. Oxford: Oxford University Press, 1976.

Picard, Liza. *Elizabeth's London*. New York: St. Martin's Press, 2003.

Prebble, John. *The Lion in the North*. Harmondsworth, UK: Coward, McCann & Geoghegan, 1971.

Salgado, Gamini. *The Elizabethan Underworld*. Phoenix Mill, UK: Sutton, 1995.

Smith, Lacey Baldwin. *Elizabeth Tudor: Portrait of a Queen*. New York: Little, Brown, 1977.

———. *The Elizabethan World*. Boston: Houghton, 1972.

Smout, T. C. *A History of the Scottish People: 1560–1830*. London: Harper Collins, 1969.

Strong, Roy. *The Cult of Elizabeth: Elizabethan Portraiture and Pageantry*. London: Pimlico, 1999.

Willson, David H. *King James VI & I*. London: Cape, 1956.

Wormald, Jenny. *Court, Kirk, and Community: Scotland, 1470–1625*. London: Edward Arnold, 1981.

Chapter 12

Charles I and the Three Kingdoms

When Charles became king in 1625 it would have taken no great soothsayer to predict that he would have problems. He had inherited the problems of not one, but three realms, and both his upbringing and personality did not bode well for his success. When his elder brother, Henry, died in 1612, Charles resolutely accepted his fate and determined that he would be the best king he could be according to his father's precepts: divine right monarchy and Anglicanism. In personality Charles was very different from his father. He was shy and cultured, but also very proud and stubborn. He was hard to know and not by any means a man of the people. He surrounded himself with courtiers who supported his outlook, and he did not understand and appeared not to care to understand the viewpoints of his subjects. Unlike his father, he did not know the Scots at all, and he assumed that the same laws and religious policies should work in all three kingdoms.

CHARLES AND THE AGE OF CRISIS

Many historians accept the concept of the seventeenth century as the Age of Crisis and in many ways it is an accurate way of describing the overall context of the era. The British Isles were not unique in their problems, but the structures of society in the three British kingdoms were very different from those in the continental kingdoms. Charles had inherited a society in which a rise in population was accompanied by lower wages and a high rate of inflation, leading to myriad social tensions. At the time of his accession a serious reoccurrence of the plague took place. (In a society that still strongly believed in signs and portents, it was noted that Stuart coronations were often accompanied by the plague.) Moreover, the late sixteenth and early seventeenth centuries have been termed the Little Ice Age, in which a climatic shift with lower temperatures meant shorter growing seasons and frequent crop failures. Revolutions are often associated with hungry, disgruntled populations who believe that the government is ignoring their problems or at least failing to adequately address them, and so it was in the seventeenth century.

Farmers and tradesmen were struggling to survive with stagnant wages and rising prices, and even the better off members of society were struggling with what one historian has called a crisis of rising expectations. The gentry (well-off landowners) expected to be upwardly mobile, but there was nowhere to go as the old aristocracy struggled to hold on to any power and privileges it still had in a rapidly changing society. Increasingly, with evolving modern institutions, there was an erosion of the influence of the old landed nobility, and it too was struggling with financial issues as revenues declined due to tenants who were unable to pay their rents.

Needless to say, the monarchy itself was in a financial crisis. Revenues had not increased since the time of Elizabeth, and with rising inflation there was no money for the expected royal services and patronage. In England, a monarch could not increase taxes without the consent of Parliament, and that is the issue that lay at the heart of Charles's troubled reign.

Charles I, by Daniel Mytens. This portrait of the king was done in 1631 prior to the outbreak of the War of the Three King-doms. It captures the king's dignified and stately bearing.

Against this backdrop of economic crisis and financial turmoil, Charles called his first Parliament in 1625. Though he was not personally disliked at that time, Parliament was not cooperative. Members were not pleased by his marriage, which had taken place in 1624. When it had become clear that, despite James's efforts, the Spanish Infanta was not about to marry an English heretic, Charles decided on a French bride, Henrietta Maria. She was the daughter of Henry IV of France (the once Protestant king, who had converted to end the French Wars of Religion) and Marie de Medici. Henrietta Maria's upbringing had been highly cultured and she probably appealed to Charles partly for that reason. However, she was Catholic, and that was enough to offend the English Parliament. (Interestingly, her marriage to a Protestant also offended the French. Instead of a state wedding, she and Charles were married by proxy outside the doors of Notre Dame.) After her arrival in England, she was allowed to hear Mass in private, and it is probable that Charles gave her assurances that he would revisit the anti-Catholic laws in Britain. Charles's mother, Anne of Denmark, had also converted to Catholicism, perhaps predisposing him toward tolerance.

In a sour mood because of the French marriage and Charles's continued reliance upon the Duke of Buckingham, Parliament voted only minimal revenues. Usually, the first Parliament of a king's reign voted to allow the collection of tonnage and poundage (essentially a tax on foreign trade). Parliament refused to grant this, although the government continued to collect it, claiming the ratification was merely an oversight.

By now, foreign policy had shifted and everyone agreed that the English should intervene in the Thirty Years War, specifically with an expedition against the Spanish. Buckingham mounted a naval expedition to take the city of Cadiz, with the intention of also capturing the Spanish treasure fleet coming from the New World. The Spanish had an excellent intelligence system and quickly learned of the plan. They evacuated Cadiz before the English arrived, removing not only valuables, but also any kind of supplies. Many of the English sailors died of starvation on the return trip, and blame for the debacle was placed on both Charles and Buckingham. Because the disastrous campaign had also been costly, Charles was forced to call Parliament again in 1626. Sir John Eliot led the Parliament in this session, calling for the impeachment of Buckingham. Charles refused and dismissed Parliament. Without money from Parliament, he attempted to force a loan from his wealthier subjects. Many refused (viewing it as a form of taxation that had not been approved by Parliament) and were imprisoned. Some money was raised through the forced loan, and Buckingham undertook another expedition, this time to relieve the Huguenots of La Rochelle. Although it was not quite as much of a disaster as Cadiz, it was at best an inconclusive campaign that wasted a great deal of money.

In 1628, the king and Parliament effected a reconciliation, but it was quickly shattered. Charles agreed to sign the Petition of Right, which declared forced loans illegal and forbade both the quartering of troops in private houses and imprisonment without specific legal charges. In light of his agreement,

Parliament granted a reasonable amount of revenue to the king, but when Eliot began again with his charges against Buckingham, Charles dismissed Parliament. Just a few months later Buckingham was assassinated. Far from ending the conflict between king and Parliament, this served only to shift it into a new direction. Without Buckingham, Charles began relying more on the advice of William Laud—a religious advocate of High-Church Arminianism (a broader interpretation of God's grace and human salvation than that found in Calvinist teachings)—whom Charles would name as archbishop of Canterbury in 1633.

Although technically Parliament could not criticize the king directly, it was clear that its objections to High-Church (what it perceived as pro-Catholic) policies reflected on the king. Although the Elizabethan settlement had taken a moderate stance on liturgy and observance, allowing for decoration of the churches, wearing of vestments, and so forth, in practice Anglicanism had been steadily moving in the direction of more Calvinist observance. Charles, with both aesthetic and religious tastes leaning toward ritual and ceremony, preferred High-Church observance, which to his critics too closely resembled Catholic practices. At the advice of Laud, and with the strength of his own convictions, Charles was appointing bishops with Arminian and High-Church outlooks and encouraging the return of some of the traditional aspects of devotional practice that had disappeared at the time of the Reformation.

THE ELEVEN YEARS TYRANNY

In the 1628 Parliament, Eliot again brought charges against forced loans and added resolutions declaring as enemies any who supported Arminianism. The king sent a messenger to dissolve Parliament, but he was forcibly restrained until a vote supporting the resolutions was cast. Parliament was then dissolved and Charles vowed to rule without it. The Eleven Years Tyranny is the name given to the time in which Charles ruled without Parliament, although the idea of tyranny was definitely in the eye of the beholder. There was no requirement that a king must call Parliament, and monarchs had ruled without Parliament before. The first act of Charles's personal rule was to imprison the most outspoken members of Parliament, including Eliot. This was more of a token gesture than actual retaliation and all but Eliot were released soon. Eliot remained in the Tower where he died in 1632. The next item, clearly, was how to rule without the customary revenues granted by Parliament. To avoid further military expenses, Charles negotiated peace terms with France and Spain and disengaged Britain from the Thirty Years War. His detractors accused him of deserting both his sister Elizabeth (the Protestant queen of Bohemia) and the Protestant cause.

Charles's financial advisors worked hard to identify sources of revenue that were not strictly speaking taxes that required the consent of Parliament. They continued to collect tonnage and poundage, and they revived a number of half-forgotten medieval customs, such as a £40 Distraint of Knighthood fee, fines for encroachment on the king's forests (which had to be surveyed to determine where the ancient forestlands had been encroached upon), and fines for those in violation of Elizabeth's laws against new construction in the city of London. Most significantly, they began collecting *ship money*. The concept of ship money was a fascinating application of constitutional theory. Technically, the Crown had had the right to demand that port cities provide additional vessels for the Royal Navy in times of crisis. Although Charles's subjects would have said that it was not a time of crisis, the government began collecting. Charles let it be known that, in lieu of ships, ports could simply pay a monetary equivalent. As the practice proved successful, it was extended to inland towns (which had no vessels to provide) and effectively it became a form of taxation, although it was not identified as such. Through such creative financing, government revenues actually improved and were better administered than they had been in the earlier years of Charles's reign. It is possible that Charles could have gone on for some time financially without having to call Parliament; however, another crisis intervened, this time from his Scottish realm.

CRISIS IN SCOTLAND AND IRELAND

Unlike his father, Charles had no personal knowledge of his Scottish subjects. He had governed, as James did, through a council in Edinburgh, and through what he thought were loyal clans in the Highlands, specifically Clan Campbell. He had a disdainful attitude toward the Highlanders and a serious lack of understanding of Scottish religion and politics. Although Charles received the Scottish crown at the same time as the English one, it was eight years before he came north for his coronation. When he came in 1633, he brought the now archbishop of Canterbury, William Laud, with him. The coronation ceremony was splendid, presided over by Laud. There was a table at the front with books and candles and behind it a tapestry of the crucifixion. The Scottish archbishop of St. Andrews, John Spottiswoode, was rebuked by Laud for not wearing a surplice (Scottish ministers wore the plain black robe favored by Genevan Calvinists). The following Sunday, Laud presided over an Anglican service at St. Giles, attended by the king. Charles seemed oblivious to the mounting dismay of the Scots. He compounded the offense by calling a Scottish Parliament (a committee elected by the Royal Council and the king's newly elected bishops) that passed 168 measures affirming the king's policies, both religious and financial.

Back in London, Charles decided to implement the uniformity in religion that James had always dreamed of, but knowing his Scottish subjects, never dared to enforce. In 1618 James VI had enacted the Five Articles of Perth (calling for such things as kneeling for communion, private baptism, and confirmation by bishops) to bring the Church of Scotland into better alignment with the Church of England. These measures were reluctantly accepted by the General Assembly in 1618, but were not ratified by the Scottish Parliament until 1621.

In 1637 Charles ordered the introduction of a new prayer book in Scotland. It was essentially the Anglican rite and had been drafted by Laud, although the archbishop of Canterbury had no jurisdiction in Scotland.

When the new *Book of Common Prayer* was first read at St. Giles, a riot ensued. The participants may have been hired, but the sentiment was genuine. It was the custom of the well-off tradesmen of Edinburgh to send female servants with "creepie stools" to hold the place for the family at church services. The story—probably apocryphal—goes that, when the reading started, one of these common women jumped up and shouted "do ye daur to say Mass at my lug [ear]?" and flung her prayer stool at the altar. More women flung stools and a general riot spilled out of the church and into the streets of Edinburgh. Whether or not the specific story is true, there was undoubtedly public reaction to the introduction of the prayer book. Shortly thereafter, a great conventicle (outdoor nonconformist meeting) was held in Edinburgh, attended by most of the burghers and gentry. Thousands of Scots took the oath called the National Covenant in 1638 to resist popery and tyranny. These Covenanters vowed to take up arms and fight against the king if necessary. The National Covenant is arguably one of the most important documents in Scottish history.

Meanwhile, in Ireland, another crisis was developing. In 1633 Charles had appointed a new governor, Sir Thomas Wentworth, later the Earl of Strafford. Part of Wentworth's mission was to increase revenues from Ireland, and he did this by playing factions off each other, alienating the New English, as well as the Old English and Old Irish Catholics. His grand scheme was the plantation of Connacht, which seriously challenged the landowning Old English of that region. Although Wentworth was Arminian in his outlook, the Irish (rightly) did not mistake his High-Church Anglicanism for pro-Catholic sentiment. As the Scottish crisis escalated, Wentworth was called back to London to serve more directly as advisor to the king. He left behind an Irish Parliament of both Catholics and Protestants temporarily united in their hostility as well as increasingly unhappy Ulster Scots who shared many of the viewpoints of the rebelling Scots. On top of that, the remaining disenfranchised Catholic Gaels of Ulster were uniting in the cause of the Highlanders, who sought to end the hated regional domination of Gilleasbuig Gruamach (Archibald the Sullen), the Earl of Argyll, who used the king's policies to confiscate the land of other chieftains to his own aggrandizement.

The rebellion in Scotland in 1639 meant that Charles had to raise an army (there were no standing armies at that time) and therefore Parliament had to be called. Wentworth had advised the king to do so, being sure that Parliament would be willing to grant money to oppose the ancient enemy, Scotland. It was called in April 1640 and Charles asked for a huge amount of money (more than twice what Elizabeth had ever been granted). In his defense the price of hiring an army would have been astronomical, given the inflation and the fact that the Thirty Years War was engaging nearly all available mercenaries. Having been ignored for eleven years, Parliament was not inclined to be beneficent, and as the new leader of Parliament, John Pym argued that the Scots were in fact fighting against the Arminianism and pro-Catholic policies that many Englishmen found objectionable as well. Frustrated and angry, Charles dismissed the Parliament after only three weeks, with no legislation passed; hence, it was given the nickname of the Short Parliament.

However, the Scots were still rebelling, and Charles could not afford to hire an army; therefore, in August 1640 he was forced to call Parliament once again. This would be known as the Long Parliament, which sat with only minor interruptions until 1659. Parliament knew that it had the upper hand and began forcing Charles to address its demands. Parliament insisted on the release of anyone who had been imprisoned (in its opinion, without cause) during the period of Charles's personal reign and it demanded the arrest, exile, or execution of anyone who had assisted Charles with his rule during that time. Many Royalists fled to the Continent, and some were indeed arrested and imprisoned. Wentworth (now Duke of Strafford) was accused of treason for his willingness to use the Irish army against any of the king's enemies (interpreted to be English as well as Scots). He denied the charge, but was executed in 1641. Laud was also sent to the Tower of London, but survived until 1645, when he too was executed. Charles was helpless to intervene, and the Long Parliament passed numerous acts that outlawed his fiscal policies and essentially eliminated the chance that a monarch could ever again govern without Parliament. On religious matters Parliament remained essentially deadlocked.

In October 1641 a new major rebellion broke out in Ireland. For anyone familiar with Irish politics, it was no surprise. In Wentworth's absence and without the appointment of a successor, the hostilities that had been just below the surface exploded. The rebellion was led by the Gaelic Irish, who saw the best opportunity in years for overthrowing English rule. Their leader was another Red Hugh O'Neill, nephew of the Great O'Neill and a thirty-year veteran of the Spanish army. He was sure that the rising would receive aid from the continental Catholics. The first effort of the Irish rebels, to take Dublin Castle, failed, but support for the rising began manifesting all over Ireland, including Ulster, where troops were led by Sir Phelim O'Neill. The Irish took Dungannon, Mountjoy Fort, Charlemont Castle, and Newry. By the end of 1641 they had retaken most of Louth and were joined, somewhat reluctantly, by the Old English of the Pale. By 1642 it had become a national rising, and the Catholic church began taking leadership of the movement, most notably under Cardinal Giovanni Rinuccini, the papal nuncio (papal representative) in Ireland. In May 1642 a provisional government, the Confederate Catholics of Ireland, was established. It met at Kilkenny to restore the rights of the Catholic church in Ireland and to maintain the king's prerogatives. Especially at the start of the rebellion, word of the atrocities committed by the rebels against the English Protestants had reached England (some were likely true and others were exaggerated), leaving Charles in a difficult position. Ostensibly the Confederation of Kilkenny was on his side, but he risked even more hostility from his English and Scots subjects if he aligned himself with a blatantly pro-Catholic movement.

By the seventeenth century Wales had already been politically integrated into the English crown and did not have separate grievances and campaigns such as those found in Ireland and Scotland. For the most part, the Welsh regarded Puritanism as an alien import; its principles did not arouse much enthusiasm outside of the border regions, which were already bilingual, more urban, and more connected to English society. In these areas support for the king was weakest. However, in contrast, because of the association between Puritanism and Anglicization, support for the king outside the towns and ports was reasonably strong.

THE WARS OF THE THREE KINGDOMS

In August 1642, any attempts at negotiation between the king and Parliament failed. The final attempt was a document called "The Nineteen Propositions." It was essentially an ultimatum from Parliament, drafted after Charles had attempted to use force to remove the most outspoken members of the opposition. Had the king accepted it, he would have been left with no authority whatsoever. He refused. Fearing the worst, he sent his wife and children to France for safety and was busy building an army, as was Parliament. On August 22, 1642, the king raised his standard over his camp at Nottingham and the English Civil War began. The superstitious noted that a storm came in the night and blew down the king's standard. It was not an auspicious beginning.

In England the divisions were based on predictable alignments. Those who supported Parliament were overwhelmingly of the middling orders, urban, and Puritan and those who supported Charles were aristocrats and gentry, those with landed estates and a High-Church perspective. The war was not, however, just an English conflict. With somewhat different motivations, but equal divisiveness, the conditions of civil war were replicated in Scotland and Ireland. Most historians now refer to the interconnected conflict as the War of the Three Kingdoms, one of the most devastating and chaotic periods in British history.

In the beginning, Charles seemed to have the advantage with his army. It was small, but made up of professional soldiers, including many who had fought in the Thirty Years War. One of his generals, Prince Rupert of the Rhine, son of his sister Elizabeth, was both a veteran and an excellent strategist. Charles's army was well armed and provisioned, in part due to the king's own revenues, but also because of assistance from his noble supporters and from continental supporters who were appalled by the idea of an anointed king being opposed by commoners. In contrast, the Parliamentary army was ragtag and amateur. It was primarily composed of Puritans who were fighting for the cause, but with little or no previous military experience.

The first battles showed the disparity. Charles won an easy victory at Edgehill and established his headquarters at Oxford. The Royalists attempted to march on the Thames Valley but the Parliamentarians managed to muster over twenty thousand men to stand against the king. The king's forces had no choice but to turn back to Oxford. Early in 1643 Henrietta Maria returned to England, bringing with her four thousand cavalry and infantry from Holland and eventually joining the king in July. Bristol surrendered to the king, and the next campaign was aimed at the city of Gloucester, which would give the king possession of the west. However, at this point the balance of power began to shift. The Royalists failed to take the city and were engaged by the Parliamentary commander Robert Devereux, third Earl of Essex (son of Elizabeth's one-time favorite) at Newbury. It was a battle decided by artillery. The king's forces had insufficient gunpowder and were forced again to withdraw. Both sides were looking for allies (the Royalists now welcomed any Irish support and the Parliamentarians looked to an alliance with the Scots). Meanwhile, a leader was emerging from the Parliamentarian ranks who meant to bring order and discipline to Parliament's army. His name was Oliver Cromwell.

Cromwell's reform of the army was nothing short of astonishing. From a ragtag group of tradesmen and farmers who knew little about fighting, Cromwell created what was in fact a model army. He insisted on the strictest of discipline, based upon Puritan precepts. His soldiers marched into battle singing psalms, and any soldier who swore could be court-martialed and executed. Unlike the mercenaries who made up most of the armies of early modern Europe, the New Model Army was made up of men who trusted in their cause and fervently believed that God was on their side. Once Cromwell implemented a sound organization and made sure that they were well armed, well trained, and paid regularly, Parliament's Army quickly became unstoppable.

SCOTLAND

As in England, the conflict in Scotland was a true civil war, with Scots divided between support for Puritanism and for the king. Additionally, Scotland was still militantly divided over the issue of episcopacy versus presbyterianism in church government. Although there had been nearly universal support for the National Covenant (except among a few recusant families) the situation began to change in September of 1643. A treaty was concluded between the Army of the Covenant and the English Parliamentarians, and a new document, the Solemn League and Covenant, was drawn up. As part of the military alliance with the Parliamentarians, this document promised to make presbyterianism mandatory in both England and Scotland. It also expressly challenged the king's authority. The terms deprived about two thousand Anglican clergy of their benefices and divided the Scots Covenanters.

Some of those who had signed the original National Covenant nonetheless believed in the authority of the king, and some believed in episcopal organization. These men now refused to sign the Solemn League and Covenant. Among them was James Graham, Marquess of Montrose. In the early days of the Civil War in England, Montrose had offered to raise an army for the king, but Charles was not interested. Meanwhile, Montrose had fought for the Covenant. He was a complex, impassioned young man, newly home from a grand tour of the Continent, and in outlook as well as the geography of his estates, he stood

James Graham, first Marquess of Montrose after Honthorst. Montrose was a strong believer in divine right monarchy and as the king's lieutenant general led a combined army of Irish and Scottish Royalists to many victories against the Covenanting Parliamentarians in Scotland. He was defeated at the Battle of Carbisdale and was later captured, brought to trial, and executed.

somewhere between Highland and Lowland politics. He was Protestant and believed the Scots should have the right to decide the structures of their religious observance and on those grounds had signed the National Covenant. As events would show, however, he believed in episcopal organization, not presbyterian, and he was an ardent believer in the rights of monarchy.

Once the Covenanting Army had effectively won the Bishops' Wars (so-called because of the central conflict over episcopal versus presbyterian religious organization), it determined that Parliament instead of the king should rule Scotland. Presbyterianism and anti-Royalism were now synonymous, and from the Highland perspective, the declaration of Archibald Campbell, eighth Earl and later Marquess of Argyll, for Covenant and Parliament meant that any of the Scottish clans and nobility who opposed the Campbell rise to power were now turned against the Army of the Covenant.

In the summer of 1641 Montrose wrote a letter to King Charles, professing his loyalty, but the letter was intercepted by Argyll, and Montrose spent the next two years in jail while Argyll received further acclaim and eventually a marquisate. Probably Argyll eventually decided that Montrose was no threat and he

Archibald Campbell, first Marquess of Argyll. Campbell, nicknamed Archibald the Sullen, supported the Parliamentarian cause in Scotland in opposition to Montrose. After the Restoration Argyll was found guilty of treason and executed.

was released to return home. Finally in November 1643, Montrose met with the king at Oxford. Charles, desperate, and perhaps recognizing the authenticity of Montrose's loyalty, granted him a marquisate and appointed him lieutenant general of the king's army in Scotland. Unfortunately the king had no troops to offer.

It could not have looked more hopeless when Montrose crossed into Scotland with two companions and four horses. The Army of the Covenant, under the Earl of Levin, controlled the Lowlands and had already hired any mercenaries who were available. Argyll was in complete control of the west with his orders of fire and sword against the loyal clans, the Mackenzies held the east for the Covenant, and the clans of the central Highlands were divided and without leadership. Montrose had stopped at Tullibardine with his kinsman Black Pate Graham when a frantic message came from an unlikely source. A small Irish army, sent by Lord Antrim, was in need of immediate help. Its commander was technically a Scot—Alasdair, son of Coll Ciotach of Colonsay in the Inner Hebrides—but he was perceived by most Scots as an Irishman.

From the days of the Lordship of the Isles Clan Donald had straddled the Irish Sea, and when his father was displaced from his Hebridean holdings, Alasdair fled to his kinsman Lord Antrim in Ulster. He was Catholic and had already been involved in the 1641 Irish Rising. He had been sent back to Scotland with a small army of sixteen hundred men to serve the Royalist cause and to launch an invasion against the Campbells. He and his men had been ravaging Kintyre and Ardnamurchan for a short time, but they now found themselves surrounded by the hostile Scottish clans of the central Highlands. In desperation, Alasdair sent a message to Montrose, whom he believed was in Carlisle. As chance would have it, his messenger happened to ask Black Pate for directions. Montrose, only twenty miles to the south, sent a message back to the astonished Irish commander, telling him he would join him at Blair Atholl. Battle was barely averted between the Irish and the hostile Athollmen by the timely arrival of the young marquess. For this occasion, Montrose wore Highland dress, and accompanied only by Black Pate, appeared between the two hostile armies. The Athollmen recognized him and a great cheer went up. They and the confused, half-starved Irish soldiers forgot their battle and all pledged their support to Montrose. The king's lieutenant general now had an army, and the connection between Irish and Scottish affairs intensified.

It has been said that only three men ever successfully united the Highlands: Montrose; another Graham, "Bonnie Dundee" of the 1689 rising; and "Bonnie" Prince Charlie, the Stuart prince of 1745. None of the three were Highlanders themselves. The Highland clans that now rallied to Montrose's cause were somewhat united in their views toward monarchy and non-presbyterian religion (some had remained Catholic and others were Episcopalian). Primarily, though, they were united in their fear and hatred of Clan Campbell. Both Montrose and Alasdair MacColla had great charisma, although in very different ways. Montrose had the poise and polished charm of a courtier—a cavalier in the best of terms—and MacColla, accompanied by Iain Lom, bard of the MacDonalds, was celebrated as a traditional heroic Gaelic chieftain. (The story goes that MacColla once asked the poet if he would fight in battle, and Iain Lom replied in a perfect quatrain, *"cathaichidh sibh-se is innsidh mise"* ["you do the fighting and I'll do the recording"].)

Montrose's army, for all of its challenges, was in some ways superior to the Army of the Covenant. It was small, probably never numbering more than twenty-two hundred, and it was chronically short on supplies. The advantage, however, was that both the Irishmen and the Highlanders were used to a hard life lived in the hills. They were in superb physical condition, and their style of fighting did not rely on large numbers or supply trains of equipment. Each soldier carried his own weapons and a supply of oatmeal for sustenance, and his belted plaid could serve him as blanket, coat, or tent as needed. Moreover, although the Lowlands and England had been without war for enough generations that retraining was essential, the Irish and the Highlanders lived lives of warfare and cattle raiding in which their military skills were well polished. Most perplexing to their opponents (as would also be the case in later campaigns), their base of operations was in the hills wherever they went, and so it could not be taken. Montrose understood and respected the peculiar virtues of his Highland army and was able to make use of it against astonishing odds. In what was termed the Year of Miracles in Gaelic poetry, Montrose was able to gain a series of victories against the mostly second-line troops of the Covenant.

By midwinter, Montrose had worked out an audacious plan to simultaneously serve the Royalist cause, strike a blow at Clan Campbell, and further unite the Highlanders and Irishmen. There was an old Campbell boast that the fortress of the chieftain was impenetrable: "it was a far cry to Loch Awe" and an even farther cry to Inveraray Castle where the Marquess of Argyll had secured himself. Argyll was confident that the mountain passes could not be crossed in winter. Suddenly, wild-eyed shepherds rushed into the streets of Inveraray town shouting that the MacDonalds were upon them. Argyll, never noted for his bravery, raced to his galley and fled down Loch Fyne as Montrose and his army swept down from Glen Shira. The army had outflanked Argyll's and Glenorchy's troops and had somehow crossed the impassable mountainous terrain of the Great Glen. The Campbells, without their chieftain, immediately surrendered. The sacking of Inveraray and the subsequent Royalist victory at the Battle of Inverlochy went a long way toward satisfying MacDonald grudges. One seventeenth century historian remarked of the Campbells that they were "stout and gallant men, worthy of a better chief and a juster cause." For the time being, the military power of Clan Campbell was broken.

More victories followed for Montrose at Auldearn, Alford, and Kilsyth. The Covenanting lords fled and it appeared that Montrose was going to be able to claim all of Scotland for King Charles. On July 14, 1645, the total defeat of the king's army in England at the Battle of Naseby meant that he was entirely dependent on Montrose. However, on September 13, Montrose's Year of Miracles came to an end. Now campaigning in the Lowlands, with unseasoned Lowland troops, Montrose suffered cataclysmic defeat at the Battle of Philiphaugh. The triumphant Covenanters celebrated by butchering the women and children who followed Montrose's army. Montrose himself fled to the north, and failing to gain support, finally escaped to Norway in July 1646.

It was a sad end for all the major participants. King Charles surrendered to the Scots Parliamentarians, perhaps believing that they would be more lenient to a Stuart king. They promptly handed him over to the English. In 1647, the brave and reckless Alasdair MacColla was killed in a minor skirmish in Ireland. He was surrounded by fourteen Parliamentarians and stabbed in the back. Montrose returned to Scotland in 1650, making one last effort in the name of Royalism. He was forced to campaign in the unfamiliar territory of Caithness with only a handful of men. He was defeated at the battle of Carbisdale and took to the hills as a fugitive. He was found and betrayed by Neil MacLeod of Assynt and taken south to Edinburgh to stand trial. The result was a foregone conclusion. In May, by orders of the Scottish Estates Montrose was found guilty of treason and sentenced to be executed. On his way to the scaffold, he passed Lord Moray's house. Inside, peeking through half-closed shutters, was his old enemy, the Marquess of Argyll. Eleven years later, by order of Lord Protector Cromwell, Argyll was himself executed and his lands confiscated. Montrose's last words from the scaffold—"God have mercy on this afflicted land"—came to have great significance during the years of Cromwell's rule in Scotland.

CHARLES'S TRIAL AND EXECUTION

The surrender of the king had come at the moment that Parliament was further fragmenting and becoming more radicalized. By this time a number of revolutionary sects had formed, indicating the range of social upheaval taking place within British society. The derisively nicknamed Quakers and Ranters worshipped in ways that were viewed as extreme by moderate Anglicans; Levelers wanted an entirely egalitarian society, whereas Diggers supported the idea of agricultural communes. The Fifth Monarchy Men saw in the events of their day the coming of the Apocalypse. Within Parliament itself there was no longer any place for moderates. The more radical Puritans gained control over the body and in 1648 locked the moderates out of the meeting rooms. The remainder, known as the Rump Parliament, was composed of only sixty men of the original five hundred of the Long Parliament. It was the Rump that controlled the trial of the king.

Charles argued that it was an illegal action. Even at this point, Charles was still talking of divine right monarchy. He refused to plead on the grounds that he was not subject to the jurisdiction of Parliament, but only to the authority of God. The trial lasted only a week. Charles was found guilty, and on the cold morning of January 30, 1649, he was executed by order of Parliament. He wore two shirts under his doublet so that he would not shiver. Whatever his shortcomings may have been, on that day Charles did not lack bravery or dignity. There was a great crowd assembled, so noisy that no one could hear the oration the king had prepared. But as the axe fell, there was a moment of silence and then a great groan burst from the crowd. Monarchs had been executed before. Charles's grandmother Mary had been executed . . . but by order of another monarch. Never before had a king been executed by commoners. The execution shook the entire foundation of both Church and state. An English minister wrote that day, "These are times of shaking, and the shaking is universal."

THE COMMONWEALTH AND PROTECTORATE

With Charles gone, rule in England was assumed by the leader of the Model Army and now leader of the Rump Parliament, Oliver Cromwell. The title he took was lord protector. Technically England was a commonwealth from 1649 to 1653 and a protectorate from 1653 to 1660. Parliament now claimed the right to all power in the land. The House of Lords was abolished and authority rested with the Rump Parliament and the Council of State. The army, led by Cromwell, remained intact. Cromwell began a pacification program aimed at subduing any lingering Royalist sentiment. Anything that suggested popery was forbidden, and one historian has called this period the Triumph of the Saints in reference to the enforcement of Calvinist godliness on the entire population. The theaters were closed; any entertainments such as dancing, singing, or gambling were deemed criminal acts; and even the celebration of Christmas was outlawed. Throughout the Three Kingdoms, complete adherence to Puritanism was the goal. Even in Wales, which had been only marginally involved in the War of the

Statue of Oliver Cromwell, lord protector of England, Ireland, and Scotland. As leader of the Parliamentarians during the War of Three Kingdoms, Cromwell founded the New Model Army and eventually defeated the forces of Charles I. After the king's arrest and subsequent execution, Cromwell took control, insisting on a Puritan regime and leading a brutal pacification campaign in the regions that had supported the king.

Three Kingdoms, Puritan tenets were forcibly extended through the establishment of English-speaking schools and radical sectarianism.

In Ireland the civil war continued and Cromwell came personally to subdue the Irish. Perhaps the most notorious and still-remembered episode was the siege and massacre of Drogheda in 1649. When the town garrison refused to surrender to Cromwell, he ordered all the inhabitants to be killed and the town set on fire. The numbers are uncertain; probably more than two thousand civilians were killed outright and several hundred more who eventually surrendered were executed after having been promised quarter. Cromwell encouraged his army to kill priests wherever they could be found, and again at Wexford he ordered the massacre of over two thousand Irish, including men, women, and children. Cromwell noted that the massacres were "a righteous judgment of God upon these barbarous wretches." The Irish finally surrendered and in 1652 a series of acts was passed confiscating the land held by Irish Catholics—about two million acres. Irish Catholics were forcibly cleared from the land, with a few being allowed to seek military service on the Continent, but many more were forcibly transported to plantations in North America and the West Indies. Those still remaining in Ireland were forcibly moved to the barren lands of the far west—"to hell or Connacht" as the saying went.

In Scotland a similar pacification program took place. Immediately upon the death of Charles, the Scots declared his son Charles II (living in exile at The Hague) as their king, reminding the English that there had been no formal union of the two kingdoms and they were free to do as they chose. Cromwell disagreed and came to Scotland with sixteen thousand men to change their minds. The psalm-singing troopers of Cromwell killed three thousand Scots and took ten thousand prisoner. Still the Scots refused to surrender. Charles II agreed to the Scottish covenants and came north to be crowned at Scone. The Scottish army was assembling at Stirling, and with great deviousness, Cromwell allowed them to believe his southern flank was unprotected. They marched into England, where they were promptly surrounded by Cromwell's army and defeated. Many were forced to surrender at Worcester, and many others were killed in the Battle of Dunbar. Charles managed to escape back to the Continent, and as with the Irish, many of the Scots prisoners were sold into slavery and deported to America and the West Indies. Cromwell thanked God for "a crowning mercy." Scotland was now occupied by an English army under General George Monck.

Back in England, Cromwell and Parliament continued to negotiate terms for the ruling of Britain without a king. (Parliament in fact offered the crown to Cromwell, but after great prayer and meditation he refused.) In May 1657 a new constitution was written, "The Humble Petition and Advice," giving Cromwell the power to name his own successor. He named his son Richard and suggested that a hereditary succession would be best. Parliament also constituted a second chamber, but because it was a mixture of noblemen, army men, and a few members chosen from the Rump, there was no agreement on what to call it. It was clearly not the House of Lords (a concept not wanted by Parliament in any case) and was usually called simply the Other House. Although he did not take the title of king, Cromwell started appearing in purple and ermine and carrying a scepter.

On September 3, 1658, Cromwell died. His son Richard succeeded him and took the title of lord protector. In personality he was very different from his father and was not particularly interested in government. He called Parliament only once in 1659. Irreconcilable differences between the army and Parliament quickly became apparent, with the army wishing to continue its dominance. Richard tried to arbitrate between the civilians and the army but with little success. He dissolved the Parliament in April and abdicated in May.

With no other leadership apparent, General Monck took the initiative. He left Scotland with a small army and headed south. Back in London he reconvened the Rump and called back as many of the original members of the Long Parliament as were still alive. (It was still a legal assembly because the original Parliament called by Charles I had never been dissolved.) The story goes that Monck galloped his horse into the assembly room and leaped on the table where he stood guard until the members that had been disbarred by the Rump could reassemble. Under the watchful eye of the army, the Convention Parliament called for the restoration of Charles Stuart. In a statement issued at Breda, Charles II agreed, promising "amnesty and oblivion" for those who had rebelled against his father and religious toleration for all. It was a triumphal return of the Stuart monarchy, but in fact, everything had changed. Charles I had never failed to point out that he was king by the grace of God. Charles II was king by the grace of Parliament and he never forgot it.

SUGGESTED READING

Ashton, Robert. *The English Civil War: Conservatism and Revolution, 1603–1649*. London: Littlehampton Book Services, 1978.

Barnard, T. C. *Cromwellian Ireland*. Oxford: Oxford University Press, 1975.

Bennett, Martyn. *The Civil Wars Experienced: Britain and Ireland, 1638–61*. London: Routledge, 2000.

Blackie, Ruth. *Montrose, Covenanter, Royalist, and Man of Principle*. Edinburgh: Birllinn, 1996.

Buchan, John. *Montrose*. Cambridge, MA: Houghton Mifflin, 1928.

Carleton, Charles. *Archbishop William Laud*. London: Routledge and Kegan Paul, 1987.

Clarke, Aidan. *The Old English in Ireland, 1625–42*. Ithaca, NY: Cornell University Press, 1966.

Fitzpatrick, Brendan. *Seventeenth-Century Ireland: The War of Religions*. Totowa, NJ: Rowman & Littlefield, 1989.

Fletcher, Anthony. *The Outbreak of the English Civil War*. London: Edward Arnold, 1981.

Gaunt, Peter. *Oliver Cromwell*. London: Blackwell, 1996.

Hibbert, Christopher. *Charles I*. New York: Routledge, 1968.

Hill, Christopher. *The Century of Revolution, 1603–1714*. Edinburgh: Nelson, 1961.

Hirst, Derek. *England in Conflict, 1603–1660*. London: Bloomsbury Academic, 1999.

Kishlansky, Mark. *The Rise of the New Model Army*. London: Cambridge University Press, 1979.

Macinnes, Allan. *Charles I and the Making of the Covenanting Movement*. Edinburgh: Donald, 1991.

Mitchison, Rosalind. *From Lordship to Patronage: Scotland, 1603–1745*. London: Edward Arnold, 1983.

Ohlmeyer, Jane, ed. *Kingdom or Colony, Political Thought in Seventeenth-Century Ireland*. Cambridge: Cambridge University Press, 2000.

Perceval-Maxwell, Michael. *The Outbreak of the Irish Rebellion of 1641*. Dublin: Four Courts Press, 1994.

Russell, Conrad. *The Causes of the English Civil War*. Oxford: Clarendon Press, 1990.

Sharpe, Kevin. *The Personal Rule of Charles I*. New Haven, CT: Yale University Press, 1992.

Stevenson, David. *Alasdair MacColla and the Highland Problem in the Seventeenth Century*. Edinburgh: Donald, 1980.

Stone, Laurence. *Causes of the English Revolution, 1529–1642*. New York: Routledge and Kegan Paul, 1972.

Chapter 13

From Restoration to Revolution

Diarist John Evelyn described the triumphal entrance of Charles II into the city of London at the end of May 1660: "[Members of the army] were brandishing their swords and shouting with inexpressible joy; the ways strewed with flowers, the bells ringing, the streets hung with tapestry, fountains running with wine." Cromwell's Rule of the Saints had come to an end, and Britain rejoiced. Yet less than thirty years later, another revolution would take place, ending the rule of the Stuart dynasty forever. What happened?

CHARLES II, THE MERRY MONARCH

Charles came to the throne at thirty years of age, having learned well many of the lessons of politics during his long exile. He understood that Parliament had truly won the War of the Three Kingdoms, and although the Stuart monarchy was being restored it was with very different terms and expectations. Unlike his father, Charles II was willing to compromise and dissemble. His moral stance was about as different as possible from the restrictive and godly rule of the Puritans. Charles's court was lavish and often dissolute. In 1662 he married Catherine of Braganza, disliked by the English because she was Catholic. She attempted to produce an heir, but after three miscarriages had no more children. She presided over a lively and fashionable court, bringing back color and style to the somber puritanical clothing of the commonwealth period. She is also credited with introducing the English to the custom of drinking tea. Charles's personal morals were notably lax, and the queen's ladies-in-waiting proved to be an excellent source of royal mistresses. Perhaps most notable was Barbara Villiers, later granted the title of Lady Castlemaine. She gave birth to Charles's son about five weeks after the queen's arrival in England. She exercised a great deal of influence over Charles during his entire reign.

Other mistresses were passing fancies. With Charles, the theaters of England, which had been closed by the Puritans, opened again, and he was fond of both the plays and the actresses. Moll Davis was a singer and actress. Diarist Samuel Pepys's wife called her "the most impertinent slut in the world." She had a daughter by the king, but was ousted from her position by Nell Gwynne, another actress. Nell became one of the king's enduring favorites, although she had a lively competition with another of the king's mistresses, Louise de Kérouaille, of French noble birth. Louise referred to Nell as "the common

Charles II from the studio of John Michael Wright. Charles II became king in 1660 through the Restoration settlement, which restored the Stuart monarchs to the thrones of England, Ireland, and Scotland.

orange wench" (for her previous career as an orange seller outside the theater) and Nell called Louise "Squintabella" for a slightly crossed eye. For the most part, the people of England (aside from the remaining Puritans) were amused and fascinated by the escapades of the royal court and often took sides in support of one mistress or another. Louise was not popular, because of both her superior attitude and her Catholicism (she was regarded, probably rightly, as trying to convert Charles). Nell was low born, but witty and good hearted. Samuel Pepys recounted that one day, as the royal coach, occupied by Nell, drove by Whitehall, the people on the streets booed. She stopped the coach and got out, saying, "Peace, good people; I am the Protestant whore!" The boos changed to cheers.

Despite the overall high spirits and exuberance of the Restoration period, there were many serious undertones in the reestablishment of government after the Wars of the Three Kingdoms. The Convention Parliament of 1660 provided for amnesty to be given to all who had fought against Charles I except the surviving twenty-six regicides, who were executed in 1660. The land settlements were complicated and often impossible to resolve. Estates that had been confiscated outright could be restored, but land that had been sold to pay taxes or raise armies and now was legally held by others could not. Some of the Royalists who had lost land in this manner sought redress through the courts but often there was no equitable solution. Some believed that Charles could have done

Samuel Pepys. Pepys is best known for his extensive diary detailing life in Restoration London. He was witness to the plague of 1665 and the Great Fire of London in 1666. Professionally he was a member of Parliament and chief secretary to the Admiralty under both Charles II and James II. He was also a member of the Royal Society.

more to aid his father's former supporters, but Crown finances still were such that he could not purchase all of the disputed lands and redistribute them.

During the 1660s, a settlement was finally reached concerning royal revenues. It was acknowledged that the king could not live on his own revenue and an annual income was assigned, although revenues still fell short of what was actually needed. New taxes were introduced (particularly on the fashionable new consumables such as tea, coffee, and chocolate, as well as wine and beer) and new property taxes were levied. Clergymen were no longer privileged (exempt from taxation), and effectively the old remnants of feudalism disappeared from the political and economic landscape of England.

Religious matters had been deferred until the election of a new Parliament. This occurred in 1661 and the assembly met continuously until 1679. It is referred to as the Long Parliament of the Restoration or the Cavalier Parliament because it was so heavily Royalist and Anglican. The religious settlement produced by this Parliament is known as the Clarendon Code, although it was not in fact written by Charles's adviser, the Duke of Clarendon. The settlement was not very tolerant of nonconformity (Catholic or Puritan). It imposed religious tests on those holding government offices, effectively excluding anyone who was not Anglican, and the Act of Uniformity enacted in 1665 as part of the Clarendon Code brought back the 1662 *Book of Common Prayer*, slightly modified but with no concessions to the Puritans. (This version remained in use in England until the late twentieth century.) Clergy were obliged to swear that they would use the *Book of Common Prayer* in conducting services and the two thousand or so who refused were dismissed from their positions. The Clarendon Code also forbade the holding of conventicles and preaching by unlicensed ministers within five miles of a town. The Clarendon Code did acknowledge for the first time the permanent existence of nonconformists and did not make these groups illegal as they had been previously. However, they were disadvantaged in terms of official positions and sometimes landholding (a particular issue in Ireland). Charles attempted to introduce a Declaration of Indulgence, which would have granted pardons to those nonconformists (both Catholic and Puritan dissenters) who violated the Clarendon Code, but he was opposed by Parliament.

RESTORATION IN THE OTHER KINGDOMS

Charles ascended the throne as king of England, Ireland, Scotland, Wales, and France. The French title was purely honorific, and effectively Wales had been long incorporated into English politics. Nonetheless, most of Wales had been a stronghold of Charles I and the Welsh continued to honor his memory and his martyrdom, particularly through commemoration of the anniversary of his execution. Many of the Welsh welcomed the Restoration in hopes of redressing their grievances toward Cromwell and his policy of enforced anglicization.

In Ireland, the fabric of land ownership and settlement had been so torn apart by Cromwell's pacification that there was little that could be done to turn back the clock. The English Parliament ratified Cromwell's confiscations, including a clause that land belonging to the Anglican church, colleges, and "innocents" (noncombatants) was to be restored. A very few Old English Catholics managed to regain part of their estates under these terms but for most of them the Restoration brought little relief. Enforcement of the Clarendon Code closed Jesuit schools, and an Irish Act of Uniformity required the use of the same *Book of Common Prayer* as in England, problematic not only to the majority recusant population, but also to many of the Ulster Scots who continued to favor the Scottish Calvinist practices.

In Scotland, the Act of Uniformity was a major problem. The return to the structures of 1633 meant that the presbyterian changes of the Solemn League and Covenant and Cromwell's subsequent regime were overturned and episcopacy was again reestablished. Scottish ministers who did not agree to these terms were dismissed, leaving vacant over a third of the Scottish parishes. These nonconforming ministers frequently continued to preach to their congregations, often in conventicles, which were outlawed under the Clarendon Code.

In Scotland, the old political rivalries and hostilities also persisted and revived. Montrose's nemesis, Archibald the Sullen, Marquess of Argyll, was executed in 1661, but his son took over his father's position and ambitions, seeking to rule the Highlands as an instrument of government. Some clans in the Highlands remained Catholic, and the failure of the Clarendon Code to provide toleration led to further disenfranchisement of the Catholic chieftains. In the

Lowlands, armed resistance by the nonconforming congregations and retaliation against those who still believed in the Covenant further divided the Scots. A poignant monument stands in the Hamilton Kirkyard, commemorating four martyrs of the Covenant who were executed in 1666. It reads, "Stay, passenger take notice what thou reads; At Edinburgh lie our bodies, here our heads. Our right hands stood at Lanark, those we want, because with them we sware the Covenant." The impassioned Scots Presbyterians continued to stand for their beliefs, and armed revolution between presbyterian and episcopal positions eventually led to the Killing Times of the 1680s, a period of sectarian violence that was arguably the lowest point of Charles's reign.

In Scotland, unlike England, the Restoration did not bring increased prosperity, but rather a slide into worsening poverty as the Navigation Acts reduced the amount of import revenue into Scotland. (The Navigation Acts formed the basis of British international trade policies for more than two centuries. One of the stipulations of the Act of 1663 was that all goods must be shipped through England. This was understood to include Wales, but not Scotland, until after the Act of Union in 1707.) Given the amount of social turmoil and economic disarray in Scotland, it is perhaps not surprising that the period from 1660 through the 1680s was notable for its witch trials, political executions, and deportations.

RESTORATION LONDON

In England the period from the 1660s through the 1680s was also turbulent. England was engaged in a series of wars against the Dutch (primarily involving Dutch demands for trade concessions). Clarendon was blamed for bungling the Second Dutch War, which resulted in the victory of the Dutch. The Treaty of Breda, signed at the end of this war in 1667, granted trade concessions to the Dutch (effectively elevating them to commercial supremacy during the seventeenth century) and transferred New Netherlands (which would become New York) to the English. Parliament began impeachment proceedings against Clarendon, but he fled to France before he could be brought to trial. After his dismissal, Charles did not appoint a single minister to govern foreign affairs, but rather assumed more direct control himself and also relied on a committee of five advisers, who became known as the *cabal*, a word formed from their initials: Sir Thomas Clifford, Lord Arlington, the Duke of Buckingham, Lord Ashley, and the Earl of Lauderdale.

In 1665 a major outbreak of plague took place. The plague had been endemic since its initial appearance in Europe in the fourteenth century so that periodic reappearances were common, but the one in 1665 was particularly virulent. At its peak, the mortality rate was around seven thousand per week. Daniel Defoe, writing his *Journal of a Plague Year* almost sixty years later, estimated the total mortality at around one hundred thousand, although a contemporary doctor estimated it at twice that number. Samuel Pepys, whose voluminous diary provides us with so much information about the Restoration period, noted his own horror-stricken reaction to the plague year. Among other observations, he recorded a journey by hackney coach on June 16. The driver started going slower and slower and finally stopped. He got out and said that he was "suddenly stroke very sick and almost blind." "God have mercy on us all," Pepys said and got into another coach.

The following year, another disaster struck. On September 1, 1666, when shutting down the great ovens at Pudding Lane, a baker somehow missed an ember. It had been an exceptionally dry summer and only a brisk breeze was needed to blow the ember into a flame. The Great Fire of London burned for four days and destroyed about four-fifths of the city of London. The king and his brother James, Duke of York, brought in sailors and other workers to try to make firebreaks and fight the fire, but all in vain. Samuel Pepys, in an agony lest his property and offices be destroyed, kept close watch on the progress of the fire, traveling up and down the river by any means possible and giving us an amazing eye-witness account. He had sent his wife, servants, and best furniture to safety up the river (and quickly buried his best wine in the garden for safe-keeping), but he lingered to watch over his remaining property. He was lucky. The Navy Office from which he worked was left standing, as was his house, but St. Paul's Cathedral was roofless, with a great charred heap of what once were houses beside it. The medieval guildhall was gone, as were the post office, Newgate Prison, and the city administration buildings. Almost the whole old city— 436 acres—"lay buried in its own ruins" and approximately 13,200 houses were gone, in addition to shops and businesses. It is not known how many people died

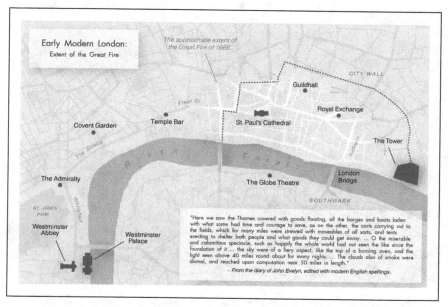

Early modern London, showing the extent of the Great Fire in 1666. This map shows many of the important buildings in London and indicates the areas that were damaged and destroyed by the fire.

in the fire because the Bills of Mortality are missing for that week. One observer wrote, "In three days the most flourishing city in the world is a ruinous heap, the streets only to be known by the maimed remainder of the churches." Sixty miles away in Oxford, Antony Wood wrote in his diary: "The wind being eastwards blew clouds of smoke over Oxon the next day . . . the sunshine was much darkened . . . the moon was darkened by clouds of smoke and looked reddish."

Although the still-superstitious Londoners were quick to blame the fire on Charles's dissolute court, or on the resident foreigners of the city, Charles simply said it was the hand of God and quickly set about trying to assist with relief efforts. The Exchequer moved its offices to Nonsuch Palace and the Navy Office kept functioning. Housing was found for those in need and the massive job began of clearing the rubble to rebuild. The site of St. Paul's was cleared completely (a huge undertaking because the remaining stone rubble had been cemented together by the lead that melted and flowed downward during the fire). The guildhall was carefully dismantled so that any timbers that were sound could be reused. London Bridge had been blocked by debris, but only the north end had burned. The bridge was quickly cleared and repaired. Shopkeepers relocated and reopened their shops as quickly as possible. The king and the Navy Office tried to provide food to the Londoners in the form of ship's

St. Paul's Cathedral, view from the southeast. This image shows the new St. Paul's, built under the direction of the architect Sir Christopher Wren after the old St. Paul's was completely destroyed in the fire, crumpling into a pile of stone fused together with the lead from the roof.

biscuit (hardtack) but it was declined. The people were not prepared to eat the unpalatable food, and because "the markets were so well supplied," it was "returned to his Majesty's stores, without any use made of it."

The rebuilding began immediately. A week after the fire, Charles promised that the city would be rebuilt—"a much more beautiful city than that consumed"—and statutes also were quickly enacted to ensure that the new buildings would meet certain specifications. Buildings were to be made of brick or stone, with no balconies jutting out over the street as had been the medieval custom. There were height regulations imposed, and street lines were surveyed. Properties not built upon within seven years could be sold. By 1671 nearly seven thousand new houses were constructed and the guildhall had been rebuilt. The rebuilding of St. Paul's took time and was not completed until 1711, but the masterful hand of the architect, Sir Christopher Wren, who oversaw all the rebuilding, was evident throughout the new city.

SCIENCE AND CULTURE

Wren was a professor at Oxford and his outlook and career illustrate a new kind of cultural and intellectual age that was emerging during the third quarter of the seventeenth century. Many historians have come to dislike the oft-used

Panorama of London, showing the skyline as it appeared following the great rebuilding. Note the prominence of Wren's great dome of St. Paul's. The rebuilding was done according to specific statutes that resulted in a much more attractive and safe city than that which had existed prior to the fire.

term Scientific Revolution. Science is a modern concept and it is highly misleading to suggest that all of a sudden Europe became scientific. The contemporary term would have been *natural philosophy*, a concept and outlook that more rightly span the Middle Ages to the eighteenth century. The natural philosophers of the seventeenth century were to some degree inventing the idea of empiricism, but they were also still greatly influenced by hermeticism and Neoplatonism (mystical systems of thought based on ancient writings and the belief that the universe could be understood through secrets contained in nature). We may find it confusing, but the thinkers of the seventeenth century saw no contradiction in intellectual systems that blended empirical observation with theology or used alchemy to understand cosmology. Robert Boyle, who conducted studies of Highland second sight (precognition), and Sir Isaac Newton, who practiced alchemy alongside his better known studies, are excellent examples of this philosophical outlook.

In November 1660, shortly after his accession, Charles provided a charter for the Royal Society of London for Improving Natural Knowledge, usually referred to as the Royal Society. It consisted of a group of men, physicians and natural philosophers, who were influenced by the new science (empirical observation) of Francis Bacon. The group had been meeting since 1645. Early members included Robert Hooke, Robert Boyle, Christopher Wren, mathe-

Robert Boyle, 1689. Boyle was an Anglo-Irish natural philosopher best known for his work on hydrostatics, optics, and chemistry. As a founding member of the Royal Society, he represented the combination of philosophy and science that characterizes the seventeenth century scientific community.

Charter of the Royal Society, detail. Founded in 1660, the purpose of the Royal Society was to bring together natural philosophers who supported the new empirical methods of investigation. Its foundation is often described as a cornerstone of the Scientific Revolution.

matician and political theorist Thomas Hobbes, and Edward Halley. In the 1680s Samuel Pepys served as president of the Royal Society. Arguably one of the greatest minds of the seventeenth century, Sir Isaac Newton was a member of the Royal Society and served as its president in 1703. His most important treatise, "The Principia," was published in 1687. The Royal Society and the growing emphasis on the natural sciences did much to transform scholarship in the seventeenth century and contributed toward the rise of the Enlightenment in the next century.

In addition to the growth of philosophy and science during this period, literature and the arts also flourished. Modern scholars regard Restoration drama as a milestone in the history of the theater. The new type of drama was more realistic than the plays of Shakespeare and Marlowe and utilized female actresses and elaborate sets. Plots were frequently comedic but highly mannered and often incorporated political satire and social observation. Authors such as Congreve and Dryden appealed to audiences with their dry wit. Similarly, in literature, the dark moralizing of John Milton gave way to the biting satire of Andrew Marvell, Daniel Defoe, and the decadent (and often scandalous) verses of John Wilmot, second Earl of Rochester. One of Rochester's more printable verses characterized Charles: "We have a pretty, witty king and whose word no man relies on, he never said a foolish thing and never did a wise one." Charles, indeed not lacking in wit, is said to have responded: "That's true, for my words are my own but my actions are my ministers'." Rochester's writings were thoroughly censored by the Victorians and have only fairly recently been rediscovered. In many ways the literarily talented and amoral Rochester in both his writings and his dissolute life (he died of syphilis at age thirty-three) illustrate well the context of Restoration society. Similarly, the biting satires exemplified by Defoe show an awareness of current events and a tolerance by the Restoration government, allowing public discussion of the issues of the day, even if they were somewhat veiled by the literary devices of satire.

THE POPISH PLOT

In August 1678 a great uproar broke out concerning an alleged plot to assassinate the king. This episode reveals the fragility of the Restoration settlement. Before Parliament Titus Oates revealed the sordid details of a plot by the king's physician to poison the king and put his Catholic brother James on the throne. Many others were implicated, including the Catholic queen, who was accused of treason and imprisoned. Charles did not believe the rumors and, for once, intervened chivalrously on the queen's behalf. Parliament, extremely susceptible to anti-Catholic hysteria, sent five Catholic noblemen to the Tower and executed more than thirty supposed participants in the plot. Titus Oates was viewed as a great hero, and in a flurry of modern-style popular media, his face was printed on lady's fans, snuffboxes, and handkerchiefs, and a grateful Parliament granted him a pension of £1,000 per year. The plot was almost certainly a fabrication, perhaps invented by Oates himself or perhaps orchestrated by someone else, with Oates serving as simply a gullible dupe. Historians view it as very likely that extremist Protestant Whigs (the increasingly strident anti-Catholic party in Parliament) manufactured the whole affair to try to stir up anti-Catholic resentment. In any case it resulted in the dismissal of the now ironically named Cavalier Parliament and soured the last years of Charles's reign.

Desperate for money, Charles was forced to call a new Parliament in 1679. This Parliament marked the triumph of the Whig Party, and Lord Shaftesbury introduced the Exclusion Act, which would debar the king's Catholic brother from inheriting. Charles refused to deny his brother's right and dismissed Parliament. In August Charles fell ill with a fever and doctors affirmed that he was dying. In a panic the Parliament realized its folly. In the event of Charles's death, civil war was virtually inevitable between the forces of his oldest illegitimate son, the popular and Protestant Duke of Monmouth, and his Catholic brother. Charles recovered and Parliament upheld the right of James. In 1681 the Tory Party (Royalist and more religiously tolerant) was in power, supported by the king. Titus Oates's pension was reduced to £2 per year and Shaftesbury was arrested for treason. The king ruled without Parliament for the rest of his reign.

CHARLES'S DEATH

Charles's English subjects had always been suspicious of his personal religious outlook, particularly in light of his Catholic wife. In 1670 Charles signed the secret Treaty of Dover with King Louis XIV of France. (Charles's sister Minette was married to Louis's brother.) The public portion of the Treaty of Dover called for English support of the French against the Dutch, in return for which Louis would grant Charles an annual subsidy. The private portion of the treaty stated that Charles would publicly profess his Catholicism and return England to the faith as soon as was expedient. If there were a rebellion, Louis would send French troops to suppress it. Given Charles's history of occasional duplicity, it is not at all clear how far he intended this to go. It may have been a reflection of his real religious feelings or it may have been merely a diplomatic move.

In 1672 Charles announced a Declaration of Indulgence, granting toleration to both Catholic and Protestant nonconformists, and also announced the beginning of the Third Dutch War. This war was not just commercial and the military expenses produced a near bankruptcy of the English Parliament. Charles was forced to cancel the Act of Indulgence and Parliament implemented the Test Acts, meant to exclude Catholics from political office. James withdrew from the admiralty at that time, publicly acknowledging his Catholicism through his refusal to swear disbelief in transubstantiation. Nothing more was disclosed concerning Charles's own religious views, but in 1685, when he had a stroke and knew he was dying, a Catholic priest was called and administered the last rites. It appeared that Charles died a Catholic, and his acknowledged heir, James, was certainly a Catholic. For the English people, the only saving grace was that James was well advanced in years and his probable heirs, his two daughters Mary and Anne, were safely Protestant.

ACCESSION OF JAMES II OF ENGLAND/VII OF SCOTLAND

James had probably become Catholic as early as 1668 or 1669, but it was not until the Test Acts of 1673 that his conversion became publicly known. He was the first Catholic monarch to take the throne since Mary Tudor (and would prove to be the last Catholic monarch of Britain). The Irish rejoiced over his accession and the Scots' Highlanders, largely Tory in sentiment, either approved of his Catholicism or at least did not object to it. Upon his accession he agreed to abide by the laws governing the established Anglican church. His coronation was conducted by the archbishop of Canterbury, although he had a private Mass celebrated following the public ceremony. His first Parliament went well, granting him generous revenues and refusing to adopt a resolution that would have required him to enforce anti-Catholic legislation.

There were, however, pockets of strong anti-Catholic sentiment, and shortly after James's accession, a rebellion broke out in the west, led by Charles's illegitimate son, the Duke of Monmouth. He had been living in Holland and his invasion in June 1685 was tiny and ineffective (with only about 150 supporters). Monmouth believed that all of England would rally to his cause, but the invasion was ill conceived and poorly executed. When the armies of the king arrived, he was found asleep in a ditch. He was promptly captured and executed. His friend, the ninth Earl of Argyll, was unsuccessful in rallying

James II, by Sir Godfrey Kneller. James II was king from 1685 until his deposition in 1688. He was the last Catholic monarch of Britain and the terms that were set forth at the time of his deposition called for the subsequent exclusion of Catholics from the British monarchy.

Covenanters to the cause and he too was captured and executed. Monmouth's few supporters in the west were badly treated. In a pacification campaign still remembered locally with horror, Judge Jeffries presided over a series of trials called the Bloody Assizes in which more than 150 men were executed and more than 800 sent into slavery in the West Indies.

James's temperament and political outlook was very different from his brother's. In his youth he had had several mistresses, and his marriage to Anne Hyde had been the scandal of the court (she was a commoner and became pregnant but he honored his promise to marry her against the advice of Charles and the court). But by his middle years, he was priggish and moralistic. He was also autocratic and lacking in any humor or personal warmth. As his reign progressed he became less tolerant of compromise and he began implementing various overt pro-Catholic actions, such as appointing Catholics to government positions and overturning the Penal Laws against nonconformists. Although many Englishmen did not like or agree with James's policies, most were content to be patient. After all, it could not be that long until he would be succeeded by his Protestant daughter Mary, who was married to the Protestant Dutch Stadtholder William of Orange.

In 1673, the widower James married a second wife, Mary of Modena. She was of the Italian house of d'Este and was, of course, Catholic. For fifteen years the marriage remained childless, and it was assumed that the aging king would produce no more heirs. However, in June 1688 a great surprise greeted the British people: Mary of Modena was delivered of a son, James Francis Edward Stuart. He was christened by Catholic ritual, and by the laws of English primogeniture he now became heir to the thrones of England, Ireland, Scotland, and Wales. Rumors began flying that the child was a changeling or that he had been smuggled into the palace in a warming pan. A comparison of portraits of the adult James Francis with James II and VII prove without doubt his Stuart ancestry. The arrival of a Catholic male heir changed everything.

In horror at the thought of a Catholic succession, seven Whig leaders, known as the Seven Eminent Persons, decided on a drastic course of action. They invited William of Orange to come to England, depose his father-in-law, and take the throne along with his wife, Mary. In September William agreed. He himself had some measure of claim to the throne: his mother was a sister to Charles II and James II, which he regarded as bolstering Mary's claim (regarded as somewhat dubious given the conditions surrounding the marriage of James and Anne Hyde, as well as the indisputable fact that her mother was a commoner). William was undeniably a Protestant (although of the Dutch Reformed church, not Anglican), and he regarded himself as a champion of the Protestants against Catholic autocrats such as Louis XIV of France (and presumably his father-in-law as well). One of his strongest motivations was international: to strengthen the position of the United Provinces against Louis XIV's France. William's forces arrived in England on November 5, 1688. Guy Fawkes Day was deliberately chosen for its symbolic significance.

Cartoon showing the rumor that James II's son (by his second, Catholic wife) was not legitimate, but was smuggled into the queen's bedroom in a warming pan. There was no real evidence of this, but the story caught the imagination of the English people and it was much alluded to in the popular press of the day.

At first James did not believe in the seriousness of William's actions. He sent his wife and baby son to France, but delayed mustering an army. In December he fled himself. He was disguised as a fisherman but was apprehended by the port authorities at Faversham. They were told to release him and not to interfere, and in a second crossing attempt he escaped to the Continent, flinging the Great Seal into the river Thames to try to avert any official government action.

THE REIGN OF WILLIAM AND MARY

The so-called Glorious or Bloodless Revolution was achieved with apparent ease in England. In James's absence, William and Mary took the throne and a new Parliament was called to uphold their accession. Technically, it could not be called a Parliament because there was no undisputed king to call it; therefore, it is referred to as the Convention Parliament. In January 1689 it convened and began hammering out the political justification and legislation to support James's deposition and William's and Mary's accession to the throne. It was

James Francis Stuart. The son of James II (the alleged "warming pan baby"), James Francis chose to remain Catholic, thus making him ineligible to succeed to the British monarchy. He was the subject of several rebellions (called the Jacobite rebellions from the Latin form of his name) that attempted to restore him to his place in the British succession.

William of Orange, by Sir Peter Lely. Dutch Stadtholder and husband of Mary, the Protestant daughter of James II, William was the victor of the so-called Glorious Revolution that debarred James Francis from succession and put William and Mary jointly on the throne.

complex and the assembly, divided by Whig and Tory, could not agree on the terms. As a group the body did not accept efforts to justify the actions on the grounds of the warming pan theory, nor would they agree to calling James senile or mentally unfit. On the grounds of old anti-Catholic legislation they might have been able to justify Mary's rule, but William demanded equality. If Mary died he intended to continue to rule; therefore, the title of prince consort would not do. At last the assembly turned to the principles of John Locke (a political theorist who never intended his theories to be applied in this manner), arguing that the rights of the people had been violated by James's appointment of Catholics and other actions contrary to their best interests. Additionally, he had fled, and so the throne was vacant, to be filled by whomever the people deemed best. William and Mary were appointed joint rulers, each to rule until death. They would be succeeded by their children, or in the event they had none, by Anne and her heirs. Parliament declared that it was inconsistent for a Protestant kingdom to be ruled by a popish prince, and thus Mary's half-brother James Francis was specifically excluded. The Bill of Rights that was part of the Revolutionary Settlement expressly forbade many of the practices of previous Stuart kings and upheld the primacy of Parliament. The Toleration Act, which was part of this package, provided for toleration of Protestant nonconformists, but new, even more stringent restrictions were placed upon the Catholics.

SCOTLAND

In Scotland the revolution was viewed as neither glorious nor bloodless. When William arrived, the Scots did not offer him their crown, only agreeing that he could administer Scotland until the Scots decided on a course of action. In March William summoned a Convention of the Estates. It was padded with Whig supporters who voted to offer the crown to William and Mary. This convention composed a "Claim of Rights and Articles of Grievances" against James and imposed new regulations on the Scots. The Regalia of Scotland (somewhat pathetic in their amount and appearance) were carried south for the coronation.

With the appallingly casual takeover of the Scottish monarchy, the unrest in Scotland now spread to armed conflict. King James's standard had already been raised by another gallant Graham, John Graham of Claverhouse, recently created Viscount Dundee and a distant cousin of the great Marquess of Montrose. Dundee was charismatic, and like his kinsman, was able to understand and exploit the potential of the Highlanders. The Highlanders were seeing their way of life increasingly threatened by the southern Whig government, and they upheld the divine right of James the Stuart king. Some of the Highland clans still maintained their Catholicism, and some were what came to be known as non-juring Episcopalians for their refusal to take an oath of loyalty to William and Mary. Neither group liked the encroachment on Scottish rights and liberties. The close alignment of the Campbells with Whiggish politics also alienated a number of the Highland clans, who chose to stand firm for King James. (Their

John Graham, First Viscount Dundee, seventh Laird of Claverhouse. Dundee led a rising of the Highlanders in 1689 in support of James Francis Stuart and in opposition to William and Mary. Depending on political perspective, he was known to his followers as "Bonnie Dundee" and to his enemies as "Bluidy Clavers."

support of the king gave them their nickname of Jacobites from Jacobus, the Latin form of the name James.)

The Jacobites met the Williamites in a great battle at the Pass of Killiecrankie in the Highlands. It was midsummer (July 27, 1689) and both armies had had a short night in which to prepare. Dundee was shaken by bad dreams and portents of failure, but went into battle with the appearance of a gallant hero. The strategy was audacious: The Highlanders remained hidden and silent as the Williamite troops marched into the long glen. Suddenly the Highlanders broke from cover high above the pass, sweeping down from the heights in a ferocious Highland charge. The Williamite troops panicked and threw themselves into the river, preferring drowning to sword blows. Others turned to flee and were caught in the fire of their own troops. When the dust settled it was a glorious Highland victory and a rout of the Williamites. However, victory was short lived. Dundee had read the portents correctly; he died of a single musket shot in the early phases of the battle. Without leadership, the Highlanders withdrew to the hills, still believing in James's cause, but unable to do anything more to oppose the revolution.

IRELAND

James reckoned rightly that his greatest support was likely to come from the Irish and he planned to mount his campaign for restoration from a base of operations in Ireland. Accompanied by a few French troops and with French aid, he landed in Ireland in March 1690. Although James and the Irish people were united in their Catholicism, they were divided by other issues. He had never paid much attention to Irish politics and so did not understand the complexity of relationships and the issues surrounding land ownership and tradition. The Irish troops were ill supplied and poorly trained, and they did not respond well to James's arrogance and autocratic commands. When the Irish force commanded by James met the English army under William's command at the Battle of the Boyne on July 12, 1690, it was a cataclysmic defeat for James and for the Irish. Williamite propaganda soon fashioned the affair into a God-given victory of the Protestants (paintings of the battle show James on a black horse and William on a white one). William entered Dublin in triumph and the Irish Catholics now faced another pacification, including executions, deportations, and the most extreme Penal Codes that they had yet endured. James fled back to France.

AFTERMATH

In England the Revolutionary Settlement provided the terms for peace and prosperity. Whig historians of the eighteenth and nineteenth centuries glorified the revolution and saw it as a triumph of constitutionalism and Protestantism. What that view overlooked were the continuing points of division produced or exacerbated by the events of 1688. Particularly in Ireland and Scotland, political and religious division was made more acute, and both regions began a steady slide into marginalization. In Scotland the Jacobite cause was not forgotten and four times more (in 1715, 1719, 1745, and 1752) the Scots (particularly the Highlanders) went to war to try to restore the rightful (in their opinion) Stuart king, James Francis Stuart. Finally after the failure of "the Forty-five," their distinctive Highland way of life and identity were crushed completely through the imposition of martial laws and the deportation and stripping of power of the remaining Highland chieftains.

In Ireland the revolution ushered in a time of even greater hardship and distress for the vast majority of the population, who remained staunchly Catholic despite the penalties imposed by the Penal Laws. Northern Ireland became even more a land of division, with intensifying hatred and conflict between Catholics and Protestants.

However, the new Britain that was forged from the events of the seventeenth century was well on the way to becoming the dominant power of the eighteenth century. Through a combination of politics, laws, and social and cultural changes, the once distinctive four kingdoms were being melded into one. In 1707 the Union of Parliaments united England and Scotland. Wales had long been incorporated into English politics, and Ireland was de facto under English control, although the relationship remained turbulent. The seventeenth century also marked the beginnings of British overseas expansion and a growing emphasis on the interconnection among trade, manufacture, slavery, and plantation economies. Although true Triangle Trade (the movement between goods and resources and markets) was a product of the eighteenth century, the economic foundations can begin to be seen during the seventeenth century. One can certainly argue for both gains and losses during this volatile time, but the British powerhouse of the modern era was taking shape, one that subsequently would be based on internationalism and an emerging empire.

SUGGESTED READING

Fitzpatrick, Brendan. *Seventeenth-Century Ireland: The War of Religions*. Totowa, NJ: Rowman & Littlefield, 1989.

Fletcher, Anthony. *Reform in the Provinces: The Government of Stuart England*. New Haven, CT: Oxford University Press, 1994.

Fraser, Antonia. *Royal Charles: Charles II and the Restoration*. New York: Knopf, 1979.

Furtado, Peter. *Restoration England: 1660–1699*. Oxford: Bloomsbury, 2010.

Harris, Tim. *London Crowds in the Reign of Charles II*. Cambridge: Cambridge University Press, 1987.

———. *Politics under the Later Stuarts: Party Conflict in a Divided Society, 1660–1715*. London: Longman, 1993.

Hill, Christopher. *The World Turned Upside Down: Radical Ideas during the English Revolution*. London: Penguin Books, 1972.

Hutton, Ronald. *Charles II, King of England, Scotland, and Ireland*. Oxford: Clarendon Press, 1989.

Israel, Jonathan, ed. *The Anglo-Dutch Moment: Essays on the Glorious Revolution and Its World Impact*. Cambridge: Cambridge University Press, 1991.

Jardine, Lisa. *Ingenious Pursuits: Building the Scientific Revolution*. New York: Doubleday, 1999.

Jones, J. R. *Country and Court: England 1658–1714*. London: Edward Arnold, 1978.

Ollard, Richard. *Clarendon and His Friends*. London: Hamish Hamilton, 1987.

Picard, Liza. *Restoration London*. London: Weidenfeld & Nicolson,1997.

Speck, W. A. *Reluctant Revolutionaries: Englishmen and the Revolution of 1688*. Oxford: Oxford University Press, 1988.

Thomas, Keith. *Religion and the Decline of Magic*. London: Penguin Books, 1977.

Westfall, Richard. *Science and Religion in Seventeenth-Century England*. New Haven, CT: Yale University Press, 1958.

Appendix

Genealogical Tables

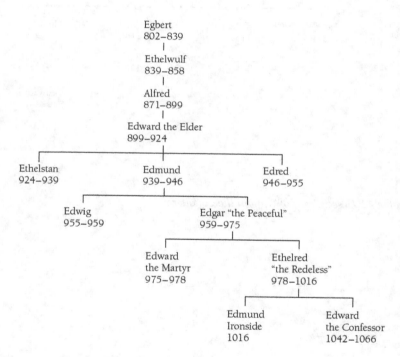

Table A.1 Kings of the House of Wessex

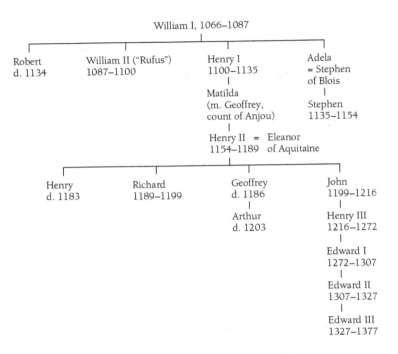

Table A.2 Descendants of William the Conqueror

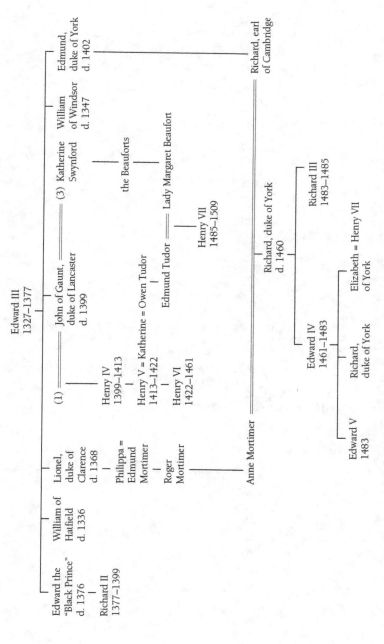

Table A.3 The English Monarchy, 1377–1485

```
               (1)  =  Robert I      = (2)
                  |   1306–1329   |

               Marjorie      David II
                  |            1329–1371
               Robert II
               1371–1390
                  |
               Robert III
               1390–1406
                  |
               James I
               1406–1437
                  |
               James II
               1437–1460
                  |
               James III
               1460–1488
                  |
               James IV = Margaret Tudor
               1488–1513
                  |
               James V      = Mary of Guise
               1513–1542  |  d. 1560

Francis II (1) = Mary, queen of Scots  = (2) Lord Darnley
of France        1542–1567            |  (3) Earl of Bothwell
                                      |

               James VI, 1567–1625
               (James I of England, 1603–1625)
```

Table A.4 The Scottish Monarchy, 1306–1625

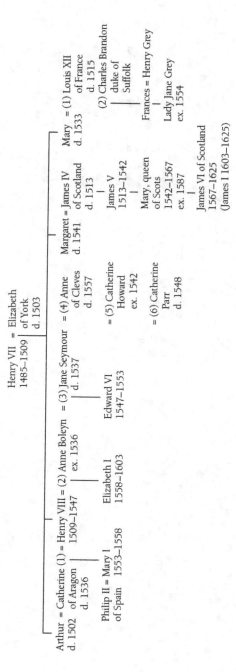

Table A.5 The Tudors

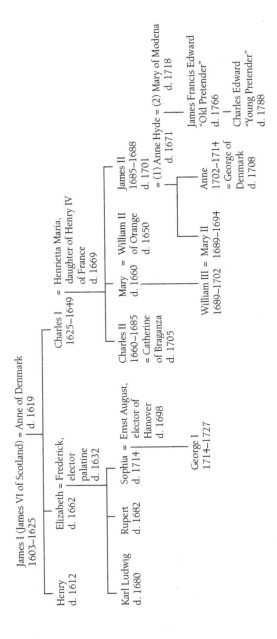

Table A.6 The Stuarts

Illustration Credits

Cover: Victoria and Albert Museum, London/Bridgeman Images.

Chapter 1

Page 7, Newgrange, a Neolithic corbelled stone structure located in the Boyne Valley in Ireland: scenicireland.com/Christopher Hill Photography/Alamy. Page 8, Stonehenge (aerial view), a prehistoric monument located on Salisbury Plain, near the middle of the south coast of England: English Heritage. Page 9, Standing stones of Callanish: Realimage/Alamy. Page 10, Knockfarrel Iron Age hillfort near Dingwall, Scotland: © Cezary Namuski. Page 12, Interior of stone house at Skara Brae, located in the Orkney Islands of Scotland: Roland Knauer/Alamy. Page 14, Replica of Iron Age dwelling from Butser Ancient Farm: Heritage Image Partnership Ltd/Alamy.

Chapter 2

Page 20, Statue of Boudicca on London Bridge: Paul Martin/Alamy. Page 22, Roman baths at Bath, England: Atlantide Phototravel/Corbis. Page 23, Hadrian's Wall, showing one of the adjoining forts: Reproduced by permission of English Heritage.

Chapter 3

Page 32, Shrine of St. Patrick's bell: Tom Bean/Corbis. Page 36, The *Cathach*, Psalter of St. Columcille: © Boltin Picture Library/Bridgeman Images. Page 39, Beehive cell, Skellig Mhicil, Ireland: National Museum of Ireland. Page 41, St. Martin's Cross, Iona, Scotland: Royal Commission on the Ancient and Historical Monuments of Scotland. Page 42, The *Lindisfarne Gospels*, written in Northumbria about 720: British Library. Page 43, The *Book of Kells*: Board of Trinity College, Dublin.

Chapter 4

Page 46, Irish round tower: © Robert Mullan/incamera stock/Corbis. Page 47, The Ardagh Chalice, early eighth century: National Museum of Ireland, Dublin/© Boltin Picture Library/Bridgeman Images. Page 51, Viking Dublin, showing excavations taking place: © Ted Spiegel/CORBIS. Page 52, Rune stone, Iona, Scotland: Crown Copyright HES. Page 53, Tombstones of the Lords of the Isles, Iona, Scotland: Crown Copyright HES. Page 55, Animatronic figure from Jorvik Viking Center, York, England: YORK Archaeological Trust. Page 59, The Bayeux Tapestry: Tapisserie de Bayeux, with special authorization from the City of Bayeux. Page 63, The Pitney Brooch: © The Trustees of the British Museum. Page 64, Sutton Hoo ship burial: © The Trustees of the British Museum.

Chapter 5

Page 67, A ceremony of homage and fealty as depicted in a medieval English manuscript: British Library. Page 74, Effigy of Richard de Clare, "Strongbow," in Christ Church Cathedral, Dublin: Eye Ubiquitous/Alamy. Page 75, Ruins of Hugh de Lacy's

Castle, Trim, Ireland: © National Monuments Service: Arts, Heritage and the Gaeltacht. Page 77, The *Domesday Book*: British Crown copyright, Public Record Office, London.

Chapter 6
Page 88, Effigies of Henry II and Eleanor of Aquitaine, Fontevrault Abbey, France: Cephas Picture Library/Alamy. Page 90, Thomas Becket: Dean and Chapter of Canterbury Cathedral.

Chapter 7
Page 96, Edward I in Parliament: Royal Library, Windsor Castle, © Her Majesty the Queen. Page 98, Llywelyn the Great and his sons, Gruffydd and Dafydd: Master and Fellows of Corpus Christi College, Cambridge. Page 101, Caernarfon Castle, Wales: National Monuments Record for Wales Collection, Royal Commission on Ancient and Historical Monuments in Wales. Page 104, The English coronation chair, Westminster Abbey: Royal Commission on the Historical Monuments of England. Page 107, The Declaration of Arbroath: Crown Copyright, National Records of Scotland, SP13/7.

Chapter 8
Page 113, Effigy of Edward III, Westminster Abbey: Royal Commission on the Historical Monuments of England. Page 116, Effigies of Henry IV and his queen, Joan of Navarre, Canterbury Cathedral: Royal Commission on the Historical Monuments of England. Page 117, English archers at Agincourt: The Stapleton Collection/Bridgeman Images. Page 118, Henry V, portrait by an unknown artist: National Portrait Gallery. Page 122, Woodcut illustration from Hans Holbein's *Dance of Death*: Private Collection/Bridgeman Images. Page 123, Page from Wycliffe's Bible: University History Archive/UIG/Bridgeman Images. Page 127, Speed's Map of Ireland (1610), detail showing the dress of the "tame" town Irish and the "wild" Gaelic Irish: British Library, London/© British Library Board. All rights reserved/Bridgeman Images. Page 132, Statue of Owain Glyn Dwr, Corwen, Wales: Warren Kovach/Alamy.

Chapter 9
Page 137, Richard III, portrait by an unknown artist: National Portrait Gallery. Page 138, Forensic reconstruction of the features of Richard III: Richard III Society. Page 143, James IV of Scotland by an unknown artist: National Galleries of Scotland. Page 149, Woodcut of the MacSweeney chieftain and his court: Private Collection/Bridgeman Images. Page 153, Lough Gur, Ireland: Matthew Fry/Alamy. Page 154, *Field of the Cloth of Gold*, anonymous artist: Royal Collection Trust © Her Majesty Queen Elizabeth II, 2016/Bridgeman Images.

Chapter 10
Page 158, Henry VIII, copied from a portrait by Hans Holbein the Younger: National Portrait Gallery. Page 160, Sir Thomas More: © The Frick Collection, New York City. Page 161, Thomas Cromwell, by Hans Holbein: © The Frick Collection, New York City. Page 162, The ruins of Glastonbury Abbey: Royal Commission on the Historical Monuments of England. Page 163, The six wives of Henry VIII: Engraving, colorized/Bridgeman Images. Page 170, Edward VI by Hans Holbein: National Portrait Gallery. Page 171, Mary Tudor, by an unknown artist: National Portrait Gallery. Page 172, *The Burning of Archbishop Cranmer*: Special Collections, University of Minnesota Libraries. Page 173, Title page of John Knox's "First Blast of the Trumpet against the

Monstrous Regimen of Women" (1571): Newberry Library, Chicago. Page 174, Mary, Queen of Scots, by an unknown artist: National Portrait Gallery.

Chapter 11

Page 182, Elizabeth I when a Princess, attributed to William Scrots: Royal Collection © Her Majesty Queen Elizabeth II/Bridgeman Images. Page 184, Elizabeth I by Marc Gheeraerts: National Portrait Gallery. Page 185, Cony catcher's pamphlet, by Robert Greene (1592): British Library, London. Page 188, Illustration of the execution of Mary, Queen of Scots: Private Collection/Bridgeman Images. Page 193, James I, by Daniel Mytens: National Portrait Gallery. Page 196, Woodcut illustration of the Lancashire witches: British Library Archive/The Art Resource, NY. Page 197, Title page of James I's *Daemonologie*: Newberry Library, Chicago. Page 198, Title page of James I's *Basilikon Doron*: University of Glascow Library.

Chapter 12

Page 208, Charles I, by Daniel Mytens: National Portrait Gallery. Page 216, James Graham, first Marquess of Montrose after Honthorst: National Portrait Gallery, London. Page 217, Archibald Campbell, first Marquess of Argyll: National Galleries of Scotland. Page 221, Statue of Oliver Cromwell, lord protector of England, Ireland, and Scotland: Royal Commission on the Historical Monuments of England.

Chapter 13

Page 225, Charles II from the studio of John Michael Wright: National Portrait Gallery. Page 226, Samuel Pepys: Royal Society of Arts, London/Bridgeman Images. Page 230, St. Paul's Cathedral, view from the southeast: Royal Commission on the Historical Monuments of England. Page 231, Panorama of London, showing the skyline as it appeared following the great rebuilding: Original engraving by the Buck Brothers, 1749. Page 232, Robert Boyle, 1689: National Portrait Gallery, London/DeAgostini Picture Library/Bridgeman Images. Page 233, Charter of the Royal Society, detail: © The Royal Society. Page 236, James II, by Sir Godfrey Kneller: National Portrait Gallery. Page 238, Cartoon showing the rumor that James II's son (by his second, Catholic wife) was not legitimate but was smuggled into the queen's bedroom in a warming pan: Private Collection/Bridgeman Images. Page 239, James Francis Stuart: National Portrait Gallery, London. Page 239, William of Orange, by Sir Peter Lely: National Portrait Gallery. Page 241, John Graham, first Viscount Dundee, seventh Laird of Claverhouse: University of Dundee Fine Art Collection.

Index

Note: Page numbers in italic indicate illustrations.

Aberconwy, Treaty of, 101
Act of 1563, 180
Act of Restraint of Appeals, 161
Act of Six Articles, 166
Act of Supremacy, 161–162
Act of Uniformity, 179, 226, 227
aes dána, 33–34, 35, 60, 128, 149
Age of Adversity, 111
Age of Crisis, 181, 207–210
Agincourt, Battle of, 115–116, *117*
Agricola, 21–22, 23
agricultural revolution, 80–81
agriculture, 4, 14–15, 108, 131
Alba, 53–54
Albigensian heresy, 121
Alexander, Duke of Albany, 142
Alexander III, 102–103
Alfred the Great, 54, 56
Allen, Walter, 183
Angevins, 80
Anglesea, 20
Anglo-Saxon Chronicle, 68, 69
Anglo-Saxons, 48–49, 56–58, 61–63
Annales Cambriae, 13
Anne of Cleves, 162, *163*
Anne of Denmark, 195, 209
Antonine Wall, 23–24
Antonius Pius, 23–24
apprentice system, 84
aqueducts, Roman, 24
Ardagh Chalice, 43, *47*
Argyll, Marquess of (Archibald Campbell),
    216–217, *217*, 219, 227
Army of the Covenant, 215–217, 218
Arran, Earl of, 167, 168

Arthur, King, 27, 29–30
Assize of Novel Disseisin, 89
Audley, Sir Thomas, 160
Augsburg, Peace of, 176, 190
Auld Alliance, 103, 146, 167
Avignonese papacy, 112, 115

Babylonian Captivity, 111–112
Bacon, Francis, 232
Bale, John, 178, 179
Balliol, John, 103–104
Bannockburn, Battle of, 106
Barbarossa, Frederick, 153–154
Basilikon Doron (James VI), 197, *198*
Battersea bronze shield, 13
Bayeux tapestry, 58, *59*, 68
Beaker folk, 10
Beaton, David, 168, 169, 172
Beaufort, Joan, 140
Becket, Thomas, 89–91, *90*
Bedford, Duke of, 116–117
Benedictines, 71, 86
Beowulf, 62–63
Bernard of Neufmarché, 76
Bible, 166, 168, 180, 183, 200
Bill of Rights, 240
Bishops' Wars, 216
Black Death, 111, 113–115, 119, *121*,
    128, 133
Bloodless Revolution, 238
Bloody Assizes, 237
bog burials, 16
Boleyn, Anne, 158, 162, *163*
Bond and Statutes of Iona, 204
Boniface VIII, 111–112

Book of Common Prayer, 179, 182, 212, 226–227, 227
Book of Durrow, 41
Book of Kells, 41, *43*
Book of the Dean of Lismore, 145
Boru, Brian, 49
Bothwell, Earl of (James Hepburn), 176
Boudicca, 19–21, *20*
Bourbon, Henry, 190
Boyd, Sir Alexander, 141
Boyle, Robert, 232, *232*
Boyne, Battle of the, 242
Boyne Valley, 7–8
Breda, Treaty of, 228
Bronze Age, 11
bronze work, 11, 13
Bruce, Edward, 109
Bruce, Robert, 103, 105–106, 139
Buchanan, George, 193–194
Buckingham, Duke of (George Villiers), 205, 209–210
burial practices, 10, 11, 15–16, 16
Butser Ancient Farm Research Center, 14–15, *14*

Cade, Jack, 135
Caesar, 12, 13, 17, 18–19
Calamitous Fourteenth Century, 111
Caligula, 19
Callanish, 8, *9*, 172
Calvin, John, 168–169
Campion, Edmund, 183
Canterbury Tales, The (Chaucer), 118–119
Caracalla, 24
Carey, Sir Robert, 199
Cassivellanus, 18–19
Catherine de Medici, 169, 188
Catherine of Aragon, 146, 157–159, 162, *163*
Catherine of Braganza, 224
Catholic threat, 183, 187
Cecil, Sir William, 186
Charles I, 205, 207–217, *208*, 219, 220

Charles II, 222, 223, 224–227, *225*, 230–231, 232, 234–235
Charles V, 159, 190
Charles VI, 116
Charles VII, 116–117
Chaucer, 118–119
Christianity
  arrival of, 29–30
  introduction of, 27
  in Ireland, 31–37
  monasticism and, 35–44
  in Wales, 30–31
  see also Reformation; religious life
chronicles, Irish, 128
Church of England, 161
Cistercian Order, 106, 179
clan structure, 12, 49, 129, *130*, 131
Clarendon, Constitutions of, 89, 90
Clarendon, Duke of, 226, 228
Clarendon Code, 226–227
Claudius, Emperor, 19
Clement VII, Pope, 158
Cluniac Reforms, 86
Cnut, 57
Cochrane, Robert, 142
Code of Adamnan, 60
coins, Roman, 26
Comyn, John, the Red, 105
Confederate Catholics of Ireland, 213
Constitutions of Clarendon, 89, 90
Convention of the Estates, 240
Convention Parliament, 225, 238
cony catchers, 185, *185*
Coronation Charter of Henry I, 93
Council of Arles, 27, 30
Council of Guardians, 103
coyne and livery, 147
Cranmer, Archbishop, 160, 162, 165, 166, *172*
Cromwell, Oliver, 215, 219, 220–222, *221*, 227
Cromwell, Richard, 222
Cromwell, Thomas, 160–161, *161*, 165, 167

cuius regio, eius regio, 176, 188, 190, 192
Culdrevny, Battle of, 36
Cunobelinus, 19
currency, 26, 183

Daemonologie (James VI), 195, *197*
Dalriadic Scots, 36, 48, 53, 102
Damian, John, 144–145
Danebury, 13–14
Danelaw, 54, 56
Darnley, Lord (Henry Stewart), 175
David I, 72
David II, 112, 129, 139
Davies, Richard, 180
Davis, Moll, 224
debased currency, 183
Declaration of Arbroath, 106, *107*
Declaration of Indulgence, 227, 235
Dee, John, 185
Defoe, Daniel, 228, 234
Derbforgaill, 73
Dio Cassio, 21
Diocletian, Emperor, 30
Distraint of Knighthood fee, 210
divorce, 61
Doctrine of the Two Swords, 86, 89, 199
Domesday Book, 76, 77, *77*
Dominicans. *See* friars
Domitian, Emperor, 23
Donald Bane, 72
Douai Bible, 183
Douglas, Archibald, 142
Douglas, Gavin, 145
Dover, Treaty of, 235
Drake, Sir Francis, 191
Drogheda, massacre at, 221
druids, 16, 20
Dudley, Robert, Earl of Leicester, 185, 186
Dunbar, Battle of, 222
Dunbar, William, 145, 146
Dundee, Viscount (John Graham), 240–241, *241*
Dutch Revolt, 190

Edict of Nantes, 190
Edinburgh, Treaty of, 173
Edington, Battle of, 54
Edmund, Duke of York, 136
Edmund Ironside, 57
education, during fifteenth century, 119
Education Act (1496), 144
Edward I, 83, 93, 95–96, *96*, 98, 100–102, 103–105, 108–109
Edward II, 106, 109–110
Edward III, 110, 111, 112, *113*, 115
Edward IV, 136, 141
Edward the Confessor, 57
Edward V, 136
Edward VI, 162, 168, 169–170, *170*, 179
eiric (honor price), 60
Eleanor of Aquitaine, 87–88, *88*, 91, 92
Eleven Years Tyranny, 210–211
Elinor (wife of Llywelyn II), 100–101
Eliot, Sir John, 209–210
Elizabeth I, 171, 174, 175, 179, 181–187, *182*, *184*, 191, 193, 201
Elizabeth of York, 138
Elizabethan Poor Law, 186
enclosure movement, 185
England
    impact of Reformation in, 164–166
    Renaissance and, 153–155
    Restoration in, 228–231
    Vikings in, 54
English succession, 115–118
Erasmus, Desiderius, 164
Eric II, 103
Essex, Earl of (Robert Devereaux), 185, 192, 215
Ethelred the Unready, 56–57
Exclusion Act, 235

Falaise, Treaty of, 102
Falkirk, Battle of, 105
Fawkes, Guy, 200
fealty, 67–68, *67*
Ferdinand II, 205
feudalism, 66–68, 93, 118, 133

Field of the Cloth of Gold, 154, *154*
Fir Bolg, 9
Fischer, John, 183
Fitzwilliam, Sir William, 192
Five Articles of Perth, 211
Flight of the Earls, 192
Fochart, Battle of, 109
Formorians, 9
forts, stone, 5, *6*, 7–9
Four Fifths of Ireland, 49
Francis I, 154
Francis IX, 171, 173, 188
Franciscans. *See* friars
Frederick of the Palatinate, 205
French Wars of Religion, 168, 171, 188,
    190
friars, Dominican and Franciscan, 120,
    157, 165, 178

Gaelic, 26, 145, 147–150, 152
gallowglasses, 128
Gearóid (fourteenth century), 153
Gearóid, eleventh Earl of Kildare, 153–
    154
geography, 1, *2*, 3–4
Geraldine League, 150
Giraldus Cambrensis, 76, 100
Glastonbury, 29–30
Glastonbury Abbey, *162*
Glorious Revolution, 238
Glyn Dwr, Owain, 131–132, *132*
Goidelic languages, 12
Golden Legend, The, 157
Gothic style, 80
Great Fire of London, *229*, 229–231, *231*
"Great Matter," of King Henry VIII, 157–
    159, 162
Great Schism, 111, 119–120
Greene, Robert, *185*
Greenwich, Treaty of, 168
Gregory VII, Pope (Hildebrand), 86–87
Gresham, Sir Thomas, 183
Gresham's Law, 183
Grey, Lady Jane, 170
guild system, 84, 119, 126

Gunpowder Plot, 200
Gwynne, Nell, 224–225

Haddington, Treaty of, 169
Hadrian, 23
Hadrian's Wall, 23, *23*
Halley, Edward, 234
Hampton Court Conference, 200
Hardecnut, 57
Hardrada, Harold, 58
Harold, Earl of Mercia, 57–58, *59*
Harold Harefoot, 57
Hastings, Battle of, 58, *59*
hellburners, 191
Henrietta Maria, 209, 214–215
Henry (Beauclerc), 77–78
Henry I, 76, 81, 89
Henry II, 73–74, *75*, 78, 80, 81, 87–91, *88*
Henry II of France, 169, 171, 188
Henry III, 86, 93, 100, 108
Henry IV, 86–87, *116*
Henry IV of France, 209
Henry of Lancaster, 115
Henry V, 115–116, *118*
Henry VI, 116, 135–136
Henry VII, 137–139, 145, 146
Henry VIII, 146, 148, 153–155, 157–160,
    158, 162, 166–167, 177
Henryson, Robert, 145
Heptarchy, 48–49, 56
Hereward the Wake, 69–70
Highland Boundary Fault, 3
Hildebrand (Pope Gregory VII), 86–87
Hobbes, Thomas, 234
honor prices, 60, 61–62
Honorius, Emperor, 24
Honorius III, Pope, 108
Hooke, Robert, 232
Howard, Kathryn, 162, *163*
Huizinga, Johan, 121
"Humble Petition and Advice, The," 222
Hundred Years War, 111, 112, 115–117
hunting, 4
Hyde, Anne, 237
Hywel Dda, 56, 60

Ice Age, 4
Iceni, 19–21
inflation, 183, 201, 207, 208
Innocent III, Pope, 92, 97
Inverlochy, Battle of, 219
Investiture Controversy, 87, 92
Iona, 37–38, *41*
Ireland
    Charles I and, 212–214
    Cromwell and, 221–222
    division of groups in, 126, *127*
    families and lordships of, *125*
    geography of, 3
    James IV/I and, 201, 203
    in late Middle Ages, 124, 126, 128
    normanization of, 73–75
    plantations of, 192, *202*, 203
    political structures of, 147–148
    Reformation in, 176–179
    Renaissance lords of, 150, 152–154
    Restoration in, 227
    saints of, 31–37, *32*, *36*
    Vikings in, 49, 51
    wars of expansion and, 106–110
    William of Orange and, *241*
Irish Parliament, 147–148, 177
Irish problem, 191–192
Iron Age, 12–17
Isabella (wife of Edward II), 109–110

Jacobites, 240–241, 242
James I, 140
James II, 140–141, *236*
James II/VII, 236–238
James III, 141–143
James IV, 139, 143–147, *143*
James IV/I, 181, 187, 193–195, 199–201,
    203–205, 211–212
James V, 167–168, 172
James VI, 176
Jeffries, Judge, 237
Joan of Arc, 117
Joan of Navarre, *116*
John (son of Henry II), 81, 91, 92–93, 97
John, Earl of Mar, 142

John of Gaunt, Duke of Lancaster, 115,
    136, 138
John XII, Pope, 86
Jorvik Viking Center, 54–55, *55*
Joseph of Arimathea, 29–30
Julius II, Pope, 145, 146

Kérouaille, Louise de, 224–225
Kildare, Earl of (Gearóid Fitzgerald), 147,
    148
Killing Times, 228
Kingdom of the Isles. *See* Lordship of the
    Isles
Kingis Quair, The, 140
Kinsale, Battle of, 192
Knowth complex, 7
Knox, Andrew, 204
Knox, John, 169, 172–175, *173*

La Tène, 5
Lamberton, William, 105
Lancastrians, 115, 135–136, 138, 141
Langside, Battle of, 187
Langton, Stephen, 92, 97
languages
    Bible and, 166, 168, 180
    Gaelic, 26, 145, 147–150, 152
    Goidelic, 12
    Latin, 26
    Picts and, 48
    during Roman occupation, 26
    in Scotland, 129, 145
    Vikings and, 52
Laoghaire, King, 33
Latin, 26
Laud, William, 210, 211, 212, 213
law, Henry II and, 89
law codes, 60
*Lebor Gabála Erenn (Book of
    Invasions)*, 9
Lepanto, Battle of, 190
Lindisfarne Gospels, The, 41, *42*
Lindow Man, 16
Linn nan creach (Age of Forays), 194
Lionel, Duke of Clarence, 136

literacy, 119
Little Ice Age, 207
livery and maintenance, 136
Llwyd, Humphrey, 180
Llywelyn ap Gruffydd, 98
Llywelyn II, 100–101
Llywelyn the Great, *98*
Locke, John, 240
London, Great Fire of, 229–231, *229, 231*
Lordship of the Isles, *53*, 73, 102, 194
Louis VII, 87–88, 91
Louis XIV, 190, 235, 237
Luther, Martin, 157, 164, 168

Mabinogion, The, 13
MacAlpin, Kenneth, 53–54
MacColla, Alasdair, 217–218, 219
MacDonald, Donald, 129
MacMurrough, Dermot, 73–74
Maeshowe, 8
Magna Carta, 93, 98
Maid of Norway, 103
Malcolm III (Canmore), 70–72, 102
manorialism, 68, 77, 133
Marcher lords, 98, 100, 102
Margaret, Queen, 70, 71–72
marriage
    early law codes on, 60–61
    feudalism and, 67–68
Marshall, William, 93, 108
Martin V, 120
martyrdoms, 30
Marvell, Andrew, 234
Mary, Queen of Scots, 167, 168, 169, 171,
    173–176, *174*, 187, *188*
Mary II, 237, 238, 240
Mary of Gueldres, 141
Mary of Guise, 168, 170, 172, 173
Mary of Modena, 237
Matilda, 78
megaliths, 5–9, *6*
mercenaries, 128
middle class, rise of, 119

Mildmay, Sir Walter, 186
Milesians, 9
Millenary Petition, 200
Milton, John, 234
Model Parliament, 96
monasteries, dissolution of, 161–162,
    165–166, 177, 178, 179
monastic reforms, 86
monasticism, 35–44, *39*, *40*, 47
    see also religious life
Monck, George, 222–223
Monmouth, Duke of, 236–237
Mons Graupius, Battle of, 21–22
Montfort, Simon de, 93
Montgomery, Treaty of, 100
Montrose, Marquess of (James Graham),
    215–219, *216*
More, Sir Thomas, 154–155, 159–160,
    160, 164
Mortimer, Roger, 109–110
Murray, Andrew, 104

Naseby, Battle of, 219
National Covenant, 212, 215–216
national monarchy, 95–97
natural philosophy, 232
Navigation Acts, 228
Nechtansmere, Battle of, 49
Neolithic period, 4
Nero, 19
Nest, 76
New Model Army, 215
Newgrange, 7, *7*
Newton, Sir Isaac, 232, 234
Nine Years War, 203
"Nineteen Propositions, The," 214
"Ninety-five Theses," 157, 168
Normans
    Battle of Hastings and, 58
    consolidation of power by, 77–78
    description of, 66–68
    influences of in Scotland, 71–73
    normanization of Britain and, 68–71

normanization of Ireland and, 73–75
uprisings against, 69–70
in Wales, 75–76

Oates, Titus, 234–235
Oath of Supremacy, 177, 182
O'Connor, Rory, 74–75
O'Donnell, Manus, 37, 150–152
O'Neill, Red Hugh, 192, 213
O'Rourke, Tiernan, 73
O'Toole, Laurence, 75
Ottomans, 190

Paleolithic period, 4
Palladius, 32
Parker, Matthew, 182
Parliament
    Addled, 204
    Cavalier, 226, 235
    Charles I and, 209–210, 212–213, 214
    Charles II and, 235
    Convention, 225, 238
    Cromwell and, 222
    Edward I and, 95–96
    Irish, 147–148, 177
    James IV/I and, 204–205
    Long, 213
    Reformation, 159, 161–162, 165, 174
    Rump, 220, 222–223
    Short, 213
    Simon de Montfort and, 93
Parr, Katherine, 162, *163*, 166
Pass of Killiecrankie, battle at, 241
Peasant Revolt, 115
Penal Laws, 242
Pepys, Samuel, 224–225, *226*, 228–229, 234
Perpetual Peace, Treaty of, 145
Petition of Right, 209
Philip Augustus, 88, 91, 92, 97, 111
Philip the Fair, 111–112
Philiphaugh, Battle of, 219
Philippa of Hainault, 115

Phillip II, 170, 191
Picts, 48, 53
Pilgrimage of Grace, 165
Pitney Brooch, *63*
plague, 111, 113–115, 119, *121*, 128, 133, 207, 228–229
Plantagenets, 80, 91–93
poetry
    Beowulf, 62–63
    of Columcille, 35
    Gaelic revival and, 149–150
    Irish epics, 43
    of James I, 140
    James IV/I and, 145
    in Wales, 131
    women and, 61
    see also aes dána
Poor Laws, 186
Popish Plot, 234–235
Poynings, Sir Edward, 147
Poynings Law, 148
Poynings Parliament, 147–148
Praesutagus, 19
predestination, doctrine of, 169
prehistoric Britain
    description of, 4–5
    geography of, 1–4, *2*
    Iron Age in, 12–17
    peoples of, 10–11
    stone forts and megaliths of, 5–9, *6*
primogeniture, 66, 147
printing press, 145, 164
privateers, 191
Protestant Settlement, 174
Pym, John, 212–213

Raleigh, Walter, 184–185
recusancy, 165, 178, 183, 187, 191, 201, 227
Redwald, king of East Anglia, 63, *64*
Reformation
    beginning of, 121
    context of, 164

Reformation (cont.)
  Henry VIII and, 157–160
  impact of, 164–166
  in Ireland, 176–179
  in Scotland, 167–176
  start of, in England, 160–162
  in Wales, 179–180
religious life
  Black Death and, 119
  cathedrals and monasteries, *85*
  Charles I and, 211–212
  in Ireland, 106–108, 191–192
  of Iron Age, 16–17
  James IV/I and, 194, 200
  in late Middle Ages, 120–121
  Queen Margaret and, 71
  reform movements in, 120–121,
    124
  religion of ruler and, 176, 188, 190
  religions of Europe, *189*
  during Roman occupation, 26–27
  during twelfth century, 84, 86–87
  see also monasticism; Reformation;
    saints
religious settlement, Elizabethan, 181–
    183, 200, 210
Renaissance, 135, 144
Restoration, 224–231, 227
Revolutionary Settlement, 240, 242
Rhys ap Tewdwr, 76
Richard, Duke of Gloucester, 136
Richard Coeur de Lion, 81, 91–92
Richard II, 115, 135
Richard III, 136–137, *137*, *138*
Rinuccini, Giovanni, 213
Rizzio, David, 175
roads, Roman, 24
Robert Curthose, 77–78
Robert II, 139
Robert III, 139–140
Rochester, Earl of (John Wilmot), 234
Romans
  baths of, *22*
  conquest by, 18–24

end of occupation by, 24
impact of, 24, 26–27
rebellion against, 19–21
towns of, *25*
Roper, William, 160
Rough Wooing, 168
round towers, *46*, 47
Royal Society, 232–234, *233*

saints
  of Ireland, 31–37, *32*, *36*
  in late Middle Ages, 121
  in Wales, 31
  see also religious life; *individual
    saints*
Salesbury, William, 180
Scandinavia, 45
  see also Vikings
scholasticism, 80
science, growth of, 231–234
Scientific Revolution, 232
Scotland
  Charles I and, 211–213
  clans and chieftaincies of, *130*
  Cromwell and, 222
  early political structures of, 48–49
  geography of, 3
  James IV/I and, 203–204
  in late Middle Ages, 128–129, 131
  Normans and, 70–73
  Reformation in, 167–176
  Restoration in, 227–228
  St. Columcille and, 36–37
  Vikings in, 52–53, *52*
  War of the Three Kingdoms and, 215–
    219
  wars of expansion and, 102–106
  William of Orange and, 240–241
Second Dutch War, 228
Septimius, 24
serfs, 68
settlement sites, 4–5
Seven Eminent Persons, 237
Seymour, Jane, 162, *163*

Shakespeare, William, 19, 115–116, 131, 137, 234
ship money, 211
Sidney, Sir Henry, 192
Sidney, Sir Phillip, 185
Silken Thomas, Earl of Kildare, 153
Simnel, Lambert, 138–139
Skara Brae, 11, *12*
Snettisham Hoard, 15–16
Solemn League and Covenant, 215, 227–228
Solway Moss, Battle of, 167
Spanish Armada, 191
Spenser, Edmund, 185
Spottiswoode, John, 211
St. Albans, Battle of, 136
St. Bartholomew's Day Massacre, 171, 190
St. Brigid, 34
St. Columcille, 35–37, 48
St. Leger, Anthony, 179
St. Patrick, 31–34
Stamford Bridge, Battle of, 58
standing stones, 8–9
Staples, Edward, 179
Statutes of Kilkenny, 124, 147
Statutes of Wales, 101–102
Stephen, 78
Stewart, James, 174
Stirling Bridge, Battle of, 104
stone circles, 8–9
Stone of Scone, 104, *104*
Stonehenge, 8, *8*
Strongbow, Richard (de Clare), 74, *74*
Stuart, James Francis Edward, 237, *239*, 240–242
Stuarts, 139–143
subinfeudation, 67, 93
succession issues
    Anglo-Saxon, 56–58, 62
    in England, 115–118
    Gaelic law and, 60
Suetonius Paulinus, 19–20, 21
surrender and regrant, 177–178

Sutton Hoo burial, 63, *64*
Sweyn Forkbeard, 56–57
Swynford, Katherine, 138
Synod of Sutrei, 86

Tacitus, 21, 22, 23, 24
Táin Bó Cúailgne (The Cattle Raid of Cooley), 13
taxation, 96, 201, 208, 226
Tertullian, 27, 30
Test Acts, 235, 236
textile production, 15
Third Dutch War, 235
Thirty Years War, 205, 209, 210
"Thirty-nine Articles," 182
three-field rotation, 81
Tinchebrai, Battle of, 78
Toleration Act, 240
tonnage and poundage, 209, 210
Tostig, Earl of Northumbria, 57–58
trade, 24, 26, 126, 129, 242–243
Trajan, Emperor, 23
Trew Law of Free Monarchies, The (James VI), 197
trial by ordeal, 62
Triangle Trade, 242–243
Troyes, Treaty of, 116
Tryggvason, Olaf, 56
Tuatha de Dánann, 9
Tudor, Margaret, 139, 145–146, 167
Tudor, Mary, 170–171, *171*
Tudor, Owen, 137–138
Twelfth Century Renaissance, 80
Tyler, Wat, 115

Ulster, 201, 203
Union of Parliaments, 242
urban revolution, 81–84, *82*
urbanization, by Romans, 22
Urnfield culture, 11

Vikings
    expansion and settlement by, 49–56, *50, 51*

Vikings (cont.)
  impact of, 58–61
  raids by, 45–47
  second wave of invasions by, 56–58
Villiers, Barbara, 224
vitrified stones, 9, *10*

Waldensian heresy, 121
Wales
  Charles I and, 214
  early Christianity in, 30–31
  geography of, 1, 3
  in late Middle Ages, 131–133
  medieval principalities of, *99*
  Normans and, 75–76
  rebellion in, 131–132
  Reformation in, 179–180
  Wars of Expansion and, 97–98, 100–
    102
Wallace, William, 104–105
Wallingford, Treaty of, 78
Walsingham, Sir Francis, 186
War of the Three Kingdoms, 214–215,
  224
Warbeck, Perkin, 139
Warham, William, 160
Wars of Expansion
  Ireland and, 106–110
  Scotland and, 102–106
  Wales and, 97–98, 100–102

Wars of the Roses, 117, 135–139, 141
wergeld (honor price), 61–62
Welsh Revolt, 97
Wentworth, Sir Thomas, 212, 213
Wessex culture, 11
white martyrdom, 35, 39
William, Duke of Normandy, 58, *59*
William II, 76
William of Orange, 237–240, *239*
William Rufus (William II), 71, 72, 77–78
William the Conqueror, 66, 68–70, 75–
  76, 77
William the Lion, 102
Wishart, George, 169, 172
witan, 57, 58, 62
witchcraft, 186, 195, *196*
Wolsey, Thomas, 154, 159
women
  in Anglo-Saxon society, 62
  divorce and, 61
  eiric (honor price) and, 60
  guild system and, 119
  property ownership and, 61
Wood, Anthony, 230
Woodville, Elizabeth, 136
Wren, Sir Christopher, 231, 232
Wycliffe, John, 121, *123*, 124

Year of Miracles, 218–219
Yorkists, 135–136

About the Authors

Samantha A. Meigs (BA, MA, University of Colorado; PhD, Northwestern University) is associate professor of history and experience design at the University of Indianapolis. Recipient of a Fulbright Fellowship for research in Ireland and an NEH Summer Grant for her research on Highland Scotland, she is author of *The Reformations in Ireland: Tradition and Confessionalism, 1400–1690*.

Stanford E. Lehmberg (PhD, LittD, Cambridge University; d. 2012) was professor of history emeritus at the University of Minnesota. He was a Fulbright Scholar and recipient of two Guggenheim Fellowships.